Speaking Against Number

Titles in the *Taking on the Political* series include:

Speaking Against Number

Heidegger, Language and the Politics of Calculation

Stuart Elden

Edinburgh University Press

Stuart Elden, 2006

Edinburgh University Press Ltd
22 George Square, Edinburgh

Typeset in 11 on 13 Sabon by
Iolaire Typesetting, and
printed and bound in Great Britain by
The Cromwell Press, Trowbridge, Wilts

A CIP record for this book is
available from the British Library

ISBN 0 7486 1981 X (hardback)

Contents

Acknowledgements

This book has its genesis in initial conversations with Michael Dillon and Morris Kaplan, who have continued to offer encouragement and suggestions throughout. Earlier versions of this manuscript have been read by Ben Anderson, Paul Harrison, Laurence Paul Hemming, Adam Holden, Mark Neocleous and Jeremy Valentine, who all offered extremely useful and challenging comments, and at times better grasped what I was striving to show than I had then realised myself. Versions of parts of this book have been given as papers at the University of North Texas, Heythrop College, Royal Geographical Society, University of Durham, University of Warwick, University of Essex, Association of American Geographers, Martin Heidegger Forschungsgruppe in Meßkirch, and the Katholieke Universiteit Leuven. Its ideas have benefited from discussion at these and other places with Charles Bambach, Babette Babich, Robert Bernasconi, Neil Brenner, Keith Wayne Brown, Jeremy Crampton, Françoise Dastur, Miguel de Beistegui, Michael Eldred, Béatrice Han-Pile, Theodore Kisiel (who also clarified some textual details regarding GA20), the late Richard Owsley, Allen Scult, Nigel Thrift and Maja Zehfuss. Thomas Sheehan most generously made available his draft translation of portions of GA21. Colleagues at the University of Durham, especially those involved in the Social/Spatial Theory research cluster, have been a constant source of inspiration. Elizabeth James provided invaluable assistance with checking the Greek and German; Hamzah Muzaini greatly assisted with the proofs and compiled the index; Susan again showed me what else counted.

Early versions of some of its ideas have appeared in the following places:

'The Place of Geometry: Heidegger's Mathematical Excursus on Aristotle', *The Heythrop Journal*, Vol. 42 No. 3, July 2001, pp. 311–28.

'Taking the Measure of the *Beiträge*: Heidegger, National Socialism and the Calculation of the Political', *European Journal of Political Theory*, Vol. 2 No. 1, January 2003, pp. 35–56.

'Reading *Logos* as Speech: Heidegger, Aristotle and Rhetorical Politics', *Philosophy and Rhetoric*, Vol. 38, 2005.

A development of some of these ideas in relation to the discipline of geography can be found in 'Contributions to Geography? The Spaces of Heidegger's *Beiträge*', *Environment and Planning D: Society and Space,* Vol. 23 No. 6, 2005.

Abbreviations

Abbreviations of Works by Aristotle

These are given by the standard page and line number method, which refers to the edition of Immanuel Bekker (ed.), *Aristotelis Opera*, Berlin: W. de Gruyter & Co., 1831. I have used the following editions and translations:

Nicomachean Ethics, Greek–English edition, translated by H. Rackham, London: William Heinemann, 1926; translated by Roger Crisp, Cambridge University Press, 2000. I have also used *Nicomachean Ethics Book Six*, with Essays, Notes and Translation by L. H. G. Greenwood, Cambridge: Cambridge University Press, 1909.

Metaphysics, introduction and commentary by W. D. Ross, Oxford: Clarendon Press, two volumes, 1924; translated by Richard Hope, Ann Arbor: University of Michigan Press, 1960.

On the Soul, Parva Naturalia, On Breath, Greek–English edition, translated by W. S. Hett, London: William Heinemann, 1936.

Physics, Oxford: Clarendon Press, 1936; translated by Robin Waterfield, Oxford: Oxford University Press, 1996.

Politics, Greek–English edition, translated by H. Rackham, London: William Heinemann, 1932; translated by C. D. C. Reeve, Indianapolis: Hackett, 1996.

The Categories, On Interpretation, Prior Analytics, Greek–English edition, translated by Harold P. Cooke and Hugh Tredennick, London: William Heinemann, 1938.

The Rhetoric of Aristotle, with a commentary by E. M. Cope, edited by J. E Sandys, Cambridge: Cambridge University Press, three volumes, 1877; translated by H. C. Lawson-Tancred as *The Art of Rhetoric*, Harmondsworth: Penguin, 1991.

The Athenian Constitution, The Eudemian Ethics, On Virtues and Vices, Greek–English edition, translated by H. Rackham, London: William Heinemann, 1935.

Abbreviations of Works by Martin Heidegger

GA   *Gesamtausgabe*, Frankfurt am Main: Vittorio Klostermann, 1975ff.

GA1   *Frühe Schriften*, 1978.

GA2   *Sein und Zeit*, 1977. Translated by Edward Robinson and John Macquarrie as *Being and Time*, Oxford: Blackwell, 1962, and by Joan Stambaugh as *Being and Time: A Translation of Sein und Zeit*, Albany: State University of New York Press, 1996. References are to the marginal pagination found in the English *and* German, which refer to the original text: *Sein und Zeit*, Tübingen: Max Niemeyer, eleventh edition, 1967.

GA3   *Kant und das Problem der Metaphysik*, 1991. Translated by Richard Taft as *Kant and the Problem of Metaphysics*, Bloomington: Indiana University Press, 1997.

GA4   *Erläuterungen zu Hölderlins Dichtung*, 1981.

GA5   *Holzwege*, 1977. Translated by Julian Young and Kenneth Haynes as *Off the Beaten Track*, Cambridge: Cambridge University Press, 2002. English pagination after /.

GA6   *Nietzsche*, two volumes, 1996.

GA7   *Vorträge und Aufsätze*, 2000.

GA8   *Was heißt Denken?*, 2002. Translated by J. Glenn Grey as *What is Called Thinking?*, New York: Harper & Row, 1968. English pagination after /.

GA9   *Wegmarken*, 1976. Translated by various as *Pathmarks*, edited by William McNeill, Cambridge: Cambridge University Press, 1998. English pagination after /.

GA10   *Der Satz vom Grund*, 1997. Translated by Reginald Lilly as *The Principle of Reason*, Bloomington: Indiana University Press, 1991. English pagination after /.

GA12   *Unterwegs zur Sprache*, 1985. Translated by Peter D. Hertz as *On the Way to Language*, San Francisco: Harper Collins, 1971. English pagination after /.

GA13   *Aus der Erfahrung des Denkens*, 1983.

GA15   *Seminare*, 1986.

GA16   *Reden und andere Zeugnisse eines Lebensweges*, 2000.

GA17   *Einführung in die Phänomenologische Forschung*, 1994.

GA18   *Grundbegriffe der aristotelischen Philosophie*, 2002.

GA19   *Platon: Sophistes*, 1992. Translated by Richard Rojcewicz and André Schuwer as *Plato's* Sophist, Bloomington: Indiana University Press, 1997.

GA20   *Prolegomena zur Geschichte der Zeitbegriffs*, 1979. Translated by Theodore Kisiel as *History of the Concept of Time: Prolegomena*, Bloomington: Indiana University Press, 1985.

GA21   *Logik: Die Frage nach der Wahrheit*, 1976.

GA22   *Die Grundbegriffe der Antiken Philosophie*, 1993.

GA24   *Die Grundprobleme der Phänomenologie*, 1975. Translated by Albert Hofstader as *The Basic Problems of Phenomenology*, Bloomington: Indiana University Press, 1982.

GA25   *Phänomenologische Interpretation von Kants Kritik der reinen Vernunft*, 1977. Translated by Parvis Emad and Kenneth Maly as *Phenomenological Interpretation of Kant's* Critique of Pure Reason, Bloomington: Indiana University Press, 1997.

GA26   *Metaphysiche Anfangsgründe der Logik im Ausgang von Leibniz*, 1978. Translated by Michael Heim as *The Metaphysical Foundations of Logic*, Bloomington: Indiana University Press, 1984.

GA27   *Einleitung in die Philosophie*, 1996.

GA28   *Der deutsche Idealismus (Fichte, Schelling, Hegel) und die philosophische Problemlage der Gegenwart*, 1997.

GA29/30 *Die Grundbegriffe der Metaphysik. Welt – Endlichkeit – Einsamkeit*, 1992. Translated by William McNeill and Nicholas Walker as *The Fundamental Concepts of Metaphysics: World, Finitude, Solitude*, Bloomington: Indiana University Press, 1995.

GA31   *Vom Wesen der menschlichen Freiheit*, 1982. Translated by Ted Sadler as *The Essence of Human Freedom: An Introduction to Philosophy*, London: Continuum, 2002.

GA32   *Hegels Phänomenologie des Geistes*, 1980. Translated by Parvis Emad and Kenneth Maly as *Hegel's Phenomenology of Spirit*, Bloomington: Indiana University Press, 1988.

GA33   *Aristoteles, Metaphysik Θ 1–3: Von Wesen und Wirklichkeit der Kraft*, 1981. Translated by Walter Brogan and

Peter Warnek as *Aristotle's Metaphysics Θ 1–3: On the Essence and Actuality of Force*, Bloomington: Indiana University Press, 1995. English pagination after /.

GA34   *Vom Wesen der Wahrheit: Zu Platons Höhlengleichnis und Theätet*, 1988. Translated by Ted Sadler as *The Essence of Truth: On Plato's Cave Allegory and Theaetetus*, London: Continuum, 2002.

GA36/37 *Sein und Wahrheit: 1. Die Grundfrage der Philosophie 2. Vom Wesen der Wahrheit*, 2001.

GA38   *Logik als Frage nach dem Wesen der Sprache*, 1998.

GA39   *Hölderlins Hymnen 'Germanien' und 'Der Rhein'*, 1980.

GA40   *Einführung in die Metaphysik*, 1983. Translated by Gregory Fried and Richard Polt as *Introduction to Metaphysics*, New Haven: Yale University Press, 2000. References are to the marginal pagination found in the English and German, which refer to the original edition, *Einführung in die Metaphysik*, Tübingen: Max Niemeyer, 1953. This was translated by Ralph Mannheim as *An Introduction to Metaphysics*, New Haven: Yale University Press, 1959, without corresponding pagination.

GA41   *Die Frage nach dem Ding: Zu Kants Lehre von den transzendentalen Grundsätzen*, 1984. Translated by W. B. Barton, Jr and Vera Deutsch as *What is a Thing?*, Chicago: Henry Regnery Company, 1967. English pagination after /.

GA42   *Schelling: Vom Wesen de menschlichen Freiheit (1809)*, 1988. Original 1971 German edition translated by Joan Stambaugh as *Schelling's Treatise on the Essence of Human Freedom*, Athens: Ohio University Press, 1985. English pagination after /.

GA43   *Nietzsche: Der Wille zur Macht als Kunst*, 1985.

GA44   *Nietzsches metaphysische Grundstellung im abendländischen Denken: Die ewige Wiederkehr des Gleichen*, 1986.

GA45   *Grundfragen der Philosophie: Ausgewählte »Probleme« der »Logik«*, 1984. Translated by Richard Rojcewicz and André Schuwer as *Basic Problems of Philosophy: Selected 'Problems' of 'Logic'*, Bloomington: Indiana University Press, 1994.

GA46   *Zur Auslegung von Nietzsches II. Unzeitgemäßer Betrachtung »Vom Nutzen und Nachteil der Historie für das Leben«*, 2003.

GA47   *Nietzsches Lehre vom Willen zur Macht als Erkenntnis*, 1989.
GA48   *Nietzsche: Der Europäische Nihilismus*, 1986.
GA49   *Die Metaphysik des Deutschen Idealismus*, 1991.
GA50   *1. Nietzsches Metaphysik 2. Einleitung in die Philosophie: Denken und Dichten*, 1990.
GA51   *Grundbegriffe*, 1981. Translated by Gary E. Aylesworth as *Basic Concepts*, Bloomington: Indiana University Press, 1993.
GA52   *Hölderlins Hymne 'Andenken'*, 1982.
GA53   *Hölderlins Hymne 'Der Ister'*, 1984. Translated by William McNeill and Julia Davis as *Hölderlin's Hymn 'The Ister'*, Bloomington: Indiana University Press, 1996.
GA54   *Parmenides*, 1982. Translated by André Schuwer and Richard Rojcewicz as *Parmenides*, Bloomington: Indiana University Press, 1992.
GA55   *Heraklit: 1. Der Anfang des abendländischen Denkens 2. Logik: Heraklits Lehre Vom Logos*, 1979.
GA56/57   *Zur Bestimmung der Philosophie*, 1987. Translated by Ted Sadler as *Towards the Definition of Philosophy*, London: Athlone, 2000.
GA58   *Grundprobleme der Phänomenologie (1919/20)*, 1993.
GA59   *Phänomenologie der Anschauung und des Ausdrucks*, 1993.
GA60   *Phänomenologie des religiösen Lebens*, 1995. Translated by Mattias Fritsch and Jennifer Anna Gosetti-Ferencci as *The Phenomenology of Religious Life*, Bloomington: Indiana University Press, 2004.
GA61   *Phänomenologische Interpretationen zu Aristoteles: Einführung in die phänomenologische Forschung*, 1985. Translated by Richard Rojcewicz as *Phenomenological Interpretations of Aristotle: Initiation into Phenomenological Research*, Bloomington: Indiana University Press, 2001.
GA63   *Ontologie (Hermeneutik der Faktizität)*, 1988. Translated by John van Buren as *Ontology: The Hermeneutic of Facticity*, Bloomington: Indiana University Press, 1999.
GA64   *Der Begriff die Zeit*, 2004.
GA65   *Beiträge zur Philosophie (Vom Ereignis)*, 1989. Translated by Parvis Emad and Kenneth Maly as *Contributions*

GA66   *to Philosophy: From Enowning*, Bloomington: Indiana
University Press, 1999.

GA66   *Besinnung*, 1997.

GA67   *Metaphysik und Nihilismus: 1. Die Überwindung der
Metaphysik 2. Das Wesen des Nihilismus*, 1999.

GA68   *Hegel: 1. Die Negativität 2. Erläuterung der »Einleitung«
zu Hegels »Phänomenologie des Geistes«*, 1993.

GA69   *Die Geschichte des Seyns: 1. Die Geschichte des Seyns 2.
Κοινόν. Aus der Geschichte des Seyns*, 1998.

GA75   *Zu Hölderlin, Griechenlandreisen*, 2000.

GA77   *Feldweg-Gespräche*, 1995.

GA79   *Bremer und Freiburger Vorträge*, 1994.

GA85   *Vom Wesen der Sprache: Zu Herder's Abhandlung »Über
den Ursprung der Sprache«*, 1999.

GA87   *Nietzsche Seminare 1937 und 1944*, 2004.

GA90   *Zu Ernst Jünger*, 2004.

The majority of texts translated from the *Gesamtausgabe* have the
pagination of the German version at the top of the page, allowing a
single page reference. Exceptions are noted above.

The following editions have been used for work not yet available in
the *Gesamtausgabe*, along with two English-language editions:

ID   *Identity and Difference/Identität und Differenz*, English–
German edition, translated by Joan Stambaugh, New
York: Harper & Row, 1969. English pagination after /.
To appear as GA11.

PIA   *Phänomenologische Interpretationen zu Aristoteles:
Ausarbeitung für die Marburger und die Göttinger
Philosophische Fakultät (1922)*, Stuttgart: Reclam,
2002. Translated by John van Buren as 'Phenomenolo-
gical Interpretations in Connection with Aristotle: An
Indication of the Hermeneutical Situation (1922)', in
*Supplements: From the Earliest Essays to Being and
Time and Beyond*, edited by John van Buren, Albany:
State University of New York Press, 2002, pp. 111–45.
English pagination after /. To appear as an appendix to
GA62.

ZSD   *Zur Sache des Denkens*, Tübingen: Max Niemeyer, 1976.
Translated by Joan Stambaugh as *On Time and Being*,

New York: Harper & Row, 1972. English pagination after /. To appear as GA14.

HC   *The Heidegger Controversy: A Critical Reader*, edited by Richard Wolin, Cambridge, MA: The MIT Press, 1993. Contains some material in GA16.

N   *Nietzsche*, translated by David Farrell Krell, Frank Capuzzi and Joan Stambaugh, San Francisco: Harper Collins, Four Volumes, 1991. Contains the lectures collected in GA6, itself dependent on material in GA43, GA44, GA47, GA48 and GA50.

Abbreviations of Works by Plato

These are given by the standard page and line number method. The following editions have been used.

Lysis, Symposium, Gorgias, Greek–English edition, translated by W. R. M. Lamb, London: William Heinemann, 1925.

The Meno of Plato, edited by E. Seymer Thompson, London: Macmillan, 1937; translated by W. K. C. Guthrie, Harmondsworth: Penguin, 1956.

Republic, Greek–English edition, translated by Paul Shorey, London: William Heinemann, two volumes, 1930.

Timaeus, Critias, Cleitophon, Menexemus, Epistles, Greek–English edition, translated by R. G. Bury, London: William Heinemann, 1929.

Theaetetus, Sophist, Greek–English edition, translated by Harold North Fowler, London: William Heinemann, 1921.

Introduction

Man as the measurer. – Perhaps all the morality of mankind has its origin in the tremendous inner excitement which seized on primeval men when they discovered measure and measuring, scales and weighing [*das Maass und das Messen, die Wage und das Wägen*] (the word 'Man [*Mensch*]', indeed, means the measurer [*Messendend*], he desired to name himself after his greatest discovery!). With these conceptions they climbed into realms that are quite unmeasurable and unweighable [*unmessbar und unwägbar*] but originally did not seem to be.
Friedrich Nietzsche, *The Wanderer and His Shadow*, § 21.[1]

Thus *aletheuin* shows itself most immediately in *legein*. *Legein*, 'to speak' [*Sprechen*], is what basically constitutes human Dasein. In speaking, it expresses itself: by speaking about something, about the world. This *legein* was for the Greeks so preponderant and such an everyday affair that they acquired their definition of man in relation to, and on the basis of, this phenomenon and thereby determined it as *zoon ekhon logon*. Connected with this definition is that of man as the being which calculates [*rechnet*], *arithmein*. Calculating does not mean here counting [*zählen*] but to reckon something, to be designing [*berechnend sein*]; it is only on the basis of this original sense of calculating [*Rechnen*] that number [*Zahl*] developed.
Martin Heidegger, *Plato's* Sophist (GA19, 17–18).[2]

The Greeks made one invention too many, either geometry or democracy.
Bruno Latour, *Pandora's Hope*.[3]

What is the relation between politics and number, between our understanding of the political as the realm in which political action occurs and the notion of calculation? How does enumerating something, holding something to account, coming to a reckoning differ from a purely linguistic description or judgement? Is there something inherently problematic in reducing complex phenomena to a question of number, an issue of quantity? In a whole range of political questions – from the abstract geometry of understandings of territory and political space more generally, to the explosion of population statistics and measures of economic standards, the popularity of utilitarianism, Rawlsian notions of justice, the notion of value, and, indeed, the very idea of political *science* – the interrelation of number and politics are demonstrated. Beyond the narrow sense of the political, dominant trends in disciplines such as history and geography have a tendency to reduce time and space to coordinates, to models of linearity and repetition. These illustrate a very real take on the political, a way of grasping it, rendering it, reducing it, measuring, controlling and dominating it.

This book, part of a longer project engaging with issues around the relation between politics and number, began as an investigation into what Heidegger could tell us about the historical ontology of geometry, the mathematics of space. The question of space was one I had examined in relation to Heidegger's thought before,[4] but I was particularly intrigued by Heidegger's suggestion that Greek thought did not have a concept of 'space' (GA40, 50), and that therefore Greek geometry cannot straightforwardly be related to the geometry understood in terms of Cartesian extension. We can conceive of place – *topos, khora* – without space. Descartes' understanding of 'space' as extension – and, moreover, of the material world as something extended in three dimensions of which geometry is the science that best allows us access to – has more than merely mathematical implications. It is behind his overall ontological casting of the world as calculable, which, in Heidegger's, account paves the way for modern machine technology. As the chapters of this study show, this has numerous political consequences.

Indeed, grasping this determination of the world – that to be, is to be calculable – is useful in understanding the modern notion of the 'political' as a whole, not sociologically, empirically, or ontically, but *ontologically*. A key question is how the rise of statistics – the description of *states* – is embedded in the transformed understanding of population that Foucault's late 1970s lectures analysed in such detail.[5] But often merely implicit in his work is how all this is related to the calculative revolution. A similar set of concerns arise in relation to contemporary attempts to rethink the question of singular and plural in political subjectivity through the notion of 'multitude'. Hardt and Negri claim that 'the entire tradition of political theory seems to agree on one basic principle: only "the one" can rule, whether that be conceived as the monarch, the state, the nation, the people, or the party'.[6] Differences are subsumed into a single body, democracy as the rule of the many becomes the rule of the people which 'syntheses or reduces these social differences into one identity'. In contrast, the multitude 'is not unified but remains plural and multiple'. As they continue, 'the multitude is composed of a set of *singularities* – and by singularity here we mean a social subject whose difference cannot be reduced to sameness . . . the plural singularities of the multitude thus stand in contrast to the undifferentiated unity of the people'.[7]

What is crucial, then, despite Hardt and Negri's over-privileging of the Hobbesian model, is a sustained investigation of the ontological determination that was required to make the people one, to reduce. What is required in order that humans, groups and organisations can be understood as either the same or different? Determining things as different and seeking to render them more equivalent, or counting them the same in the first place, requires a number of important moves: most importantly, recognising things as sufficiently similar in their essence that they can be summed or evaluated against each other. In other words, while examinations of these issues are necessary, what would make them more sufficient is an examination of their conditions of possibility. This would be to examine how mathematics and politics intersect, through an examination of how calculation, the taking of measure, is key to the *constitution* of the modern state.[8]

One of the other ways in which this is important is in the notion of 'territory', which in terms of the modern state system of bounded geographical territories is usually said to have begun with the Peace of Westphalia in 1648. This is some eleven years after Descartes' *Discourse on the Method* and the *Geometry*, seven after the *Meditations*, and the negotiations were just beginning when the *Principia Philosophiae* appeared in 1644. Though the peace and the writings are not directly linked, it is perhaps symptomatic that a philosophical justification for demarcated, controllable, calculable space is made at the same time this is put into practice.[9] Modern technology requires a view of space as mappable, controllable and capable of domination; modern politics is able to fully exploit this. While this is a much more complicated story than can be noted here – the importance of Westphalia is moot, with colonial divisions of the world such as the Treaty of Tordesillas, Renaissance politics and the Diet of Augsburg all perhaps better examples; and Descartes' break from Greek geometry is rather the culmination of a number of small changes with scholastic debates, for example – the guiding theme emerges from thinking this question of the politics of calculation. How do political conceptions of space relate to mathematical-philosophical ones? This geometry of the political is therefore a historical inquiry. Geometry does not, *contra* Husserl,[10] have *an* origin [*Ursprung*], but rather a descent [*Herkunft*], an emergence [*Entstehung*]. Husserl's *Ursprung* would be the *Evidenzen* or conditions of possibility for geometry – a putatively historical examination that is essentially anti-historical. But this inquiry would be genealogical. It is not a question of (funda-mental) ontology, but of historical ontology.[11]

The work here, though, concentrates on an engagement with the question of the politics of calculation through a reading, exegesis and critique of the work of Martin Heidegger. It is therefore a very limited engagement, but one that I believe opens up the problems in a useful way. Heidegger is important here because his work both critically examines the importance of mathematics in terms of determining thought, and investigates the role played by understandings of calcu-lation in terms of politics. It is his insistence on working through to the ontological determination that conditions the particularities of its consequences that is so fundamental to what he can contribute. And yet Heidegger's own politics and the way in which he harnessed his thought to political action mean that any straightforward appro-priation of his work is impossible. We simply cannot read Heidegger neutrally. Indeed, as I aim to show here, several seemingly apolitical concerns are inherently political.

The book therefore contains three substantive chapters which make use of the range of Heidegger's writings in order to provide a detailed analysis of the relation between language, politics and mathematics in his work. Although it does not claim to be exhaustive in its treatment, it attempts to provide a fairly comprehensive overview of Heidegger's work on these issues. This takes in early lecture courses on Aristotle and Descartes, courses and unpublished writings from the Nazi years, including the famous *Beiträge zur Philosophie: Vom Ereignis*, and, to a lesser extent, post-war works on technology. While some of Heidegger's writings on these questions, such as the essays 'The Age of the World Picture' and 'The Question Concerning Technology', are well known, these are not, to my mind, the most productive places to examine. Rather, a number of other analyses are made, specifically of work where the philosophical inquiry is sharper and the political nature more explicit. The publication of this material means we are now in a position to undertake a much deeper and careful analysis of Heidegger's thought than was possible even a few years ago.[12] The main chapters encounter various texts of Heidegger's, and though there is a definite chronological sense to the argument, they are thematically divided rather than slavishly linear. In doing this, different slices of Heidegger's thought can be examined. While there is both continuity and contrast between his early and late positions, it is revealing that themes mentioned only in passing in early work are returned to and developed in later writings.

The concluding section asks questions of Heidegger's work taken as a whole to examine how this reading works as a means of taking on the political, of making problematic the link between politics and calculation, through speaking against number. As such the detailed textual analysis in Chapters One, Two and Three provides a springboard into the matters themselves, both in the conclusion and for future work.

Writing about Heidegger and politics, rather than Heidegger's politics, presents a number of difficulties. Heidegger's membership of the Nazi party, and his role as Rector of Freiburg University between 1933 and 1934, has led to a debate which has been played out in many times and places – the late 1980s being only the most recent. Some of this has been so comprehensively explored in recent years that one might wonder if there is anything left to be said. Although it is sometimes unavoidable, I will generally not go into detail about the facts here. There are many places those interested can go for this information.[13] Instead, I will approach this question from another direction, that of the relation between the politics and the thought. We should note, of course, that Heidegger's political involvement goes beyond merely his membership of the party, and includes his grasp of the political more generally. Perhaps inevitably, given the collision in one person of Nazism and continental philosophy, a cautious, balanced approach has seldom been taken. What has been notable is that much of the existing literature takes one of two main strategies – exonerating Heidegger through a separation of the man from the thought, or simply damning his thought because of the actions.[14]

As some of the better recent literature has recognised, neither exoneration nor outright dismissal is adequate to the matter at hand: rather, we need to investigate how the thought relates to the political. Two approaches are taken – either to work entirely textually, to examine the writings themselves, a position of immanent criticism; or to work contextually, relating Heidegger to his time, to the material in archives that shed light on his politics. While both have much to commend, neither alone is sufficient.[15] The work of Hugo Ott and, to a substantially lesser extent, Victor Farías, is important in uncovering materials that will not appear in the published corpus; but it is the work of interpreters of Heidegger's writings that shows us why this is important. Put simply, while Heidegger's political action is central to understanding his thought, it is only of interest because of his thought. His actions take on a significance because of his thought, not the other way round. If Heidegger's thought did not open up numerous possibilities in philosophy and other disciplines, he would simply be yet another minor bureaucrat in the Nazi machine: neither blameless nor worthy of particular attention.

One of the attempts to think through Heidegger's thought for a possible ethics and thereby politics is found in Olafson's work on *Mitsein*. Olafson contests any straightforward attempt to make the thought and the action part of a whole. We can see this both in his criticisms of Derrida's work on the role spirit plays in Heidegger's work, and most explicitly in the separation of *Being and Time* from the later politics.

> Heidegger is not the only great philosopher whose conduct in the arena of public affairs has been contemptible but who nevertheless made important and original contributions to thought. Although we inveterately want our heroes and villains to be all of a piece, that simply is not the way things work. In this respect, philosophers can be just as disappointing as the rest of us; the associations of philosophers, beginning with Plato and Aristotle, with the world of power have always been suspect and their judgements often deplorably misguided. In our own day, to cite just one example from the other end of the political spectrum, Sartre was apparently unable to recognise the Communist regimes of Eastern Europe for the tyrannies they were. But if this fact is irrelevant, as I think it is, to an assessment of *Being and Nothingness*, how can Heidegger's implication in Nazism dictate a judgement on *Being and Time*?[16]

The opening statements Olafson makes here, if banal, in no way validate the concluding clause. In a sense, the question is the other way round: how can *Being and Time* help with an assessment of Heidegger's implication in Nazism? Heidegger's politics does not dictate a judgement, but it does, rightly, make us sceptical. Rather than assuming, as Olafson seems to do, that *Being and Time* can rise above the politics, we need to see to what extent *Being and Time*, and the lecture courses that were central in its development, are already political. Olafson makes the suggestion that 'what is true is that Heidegger's one attempt to formulate a social philosophy was not only a disastrous failure but betrayed the best inspiration of his own thought as well'.[17] For *this* judgement to be true, the level of engagement with both needs to be much more sustained.

Better examples that could be given here are Jacques Derrida's painstaking examination of Heidegger's use of the word *Geist* (that Olafson criticises), Charles Bambach's analysis of notions of autochthony, and Janicaud and de Beistegui's more general studies.[18] Superficially similar are Young's attempts to suggest that Heidegger's thought can be consistent with liberal democracy;[19] and, at the other end of the scale, Ernst Nolte's biography, which does not merely admit the Nazi affiliation, but suggests that it was the only valid response to the problems of the times.[20] As Sheehan acidly notes, 'with friends like Nolte, Heidegger may not need enemies'.[21]

In aspiration at least, this book is closer to the first four, and in large part this study is undertaken through a contextualised textual reading, examining the words and ideas Heidegger uses, and the situation in which he was speaking. It is for this reason that there is such an emphasis on language in this study – both as a topic of concern, and as a method of inquiry. This text is, it has to be said, littered with Heidegger's German and Aristotle's Greek. But this emphasis on words is not arbitrary. As Klemperer points out, 'Nazism permeated the flesh and blood of the people through single words, idioms and sentence structures which were imposed on them in a million repetitions and taken on board mechanically and unconsciously . . . Words can be like tiny doses of arsenic'.[22] Heidegger's use of words is one of the most important aspects of his thought, and his analysis of words one of his ways of coming to terms with the Nazi regime. As Bourdieu puts it, 'we must abandon the opposition between a political reading and a philosophical reading, and undertake a simultaneously political and philosophical *dual reading*'.[23]

There are a number of ways such a political and philosophical reading can be done – one would be to investigate why Heidegger allied himself to National Socialism in the first place; another why he continued to believe it had potential for 'greatness'; a third why he felt it had, in practice, failed. Each of these will receive some treatment in this study. It is, of course, important to recognise that 'National Socialism' was never a unified body of action or thought, and that, as Sluga notes, not only did a range of philosophers commit in some way to National Socialism, 'they did so for a number of different and mutually incompatible philosophical reasons'.[24] This should make us guard against a straightforward case of thinking that because

Heidegger criticised or distanced himself from some aspect of National Socialism, that this was a straightforward rejection. Criticism of National Socialism could come from within as well as without. As Gillespie suggests, 'Heidegger himself had no doubts that his earlier thought was compatible with at least some idealised version of Nazism'.[25] Gillespie continues to suggest that Heidegger 'never abandoned his support for the ideals of National Socialism' and that, 'coupled with his unremitting criticism of other contemporary political possibilities, there is little doubt that Heidegger continued to regard the Nazi movement as the most promising political development of his time'.[26] While I would broadly support this interpretation, what is in danger of being missed here is why Heidegger offered 'unremitting criticism' of other political positions – notably Bolshevism and Americanism – and why National Socialism in practice, *if not in theory*, was equally a failure. Here, then, the continual stress will be more on the thought than the politics, but with a recognition that this treatment of the thought must be understood to include the *political* thought. Indeed, as Sheehan has suggested, 'major elements of his philosophy are deeply flawed by his notions of politics and history – and that this is so quite apart from the fact that he joined the Nazi party and, for whatever period of time, ardently supported Hitler'.[27]

Equally, if the relation of his thought to his political career has been less well examined, even more rare – for obvious reasons – have been attempts to utilise his thought for political purposes. For even when Heidegger is profoundly wrong, he is never less than interesting. The book will insist that questions of language and calculation in Heidegger are inherently political, and that a far broader range of his work is therefore concerned with politics than is usually admitted.

One of the key issues that runs through this book is the understanding of *Mitsein*, of being-together. This is both an issue in relation to the being-together of humans both in the world, generally, but more specifically in community, and the mode of connection of the material world itself. While there are a similar set of issues at play in both, the recurrent theme here is that which divides Heidegger's major work, *Being and Time*. As Chapter One will outline at length, this work can be profitably understood as structured around the Aristotelian distinction between *poiesis* and *praxis*, between making and doing. In the *Nicomachean Ethics*, Aristotle both differentiates these modes of activity, and the character of the intellectual reflection that informs them, namely *tekhne* and *phronesis*. *Poiesis* is concerned with things in the world, which do not share our mode of being, such as equipment, matter and nature; *praxis* with things which do share our mode of being, other humans. As this book will show, it is useful to read *Being and Time* as concerned with the *tekhne* of *poiesis* in the first part of Division I; and in the second part of that Division and Division II, with the *phronesis* of *praxis*.

Chapter One deals with the second issue, which although secondary in *Being and Time* informs a wide range of Heidegger's early lecture courses. It therefore deals with *speaking*, as Heidegger's privileged example of how humans interconnect, both as beings-in-the-world and beings-in-the-*polis*. Heidegger reads Aristotle's definition of the human as the *zoon ekhon logon*, as that being that has the *logos*, as the being that has language, the being that *speaks*. In this he criticises understandings of the human as the rational animal, suggesting that logic or *ratio* are narrow and particular ways of reading the notion of *logos*. Reading the full range of Heidegger's early lectures on Aristotle, but concentrating on the one from Summer Semester 1924, the first half of the chapter shows how the privileged political text for Heidegger is the *Rhetoric*. However, the speech community envisaged, a being-in-the-*polis*, highlights some problematic issues concerning leadership and exclusion which, while in themselves seemingly neutral, open up a number of crucial problems.

These problems are pursued in the second half of the chapter, which moves to the next course Heidegger delivered, where he devoted the first half to a painstaking analysis of the *Nicomachean Ethics*. The concentration here is on the notion of *phronesis*, suggesting that it is symptomatic that Heidegger neglects to analyse a short but telling passage where Aristotle shows how this virtue functions in three domains: concerning the self, the *oikia* and the *polis*. In this reading, Heidegger strips out the ethical in order to reach the ontological issues, and thereby opens himself up to the political problems that would later entangle him, particularly in the notion of being-together politically. This is especially evident through his inability to distinguish leading from guiding.

Chapter Two analyses the material in which Heidegger works out the implications of the tensions in his thinking of political community. Beginning with a reading of Heidegger's work on truth, it shows how Heidegger moved to an understanding of politics as *polemos*, as struggle, *Kampf*, and as war, *Krieg*, orientating himself and the German *Volk* in terms of a position *against*. Reading Heidegger shows how he was very much a novice in political theorisation, and how his explicit political involvement was founded on his deeply problematic sense of just what politics was.

This is particularly pursued through an examination of two lecture courses Heidegger gave under the title of *The Essence of Truth*, from 1931–32 and 1933–34, that is before and during the Rectorial period. Taking Heidegger's 1935 assertion of the 'the inner truth and greatness of National Socialism' as its themes, it shows how a particular reading of Plato's myth of the cave in the *Republic* led him to a view of what the role of the philosopher actually was. This, then, is the pivotal section of the book. If Heidegger's violent interpretation of politics as struggle is difficult to see as separate from Hitler and Schmittian conceptions of the political, immediately following the resignation things begin to get much more complicated. The second half of the chapter therefore examines a lecture course on language and the *Volk*, along with material on Hölderlin, which demonstrates the equivocal position he was now in. While on the one hand the deeply problematic claims remain, on the other we find him struggling to break free from at least some aspects, as an attempt to think through the problems of his grasp of the political.

Chapter Three suggests that this rethinking was most successfully done in terms of a thinking about *number*. Initially, this chapter returns to earlier work of Heidegger on mathematics, notably the excursus on Aristotle, arithmetic and geometry in the *Plato's* Sophist course. It suggests that here Heidegger thinks through some fundamentally important issues about the mode of connection of the world, but that though these inform the first division of *Being and Time* in some central ways, he does not continue the project in anything like systematic form. From around 1935, however, with the skies darkening, Heidegger consistently argues that modern understandings of politics are overdetermined through their relation to calculation.

Although it is doubtless invidious to single out a representative figure, Descartes plays just such a role in Heidegger's thought. Particularly in his *Geometry*, the distinction Aristotle proposed between the mode of connection of units and points, between arithmetic and geometry, is collapsed, thus rendering the material, external world – *res extensa* – as amenable to calculation and division. The analysis here is particularly of crucial 1930s texts such as the *Question of the Thing* course on Kant, the Nietzsche lectures, the *Beiträge zur Philosophie* and other manuscripts. Although these ideas would find most obvious expression in the later work on technology, it is in these earlier writings that we find their most explicit political context. Here we find Heidegger engaging with a context that includes *Gleichschaltung*, mechanisation, total mobilisation and the four-year plan. The reduction of the world to calculability, to measurability, is the modern malaise, and Nazism its most obvious symptom. The interrelation of machination, calculation and *tekhne* is explored here in order to concentrate on the implications this work has for Heidegger's understanding of space, politics and the globe.

The conclusion will bring together the three main strands of the book, evaluating the political implications of Heidegger's work. It will suggest that although much more of his own thought is political than usually noted, a thorough recognition of these interrelations has powerful potential. Noting how his work in the area of calculation has proved important in other studies, it will suggest that it is possible to take this forward in productive ways. Overall, the book intends to show that there is a way of using Heidegger's thought for political purposes that is not blind to the way it was employed by him, but that this is only possible through a sustained engagement with his political thought. An inquiry into the question of measure and the mode or order of connection is only one way into, through and beyond Heidegger's texts, but it is a revealing one. Taking on the political, and yet distancing itself from an understanding of the political as polemical, this book contributes to understanding of the relation of calculation to the political. In thinking the relation of calculation to politics, it opens up new ways of thinking about the political, through, as the conclusion suggests, taking the measure of the political.

Notes

1. Friedrich Nietzsche, *Menschliches, Allzumenschliches II. 2 Der Wanderer und sein Schatten*, in *Samtliche Werke: Kritische Studienausgabe*, edited by Giorgio Colli and Mazzino Montinari, Berlin and München: W. de Gruyter and Deutscher Taschenbuch Verlag, fifteen volumes, 1980, Vol. 2, p. 554; translated by R. J. Hollingdale as *The Wanderer and His Shadow*, in *Human, All-Too-Human*, Cambridge: Cambridge University Press, 1986, pp. 310–11. See also *Zur Genealogie der Moral*, II, §8, in *Samtliche Werke: Kritische Studienausgabe*, Vol. 5, p. 306; translated by Carol Diethe as *On the Genealogy of Morality*, Cambridge: Cambridge University Press, 1994, p. 49.

2. The *Gesamtausgabe*, Frankfurt am Main: Vittorio Klostermann, 1975ff, from which almost all references to Heidegger's work will be taken, will be referred to in the text as GA followed by volume number. See the list of abbreviations and volume numbers at the beginning of this volume.

3. Bruno Latour, *Pandora's Hope: Essays on the Reality of Science Studies*, Cambridge, MA: Harvard University Press, 1999, p. 252.

4. See Stuart Elden, *Mapping the Present: Heidegger, Foucault and the Project of a Spatial History*, London: Continuum, 2001, Chapters One to Three.

5. See Michel Foucault, *Sécurité, Territoire, Population: Cours au Collège de France (1977–1978)*, Paris: Seuil/Gallimard, 2004; *Naissance de la biopolitique: Cours au Collège de France (1978–1979)*, Paris: Seuil/Gallimard, 2004.

6. Michael Hardt and Antonio Negri, *Multitude: War and Democracy in the Age of Empire*, New York: The Penguin Press, 2004, p. 328.

7. Hardt and Negri, *Multitude*, p. 99. Compare Paolo Virno, *A Grammar of the Multitude*, Los Angeles: Semiotext[e], 2004, especially p. 76: 'Multitude signifies: plurality – literally: being many – as a lasting form of social and political existence, as opposed to the cohesive unity of the people. Thus, multitude consists of a network of *individuals*; the many are a *singularity*'.

8. Some of Jacques Derrida's last works attempted to think the relation of calculation to the political. See, for example, 'The "World" of the Enlightenment to Come (Exception, Calculation, Sovereignty)', *Research in Phenomenology*, Vol. XXXIII, 2003, pp. 9–52.

9. Although there are numerous links. Descartes was originally a gentleman soldier in Prince Maurice of Nassau's army, and, following his attendance at the coronation of the Emperor Ferdinand II at Frankfurt in 1619, was held up by the onset of winter in the Duchy of Neuburg, where he remained in a stove-heated room for a day and began the process of thought that led to the *Meditations*. He was given lands by the Swedish Queen Christina that she had gained through the Peace of Münster, and apparently wrote the libretto for a ballet commemorating the event – *La Naissance de la paix* – although the text that exists is almost certainly not by Descartes. See John Rockford Vrooman, *René Descartes: A Biography*, New York: GP Putnam's Sons, 1970; and Stephen Gaukroger, *Descartes: An Intellectual Biography*, Oxford: Clarendon Press, 1995.

10. See Edmund Husserl, *The Crisis of European Sciences and Transcendental Phenomenology: An Introduction to Phenomenological Philosophy*, translated by David Carr, Evanston: Northwestern University Press, 1970.

11. See Stuart Elden, 'Reading Genealogy as Historical Ontology', in Alan Milchman and Alan Rosenberg (eds), *Foucault and Heidegger: Critical Encounters*, Minneapolis: University of Minnesota Press, 2001. Some initial steps have been taken in 'Another Sense of *Demos*: Kleisthenes and the Greek Division of the *Polis*', *Democratization*, Vol. 10 No. 1, Spring 2003, pp. 135–56; and 'Missing the Point: Globalisation, Deterritorialisation and the Space of the World', *Transactions of the Institute of British Geographers*, Vol. 30 No. 1, March 2005, pp. 8–19.

12. This inquiry is made possible by the publication of Heidegger's *Gesamtausgabe*, the collected edition of his published writings, lecture courses and manuscripts, begun in 1975 shortly before his death. This is still ongoing, but at the time of writing only three of his lecture courses are unpublished, and the majority of unpublished volumes are those of his manuscripts, occasional lectures, seminars, letters and notebooks. While there will undoubtedly be much important and interesting material in these, what we have allows a very detailed analysis of his concerns. It is worth noting, though, that, in addition to the unfinished nature of this edition, there are serious problems with the edition itself. As various scholars have highlighted, there are a number of contentious editorial decisions being made, and, supposedly following Heidegger's own direction, this is not a historical-critical edition, but *Ausgabe der letzer Hand*, an 'edition of the last hand', where the materials are published as they were left, rather than as originally composed. See Thomas Sheehan, 'Caveat Lector: The New Heidegger', *New York Review of Books*, Vol. 27 No. 19, 4 December 1980, www.nybooks.com/articles/7216; Daniel Dahlstrom, 'Heidegger's Last Word', *Review of Metaphysics*, Vol. 41 No. 3, March 1988, pp. 589–606; and Theodore Kisiel, 'Heidegger's *Gesamtausgabe*: An International Scandal of Scholarship', *Philosophy Today*, Vol. 39 No. 1, Spring 1995, pp. 3–15. However, access to the original manuscripts is strictly controlled and I would lack the necessary philological skills, particularly concerning Heidegger's use of the *Sütterlinschrift* style of writing (for a sample, see http://www.freewebs.com/

m3smg2/Auf1.jpg). Despite their undoubted scholarly weak-nesses, the *Gesamtausgabe* volumes are extremely rich sources for the examination of these questions.

13. Among many others, see Richard Wolin (ed.), *The Heidegger Controversy: A Critical Reader*, Cambridge, MA: The MIT Press, 1993; Victor Farías, *Heidegger and Nazism*, translated by Paul Burrell and Gabriel R. Ricci, Philadelphia: Temple University Press, 1989; Hugo Ott, *Martin Heidegger: A Political Life*, translated by Allan Blunden, London: HarperCollins, 1993; and Hans Sluga, *Heidegger's Crisis: Philosophy and Politics in Nazi Germany*, Cambridge, MA: Harvard University Press, 1993.

14. See Pierre Bourdieu, *The Political Ontology of Martin Heidegger*, translated by Peter Collier, Cambridge: Polity, 1991, p. 3.

15. For a discussion, see Frank Edler, 'Roping in Heidegger – Philologically Speaking', *Janus Head*, Vol. 6 No. 1, 2003, pp. 159–64.

16. Frederick A. Olafson, *Heidegger and the Ground of Ethics: A Study of* Mitsein, Cambridge: Cambridge University Press, 1998, p. 14. The very debatable criticisms of Derrida can be found at pp. 6, 100–1, n. 4.

17. Olafson, *Heidegger and the Ground of Ethics*, p. 101, n. 4.

18. Jacques Derrida, *Heidegger et la question: De l'esprit et autres essais*, Paris: Flammarion, 1990; Charles Bambach, *Heidegger's Roots: Nietzsche, National Socialism, and the Greeks*, Ithaca: Cornell University Press, 2003; Dominique Janicaud, *L'ombre de cette pensée: Heidegger et la question politique*, Grenoble: Jérôme Millon, 1990; Miguel de Beistegui, *Heidegger and the Political: Dystopias*, London: Routledge, 1998. See also Richard Wolin, *The Politics of Being: The Political Thought of Martin Heidegger*, New York: Columbia University Press, 1990; Alan Milchman and Alan Rosenberg, 'Resoluteness and Ambiguity: Martin Heidegger's Ontological Politics, 1933–35', *The Philosophical Forum*, Vol. XXV No. 1, Fall 1993, pp. 72–93.

19. Julian Young, *Heidegger, Philosophy, Nazism*, Cambridge: Cambridge University Press, 1997.

20. Ernst Nolte, *Martin Heidegger: Politik und Geschichte im Leben und Denken*, Berlin: Propyläen, 1992.

21. Thomas Sheehan, 'A Normal Nazi', *New York Review of Books*, Vol. XL Nos 1–2, 14 January, 1993, pp. 30–5.

22. Victor Klemperer, *The Language of the Third Reich: LTI –*

Lingua Tertii Imperii: A Philologist's Notebook, translated by Martin Brady, London: Athlone, 2000, p. 15. See Berel Lang, *Act and Idea in the Nazi Genocide*, Chicago: University of Chicago Press, 1990, Chapter Four; Henry Friedlander, 'The Manipulation of Language', in Henry Friedlander and Sybil Milton (eds), *The Holocaust: Ideology, Bureaucracy and Genocide: The San José Papers*, Millwood, NY: Kraus International Publishers, 1980, pp. 103–29; Gordon A. Craig, *The Germans*, Harmondsworth: Penguin, 1982, pp. 322–8; George Steiner, *Language and Silence: Essays 1958–1966*, London: Faber & Faber, 1967; and John Wesley Young, *Totalitarian Language: Orwell's Newspeak and its Nazi and Communist Antecedents*, Charlottesville: University Press of Virginia, 1991.

23. Bourdieu, *The Political Ontology of Martin Heidegger*, p. 3.
24. Sluga, *Heidegger's Crisis*, p. 9.
25. Michael Allen Gillespie, 'Martin Heidegger's Aristotelian National Socialism', *Political Theory*, Vol. 28 No. 2, April 2000, pp. 140–66, p. 140; see Kathryn Brown, 'Language, Modernity and Fascism: Heidegger's Doubling of Myth', in John Milfull (ed.), *The Attractions of Fascism: Social Psychology and the Aesthetics of the 'Triumph of the Right'*, Oxford: Berg: 1990, pp. 137–54, p. 147. For a more penetrating analysis of Heidegger's relation to the movement, see Bambach, *Heidegger's Roots*.
26. Gillespie, 'Martin Heidegger's Aristotelian National Socialism', p. 140.
27. Thomas Sheehan, 'Heidegger and the Nazis', *The New York Review of Books*, Vol. XXXV No. 10, 16 June, 1988, pp. 38–47, p. 38.

One – Speaking: Rhetorical Politics

Logos, Logic and Speech

In its treatment of the question of being, *Being and Time* spends the first division of the first part on an analysis of Dasein, before moving in the second division to the relation of Dasein to temporality. As Heidegger makes clear in the introduction, the purpose of 'the analytic of Dasein remains wholly orientated towards the guiding task of working out the question of being'. It therefore does not provide 'a complete ontology of Dasein', and cannot be confused with anthropology, biology or psychology precisely because of this *ontological* focus (GA2, 17, see 45). This should doubtless be remembered when Heidegger is criticised for neglecting some key issues in *Being and Time*, such as the body, gender and so on. Nonetheless, given that he moved beyond the concentration on being itself, most explicitly in relation to politics, certain absences become both more marked and remarkable.

Language has a privileged place in *Being and Time*. Questions of speech and poetry undoubtedly play an important role throughout Heidegger's career, but even in this early period he tells us that speaking 'is what basically constitutes human Dasein' (GA19, 17–18). 'Speaking' here is his translation of the Greek *legein*, 'to speak', *Sprechen*. Speaking is a way of human expression, indeed the way of human expression, 'speaking about something, about the world' (GA19, 17–18; see GA2, 161). Because this was such a commonplace, everyday, indeed fundamental way of being, the human is defined by it, hence Aristotle's famous definition of the human as the *zoon ekhon logon* (*Politics*, 1253a9; see *Nicomachean Ethics*, 1098a3–5, 1139a5–6), the animal that has the *logos*. For Heidegger, *logos* is thus 'the *fundamental* determination [*Bestimmung*] of the being of humans as such (GA18, 18).

Heidegger suggests that '*logos* gets translated (that is always interpreted) as reason, judgement, concept, definition, ground or relationship [*Vernunft, Urteil, Begriff, Definition, Grund, Verhältnis*]' (GA2, 32). Naturally, to try to render such a putatively polysemantic word with a simple equivalent is problematic, and he recognises that his suggestion of *Rede*, discourse or talk, is insufficient as a translation unless we work through what it means. It is important to note that this is not 'language', for which Heidegger tells us the Greeks had no word, rather they 'understood this phenomenon "in the first instance" as *Rede*' (GA2, 165; GA20, 365; GA21, 6; GA29/30, 441; GA54, 103). Rather than laboriously detailing what is wrong with all the other translations, Heidegger suggests that what we find in *Rede* is the way in which what is being talked *about* is revealed through the talking, either for the speaker or those listening to them (GA2, 32–3). In a series of opaque comments, Heidegger then outlines how the other ways of translating this term are all related, at base, to this sense of *logos* as *Rede*.[1] Leaving his readers somewhat at sea, Heidegger contends that 'this interpretation of "apophantical discourse" may suffice to clarify the primary function of the *logos*' (GA2, 34). Apophantical is a straightforward rendering of the Greek *apophansis*, and means 'letting a being be seen from itself', an assertion which points to something, an indication, deriving from the verb *aufzeigen*, to point out or show.[2] Saying that 'the hammer is too heavy' does not *mean* but rather *discloses*, and not just by way of a representation of the hammer, but the very being itself. This is the very meaning of *logos* to the ancients, as 'the only clue for obtaining access to that which properly is [*zum eigentlich Seienden*], and for defining the being of such beings' (GA2, 154, see 157, 159ff).

This is a dense and contentious set of claims. *Logos* is undoubtedly related to the verb *legein*, but there is something singularly important in Heidegger according this this the fundamental meaning of discourse, of speaking.[3] In a more traditional reading, *logos* is reason, logic, rationality. Heidegger argues that the *theoretical* sense of *logos* for the Greeks was the proposition, apophantical *logos*, but this has been taken by Western philosophy to be the *only* sense, leading to varieties of propositional logic (GA19, 252–3; GA21, 153–4; GA29/30, 474). There is more, for Heidegger, in that it is a peculiarly practical sense of speech that is stressed, a sense that finds its ultimate outcome in what speech *does*, of which rhetoric is a privileged form. This is why the concentration on speaking, on language, is at the basis of Heidegger's rhetorical *politics*, because in the early 1920s, his determination of the political is fundamentally grounded upon this distinction. This raises the question of what being-together politically is, a problem that this chapter argues Heidegger fails to conceptualise adequately, and that he later attempts to resolve in two essentially different ways, explored in Chapters Two and Three respectively. Heidegger repeatedly notes how the *zoon ekhon logon* is the Greek determination of the human being which is, in this early period, explicitly equated with the *zoon politikon*, commonly translated as the 'political animal'. in other words, as we shall see, the political is founded upon language.

Although he therefore wants to pursue the particular insight that *logos* is speech, Heidegger's interest in logic in a more traditional sense is a continual one, finding expression in a number of key lecture courses centred on the question, and in extensive discussions elsewhere. Early in his career Heidegger had written on questions of logic, such as the paper '*Neuere Forschungen über Logik* [New Research on Logic]' (1912) and his dissertation '*Die Lehre vom Urteil in Psychologismus: ein kritisch-positiver Beitrag zur Logik* [The Lesson of Judgment in Psychology: A Critical-Positive Contribution to Logic]' (1913) (GA1, 17–43; 59–188). In 1915 he suggests that the work of his *Habilitationsschrift* – a post-doctoral dissertation to allow him to teach – on Duns Scotus (GA1, 189–412) has led to a future plan 'of a comprehensive presentation of medieval logic and psychology in the light of modern phenomenology, partnered by a consideration of the historical situation of individual medieval thinkers' (GA16, 39).[4] Although this was not undertaken, in his later career Heidegger is particularly interested in questions of logic in their usual sense in relation to Kant (GA21, GA25), Husserl (GA17, GA21) and Leibniz (GA26).

Indeed, *Being and Time*, in its originally conceived plan, is not unconcerned with the question of logic. While the references to 'logic' in a modern sense are few, the crucial course *The Basic Problems of Phenomenology*, which is understood as 'a new elaboration of Division 3 of Part 1 of *Being and Time*' (GA24, 1), contains a detailed discussion of logic and its history within the tradition (GA24, 252–320). Heidegger considers that Kant and Hegel brought logic back into the central preoccupations of philosophy, without managing to avoid its slip back into merely 'academic logic'. In this course the positions of Aristotle, Hobbes, John Stuart Mill and Hermann Lotze, among others, are discussed, along with the more recent – at the time – work of Emil Lask and Husserl.[5] Similar themes had been discussed in earlier lecture courses, notably 1919's *Phenomenology and Transcendental Philosophy of Value* (GA56/57). The discussions of logic in themselves need not delay us unduly here, but do need to be read in a dual sense as part of Heidegger's work on the destructuring of the tradition; and as part of his retrieval of the ontological. The explication of Kant's use of logic in the Winter Semester 1927–28 course, for example, relates the different senses of logic found in the *Critique of Pure Reason* to the *Lectures on Logic*, stressing particularly transcendental logic, or ontological logic (GA25, 169–70).[6]

But even here he wants us to return to Aristotle, and the fundamental determinations of *logos* as speech he finds in *De Anima* and elsewhere (GA25, 171). In this he finds substantial support in Kant's lectures, which give 'a brief sketch of the history of logic, which shows that in his view logic since Aristotle has not made a single step forward and also does not need to' (GA25, 180; see GA40, 143–4). While traditional logic 'gave the impression that everything had been put to order', Kant demonstrates this is not the case (GA25, 181). Even Hegel's *Logic* is described as 'meant to give nothing but an ontology worked out on the basis of a presumably radicalised Kantian position' (GA25, 294).[7] This is a book, suggests Heidegger, rather unfairly, which 'lives from the tables of others . . . simply assimilates and reworks the one traditional form of logic' (GA63, 45). An indication of the limits of the tradition can be found right at the beginning of the introduction to *Being and Time*, where Heidegger suggests that the question of being is one which exercised Plato and Aristotle, but then falls into disrepair down until Hegel's *Logic* (GA2, 2).[8] Indeed, in the early Heidegger, it is Hegel – rather than, as later, Nietzsche – who is 'the last great metaphysician in Western metaphysics', and for whom 'metaphysics coincides with logic as the science of reason' (GA29/30, 420, see 508).[9]

In the course that followed, explicitly intended to deal with the metaphysical groundings of Leibniz's proposition that 'nothing is without reason', Heidegger again makes a similar set of moves. He begins by noting that while logic is an abbreviation of the Greek *logike*, it is really an abbreviation of the *episteme logike*, the science or knowledge [*Wissenschaft*] that deals with *logos* (GA26, 1; see GA21, 1). Something similar can be said of the *Wissenschaft* that deals with *phusis* or that which deals with *ethos*, but while the former deals with the world and the latter with humans, that which deals with *logos* is the more fundamental, indeed it is a connection [*Seinszusammenhang*] between the other two universals (GA21, 3). What is interesting is that in a number of languages the science of something will later be rendered from the root of *logos* itself – biology, theology, technology.[10] Again he moves to Aristotle (GA26, 29–32), repeating many of the points of previous semesters' courses. More explicit here, perhaps, is the sense that this is preliminary to the real or actual theme of the course – the metaphysical foundations (GA26, 32–3).

Indeed, it seems that whenever Heidegger engages with the tradition it is to serve his primary purpose of regaining the more originary sense of logic he finds in his readings of Aristotle (for example GA20, 115–16, 364–5; GA21, 25); or of outlining how the fallen sense of logic as proposition emerged (for example, GA20, 344). Heidegger's insistent claim is that the problem of logic is today understood too narrowly, and that the notion of *logos* is reduced to this narrow understanding. Indeed, he claims that 'philosophy, after Aristotle, no longer understands the problem of genuine logic', it has been reduced to formal, academic logic (GA61, 20; see GA1, 17–43).[11] Despite this, Heidegger wants to reclaim the original sense of logic (GA20, 2), a logic that would not be an ontic logic, a school logic, but a hermeneutically ontological logic, looking at the interaction of being, truth and language (GA21, 12–19; GA18, 9). 'Scholastic logic' is a 'form of laziness . . . a fraud' (GA21, 12). Logic for Heidegger was always a logic of logic: ontology was the science of being, *logos* was the way of access to the being of beings (GA19, 438; see 205, 529, 626 Supplement 25; GA1, 288); logic was a science of the ways being was addressed and articulated.[12] The *logos* of the *on* – in other words, ontology in its root form – means 'the addressing [*Ansprechen*] (*legein*) of beings as beings, yet at the same time it signifies that *with respect to which* beings are addressed (*legomenon*)' (GA9, 132/104; see GA29/30, 521). In a marginal note added to a transcript of the *Plato's* Sophist course, Heidegger suggests that 'logic' comes 'precisely from onto-logy; the "logy" more original than logic' (GA19, 438, n. 3).

Reading Aristotle

It is therefore clear that, as with so much else in his early career, it is through a detailed engagement with Aristotle that Heidegger pursues these claims concerning logic and ontology. Indeed, the publications in the *Gesamtausgabe* have made it apparent just how much time he spent on this topic, in lectures, seminars and intended publications. For Heidegger, Aristotle deserves an honoured place in Greek thought and even the entire Western philosophical tradition (GA18, 5).[13]

Initially beginning with a seminar exercise on *De Anima* in 1921, the first full course was given in the Winter Semester 1921–22, and was entitled *Phenomenological Interpretations: Initiation into Phenomenological Research*. This appeared in the University catalogue as 'Phenomenological Interpretations (Aristotle)' (GA61),[14] and has been published as *Phenomenological Interpretations of Aristotle*, although more accurately this would be *Phenomenological Interpretations to* [zu] *Aristotle*. Indeed it was a course that Heidegger always referred to merely as 'Introduction' (see GA63, 47),[15] intended to pave the way for work *on* Aristotle, which came in huge detail in the following semester's course, as yet unpublished (Summer Semester 1922 – to appear as GA62).[16] This was under the title of *Phänomenologische Interpretationen ausgewählter Abhandlungen des Aristoteles zu Ontologie und Logik* [Phenomenological Interpretations of Various Treatises of Aristotle on Ontology and Logic]. The next semester was one of the very few during which Heidegger did not lecture, but he began a monumental seminar, continuing into the next semester, while revising some of his notes towards a book he was planning on writing on Aristotle. The introduction to this book, never completed, but circulated for employment purposes, is the now famous *Phenomenological Interpretations to Aristotle: Indication of the Hermeneutic Situation* piece (PIA). Aristotle plays an important role in the next two courses (GA63 and GA17), before the central *Grundbegriffe der aristotelischen Philosophie* [Basic Concepts of Aristotelian Philosophy] (GA18), and a major part of the *Plato's Sophist* course (GA19) is devoted to him. (We should also note a further seminar on the *Nicomachean Ethics* in Summer Semester 1922, and one on *Physics* Book B in Winter Semester 1923–24, to appear as GA83).[17]

A wealth of material, then, much of which will be analysed throughout this chapter, and returned to in a different context in Chapter Three. We can see the contours of his overall project very clearly in the draft of the Aristotle book introduction. Heidegger suggests that 'the following investigations serve a history [*Geschichte*] of ontology and logic' (PIA, 7/111), the two categories of the course due to appear as GA62. Aristotle provides the basis, the ground, for an investigation into these crucial categories:

> The problematic of philosophy has to do with the being of factical life. In this regard, philosophy is principal *ontology* . . . The problematic of philosophy has to do with the being of factical life in the how of its being-claimed and being-interpreted at any particular time [*im jeweiligen Wie des Angesprochen- und Ausgelegtseins*]. This means that philosophy,

as the ontology of facticity, is at the same time the categorical interpretation of the claiming and interpreting; that is, *logic*.

Ontology and logic are to be brought back into the primordial unity of the problematic of facticity and are to be understood as the expressions of principal research; which can be described as the *phenomenological hermeneutics* of facticity. (PIA, 29/121)

We can see here how the interpretation of *logos* as speech is crucial to understanding the overall project of a hermeneutics of facticity, of existence. This 'translation', then, is not merely a means of distancing himself from the tradition, nor simply a gloss on Aristotle. Rather, it is a rendering which goes to the very heart of his inquiry.

With this there is indicated the *visual stance* [*Blickstand*] which the following interpretations, as phenomenological and as investigations into the history of ontology and logic, will take. The idea of the phenomenological hermeneutic of facticity includes within it the tasks of: formal and material object-theory [*Gegendstandslehre*] and logic; the theory of science [*Wissenschaftslehre*]; the 'logic of philosophy'; the 'logic of the heart'; the logic of 'pre-theoretical and practical' thought; and it includes these within itself, not as some unifying collective concept, but rather according to its own effective force as the principal approach of the philosophical problematic. (PIA, 31/122)[18]

One of the key reasons behind Heidegger's concern with *logos* comes in the context of a discussion of the root of phenomenology, his mode of investigation. Heidegger wants to trace a history of these 'two originary words of Greek philosophy', namely *phainomenon* and *logos* (GA17, 1–2).[19] The Greek notion of *logos* was understood, he suggests, as 'discourse' about being. In this respect logic was hermeneutics, not understood in its common usage, but in the particular sense Heidegger gives it both in the book introduction and in the subtitle of one of his courses, *Hermeneutics of Facticity* (GA63).[20] Hermeneutics indicates, therefore, 'in connection with its original meaning . . . a definite unity in the actualising of *hermeneuein* (of communicating), i.e., of the interpreting of facticity in which facticity is encountered, seen, grasped, and conceptualised' (GA63, 14; see GA2, 37).

Heidegger pursues this through readings of some works of Aristotle, notably *Peri Psuches*, and *Peri Hermeneias*. *Peri Psuches*, sometimes known by its Latin title *De Anima*, is usually translated as 'On the Soul'. But Heidegger cautions that this title is already misleading, if we simply stop here, because it fails to take into account the central role of language, *Sprache*. Heidegger argues that 'perception [*Wahrnehmung*], thinking, and desiring [*Wollen*] are for Aristotle not experiences [*Erlebnisse*]'. Accordingly, *Peri Psuches* 'is not psychology in the modern sense, but deals with the being of humans (that is, of the living person [*Lebendem*] in general) in the world' (GA17, 6; see GA19, 26–7).

It is the same with speaking, so we need to be equally careful in our interpretation of the notion of *logos*. '*Logos* is phonetic [*lautliches*] being, that means it is voice [*Stimme*]' (GA17, 14). The classic place to look for this is *Peri Hermeneias* (*De interpretatione* or *On Interpretation*) Book 4, where Aristotle provides a definition of *logos*: '*Logos de esti phone semantike*' (16b26). A standard English translation has this as 'a sentence is significant speech', although *phone* is more usually voice or sound. Heidegger does not really translate this phrase, but poses a number of questions: 'The first question is now: What is *phone*, then *phone semantike*, finally: what is *logos*?' (GA17, 14; see GA19, 18). For Aristotle, 'the *phone* is a noise that pertains essentially only to a living being' (420b6–7); so while only animals can produce voice, the *phone semantike*, that is the *logos*, is particular to humans. Aristotle makes it clear in this classic definition that though all sentences have this meaning, this *semantike*, this does not mean that they are all propositions, that we could ascribe truth or falsehood to them. In sum, all *logos* are *semantikos*, that is *phone semantike*, but not all *logos semantikos* are *apophanitikos*: not all forms of signifying speech are apophantical (GA29/30, 448–9). A request or a prayer, for example, is a *logos*, but does not have a characteristic of either *alethes* or *pseudes*, truth or falsehood (17a1–6). Heidegger adds questions, instructions, requests or calling attention [*Aufmerksammachen*] to this category – they are not 'true or false', so it makes no sense to call them judgements. Whilst they may be *aletheuein*, a mode of being-true, of uncovering, not all instances of *logos* are (GA17, 20; see GA21, 129–30). Instead of seeing truth in terms of propositions, we should see propositions in terms of truth.[21] 'Speaking is being with the world, it is something originary and situated before judgement' (GA17, 20–1).

Heidegger therefore suggests that Aristotle's *De interpretatione* 'deals with *logos* in terms of its basic accomplishment of uncovering and making us familiar with beings' (GA63, 10). *Logos* has a fundamental property of *aletheuein*, that is, 'making what was previously concealed, covered up, available as unconcealed, as there out in the open' (GA63, 11). The *Genesis* of words is therefore not the physio-logical being of humans, but their proper existence [*eigentlichen Existenz*]. As long as the human is in the world, it has need of speech: 'it speaks, insofar as the world is discovered as a matter of concern [*Besorgbares*] for it and in the "for it" sees itself' (GA17, 16). This does not mean that the word is simply there like a work-tool [*Werkzeug*], an organ [*organon*] (17a2), as, for example, the hand is. Rather, 'speech is the being and becoming [*Werden*] of humans themselves' (GA17, 16). Heidegger goes on to relate this to the question of time, and our experience of this (GA17, 16–17).

Whilst we therefore have some sense of what *logos* is, this is a mere *Vormeinung*, a pre-opinion. We still have no idea what the concept of *logos* meant for the Greeks, in its natural state of Dasein. Hellenism – that is, later Greek thought – has turned this into linguistics and grammar, 'a doctrinaire treatment and theory' (GA17, 17; see GA29/30, 451). All modern language formulations come from this, as indeed does the theory of knowledge and other related issues, so that the question of how the Greeks lived in their language is no longer asked. But, Heidegger suggests, 'the Greeks lived in their language in an excellent way, were lived by it; and they were conscious of this' [*ausgezeichneten Weise in der Sprache und wurde von ihr gelebt; und war ihm bewußt*]. It is this understanding that Heidegger claims is behind Aristotle's observation that the being of humans can be defined as *logon ekhein*, as having speech (*Politics*, 1253a9). This is grounded on 'the responding and discussing ability of the meeting of world and self, which requires no philosophy' (GA17, 17–18; GA22, 310).

Because of this, Heidegger suggests that:

> We should be wary of the concept of a 'being endowed with reason' insofar as it does not capture the decisive meaning of *zoon logon ekhon*. In the paragon academic philosophy of the Greeks (Aristotle), *logos* never means 'reason', but rather discourse, conversation [*Rede, Gespräch*] – thus man is a being which has its world in the mode of something addressed (GA63, 21–2).

This traditional definition has become that of *animal rationale* (GA63, 26; GA18, 13), which covers up the phenomenal basis for this definition of 'Dasein' (GA2, 165). This means that though the Greeks understood this in a fundamental way, the term has become something entirely other:

The position which looked at the human with the definition 'animal rationale' as its guide saw them in the sphere of other Daseins [*Daseinenden*] with them in the mode of life (plants, animals) and indeed as a being which has language (*logon ekhon*), which addresses and discusses its world – a world initially there for it in the dealings it goes about in its *praxis*, its concern taken in a broad sense. The later definition '*animal rationale*', 'rational animal', which was indifferently understood simply in terms of the literal sense of the words, covered up the intuition which was the soil out of which this definition of human being originally arose (GA63, 27–8).

In addition, in reading the term *zoon ekhon logon*, we should bear in the mind that to say that the human is the animal or being which *has* language is not to say that they merely possess it, but that they are, at the same time possessed by it. As Aristotle notes in the *Metaphysics*, having means both an activity of the haver and the thing had, and a disposition or comportment (1022b4–14, see 1023a8–25; GA33, 151/129). Having is akin to holding, in the way that a fever has hold of a man, or a tyrant has hold of a city (1023a10). The verb is, as Hatab puts it, in between the haver and the thing had.[22]

Speaking [*das Reden*] is therefore not a characteristic [*Eigenschaft*] like 'having hair', but 'constitutes the specific existence [*Existenz*] of humans', because 'the human is in the world in such a manner that this being with the world is what it speaks about' (GA17, 21). This is a fundamental definition of being-human, a life in the possibility of dealings [*Umgänge*] with *pragmata*, the world as a matter of concern [*besorgbaren*], such that in its being it speaks. 'The being is in its *praxis* essentially characterised by speech' (GA17, 21–2). *Logos* is a possibility of human being, which brings it to the highest possibility of its being, the *eu zen* (*De Anima*, 420b20). But this is no longer mere *logos*, but *dialektos*, speaking with others, *hermeneia* (420b19), moving toward an understanding with others (GA17, 21–2). Speaking is therefore at one with the mode of hearing, listening. It should therefore not be understood in isolation, but as part of an exchange, what we might call a speech community (GA17, 28).[23]

In this last formulation we are getting ahead of ourselves, as this notion is discussed in much greater detail in the following semester's course, and forms the basis of discussion in the next section of this chapter. What has been clearly established is that for Heidegger, in his reading of Aristotle, the human can be defined as that being that has the *logos*, that has speech. Indeed, this is how the question of 'logic', in the sense of *logos*, is discussed in *Being and Time*. The second half of the introduction, for example, is very closely concerned with this originary sense of *logos*. From this position of having read Heidegger's early lecture courses, we can see just how much work is behind his claim that 'Dasein, the being of humans, is "defined" as the *zoon logon ekhon* – as that living thing whose being is essentially deter-mined by the potentiality for discourse [*Redenkönnen*]' (GA2, 25).[24] It is worth noting that the idea that the human is the *zoon ekhon logon* is one of the two clues Heidegger notes are crucial to philosophical anthropology – this one, which sees the human as 'rational animal', and a theological one: 'And God said, let us make man in our image, after our likeness' (Genesis I:26). In their traditional interpretations, as Heidegger makes clear, neither the question of being, or what might be actually meant by the claims is interrogated (GA2, 489).[25] For Heidegger, though, '*legein* is the clue for arriving at those structures of being which belong to the entities we encounter in addressing ourselves to anything or speaking about it' (GA2, 25). What we also find here is that Heidegger folds *legein* into *noein*, to think or to know (GA2, 25–6, see 44). As he later makes clear, 'knowing the world (*noein*) – or rather addressing oneself to the "world" and discussing it (*logos*) – thus functions as the primary mode of being-in-the-world, even though being-in-the-world is not understood as such' (GA2, 59). It is difficult to see how this could be any more central to Heidegger's inquiry.

The Importance of Rhetoric

Three key political topics emerge from this set of concerns, all closely related, and all found in Heidegger's work on Aristotle from this period. Although references will be made to other texts, the concen-tration here is on what two courses can contribute to our under-standing of these topics: rhetoric; political community or the issue of *Mitsein*, being together; and the question of leadership. The first course is *Basic Concepts of Aristotelian Philosophy*, or, as it is listed in some places, *Aristotle's* Rhetoric (GA18); the second is entitled *Plato's* Sophist (GA19). These two courses, together with their suc-cessor course *History of the Concept of Time* (GA20), are from the years 1924 to 1925, and, as Kisiel has shown, are the furnace from which *Being and Time* was forged.[26] But while large sections of *History of the Concept of Time* – such as the analyses of worldhood, being-in-the-world, everydayness, care and spatiality – are self-evidently very close to *Being and Time*, the relation of the other two courses is more difficult to discern. What emerges from close reading is that many of the keywords of *Being and Time* are actually Heidegger's renderings of terms in Aristotle's thought.

As I will show in detail later in this chapter, it has long been recognised that the *Nicomachean Ethics* is central here, but what we find in *Basic Concepts of Aristotelian Philosophy* is that the *Politics*, and most explicitly the *Rhetoric*, are also very important. *Basic Concepts of Aristotelian Philosophy*, despite hiding behind a bland title, is one of Heidegger's most remarkable courses, not least because it is explicitly political, perhaps beyond anything else Heidegger wrote before 1933.[27] As Heidegger confessed to Karl Löwith, this course, which was originally slated to have been on Augustine, was changed to this topic in order to have one final attempt at getting the Aristotle book into print.[28] But the question immediately arises as to why a course devoted to Aristotle's 'basic concepts' should accord the *Rhetoric* such a privileged place, alongside more obvious texts such as the *Physics*, *Metaphysics*, *Politics* and *Nicomachean Ethics*?

Aside from this course, there are but a few references to the importance of the *Rhetoric* in Heidegger's works. One of them comes in *Being and Time*, where Heidegger suggests that 'contrary to the traditional orientation, where rhetoric is considered as something we learn in school, Aristotle's work must be taken as the first systematic hermeneutic of the everyday character of being-with-another [*Miteinanderseins*]' (GA2, 138). In the *Sophist* course, he states that Aristotle's advantage over Plato is that by 'penetrating through to the proper structure of *logos* [he] made it possible to institute a genuine investigation of *logos* itself. It likewise makes it possible for the *logos* that is not theoretical, i.e. for speech that is not in service to *dialegesthai*, to receive a certain justification within the context of everyday Dasein'. Speaking does not have to aim for *aletheia*, but pertains to everyday Dasein: this is Aristotle's 'genuine discovery' (GA19, 339).[29] As he had suggested somewhat earlier in that course, 'only on the basis of a positive understanding of the phenomenon of *legein* within life (as can be found in the *Rhetoric*)' did Aristotle really come to terms with this phenomena (GA19, 199–200).[30] In 1925 Heidegger suggests that rhetoric is the first part of logic properly understood, that is, as *speech* (GA20, 364).

The Hellenistic period and the early Middle Ages have demeaned rhetoric to be a school-discipline, just as they have with logic. But actually, for Aristotle, Heidegger suggests, 'rhetoric is nothing other than the interpretation [*Auslegung*] of concrete Dasein, the hermeneutic of Dasein itself', indeed the discipline where this self-interpretation explicitly takes place (GA18, 110; see GA20, 365). As Scult notes, it is 'the very concreteness of its focus that makes the *Rhetoric* the perfect site for the realization of certain key aspects of Aristotle's ontology'.[31] We can see this exhibited most explicitly in the discussion of the emotions or passions at the beginning of Part Two of the *Rhetoric* (1377b–1388b; see GA20, 393).[32]

The passage from *Being and Time* concerning the *Rhetoric* is explicitly in relation to what Heidegger finds in Aristotle's discussion of *pathe*, as is the reference in the *History of the Concept of Time* course, which, in both cases, later informs his discussions of fear (GA2, 342; GA20, 393ff). It is indeed to Book II of the *Rhetoric* that Heidegger devotes much attention in *Basic Concepts*, albeit with productive detours through the *Ethics*, *De Anima*, *Parts of Animals* and other texts (see, especially, GA18, 161–72, 179, 183, 246–61). What Heidegger finds remarkable is that this interpretation of affects – and he uses the German word *Affekt* here to translate *pathe* – is not psychology, but is concerned with the moods created through rhetoric and the moods that create rhetoric: 'it is into such a mood and out of such a mood that the orator speaks. He must understand the possibilities of moods in order to rouse them and guide them aright' (GA2, 138–9; see GA18, 122, 197). Mood here is the difficult term *Stimmung*, which is also sometimes rendered as attunement, and is analysed in *Being and Time* in relation to fear and angst, and in *The Fundamental Concepts of Metaphysics* to boredom. Scult makes much of this insight:

> Thus, for Heidegger's Aristotle, the situations in which we find ourselves, which comprise the world in which we live, call us to live our particular lives by imposing themselves upon us as highly charged emotional moods; and we move about in the world, becoming ourselves, by articulating responses to those moods that seem 'appropriate' in our life with others.[33]

Despite its central role, it is worth noting that the point of this course is not explicitly to think about rhetoric, but to illuminate the basic concepts of Aristotle's philosophy, conceptually, listed as the thirty we find discussed in the *Metaphysics* Book V (1012b–1025a; GA18, 3–4). Many of these concepts were philosophically nuanced readings of everyday Greek terms. Heidegger is concerned with precisely the same kind of move. Except that goal is not the concepts in themselves, but their conceptuality, their *Boden*, literally their soil, that is their ground or basis (GA18, 4). In other words the underlying structure, hermeneutically, of Aristotle's thought. The two most central for Heidegger are the seventh and eighth, *on* and *ousia*. The first is being, the second he glosses as *Dasein* (GA18, 3; see 25). '*Ousia* is the expression as such for the basic concept of Aristotelian philosophy' (GA18, 22). In this course, the means of access into the question is through the human as the being possessing speech. As Kisiel summarises:

> Hence, many themes that were given short shrift in BT [*Being and Time*], according to critical readers, are dealt with in great detail in SS 1924: animality, corporeality, the life of pleasure, Dasein both as consumer and as producer; speech in its full amplitude of possibilities, authentic as well as inauthentic, practical as well as theoretical; being-with as speaking to one another toward communal ends, with special attention to the problem of political rhetoric.[34]

Most important for our current purpose is the way the notion of being-with-another, *Miteinandersein*, is understood as coming about through speech, and the concomitant listener (GA18, 45–7, 123, 134). In an important early passage of this course, Heidegger notes that all speaking is a speaking about something, and a speaking to someone. Language is something concrete: humans do not solely exist, but constitute themselves through their speaking with others. 'All speaking is, especially for the Greeks, a speaking to one or with another, with itself or to itself' (GA18, 17). All 'life is being-in-a-world, animal and human are present [*vorhanden*] not beside another, but with another [*nicht neben anderen, sondern mit anderen*]'. The difference is that, for the human, they constitute each other mutually through speech (GA18, 21). This is why the Greeks perceive the human as *zoon ekhon logon*, not only philosophically, but in their concrete lives. Language is a fundamental determination of human being-in-the-world; it is what separates us from the animals' way of being-in-the-world (GA18, 17–18, 49).[35] A living being [*ein Lebendes*] is not to be understood physiologically, but as one that has its proper existence [*eigentliches Dasein*] in 'conversation and in discourse' (GA18, 108). As an approximate contemporary (1924), and perhaps explicitly German, translation of the *zoon ekhon logon*, Heidegger offers the idea that 'the human is a living being that reads the newspapers' (GA18, 108).

Heidegger gives some time over to an analysis of animality and its being-in-the-world, and what distinguishes it from the humans' way of being-in-the-world (for example, GA18, 53–62). In doing so, a whole range of the issues familiar to us from *Being and Time* begin to emerge – care, everydayness, the one [*das Man*], to name the most obvious. As was intimated earlier, these and other terms familiar from *Being and Time* emerge through an engagement with Aristotle, not just from the *Nicomachean Ethics*, but also the *Politics* and the *Rhetoric*.

The crucial point about speech is the interpretation of concrete Dasein: 'That is for Aristotle the intended sense of rhetoric. Speaking in the manner of speaking-in-discourse [*Sprechens-in-der-Rede*]: in the people's assembly [*Volksversammlung*]; before the court; celebratory rhetoric [*bei feierlichen Gelegenheiten*]'. What is interesting for Heidegger is that 'these possibilities of speaking are definite [*exponierte*] examples of ordinary speaking, how it speaks into Dasein itself [*wie es im Dasein selbst spricht*]' (GA18, 110). It is through rhetorical activity, 'everyday speech', that human beings 'show themselves with the kind of access which genuinely belongs to them' (GA2, 61).[36] The Greeks therefore take their view of existence from everyday life and not outside, and it is clear how Aristotle comes up with his primary definition of the human as that being which has the *logos*, understood as speech (GA18, 110). It is not something arbitrary, not an invention, but the essential character of Dasein, to be speaking about something, *logos ousias*, speaking about beings, *Sprechen mit den Sachen selbst*, speaking about the matters themselves – that Husserlian motto for phenomenology (GA18, 109–10).

The examples Heidegger gives of rhetorical speech – in the assembly, before the court and in praise of something – are Aristotle's examples: forms of public discourse that necessarily have political issues.

1. The political speech aiming to lead a popular body, for Heidegger the *Volksversammlung*, to resolve a decision – *deliberative* rhetoric, *sumbouleutikon*.
2. The judicial speech before a court of law – *forensic* rhetoric, *dikanikon*, speech for the accused and the defendant.
3. The festive speech, *display* rhetoric, *epideiktikon*, a speech to praise (see 1358b8–9; GA18, 125).

Deliberative rhetoric can be either *exhortation* or *deterrence*, to persuade either for or against; forensic rhetoric can be *prosecution* or *defence*; display is either *praise* or *denigration*. Deliberative speakers speak of such concerns as revenue, war and peace, the defence of the realm, imports and exports and legislation (1359b–1360a). Each of these kinds of rhetoric also has a temporal relation – to the future for deliberative; to the past for forensic; to the present (and to an extent the past) for display (see GA18, 125–6). They equally have different objectives, *advantage* or *harm*; *justice* and *injustice*; *nobility* and *baseness* (1358b). As Kisiel notes, all of these kinds of speech are extremely politically charged in 1920s Germany – debates about the November criminals of the Weimar Republic; Hitler's famous speech to the jury following the Munich Beer Hall *Putsch*; praise speeches originally given to celebrate the victories in the Olympic games – but in 1924 are more relevant to the elegies to war heroes (of which Heidegger would give some of his own later).[37]

Being Together Politically

For Aristotle, and Heidegger following him, 'rhetoric is a kind of offshoot of dialectic and the study of ethics, and is properly characterised as political. It is therefore subsumed under the schema of politics' (*Rhetoric*, 1365a29–33). Rhetoric and, indeed, ethics are part of the wider realm of *politike* (*Ethics*, 1094a11–12), which is why the *Nicomachean Ethics* should be supplemented with the *Politics*, with which it forms a continuous inquiry, and why the *Rhetoric* is a thoroughly political text. Aristotle suggests that *strategike*, *oikonomika* and *rhetorike* – strategy, householding and rhetoric – are all subordinate to *politike* (1094b3–4), and all have their ultimate end in the good of man [*agathon tanthropinon*], which is the *telos*, the *hou heneka* – the final cause, the 'for the sake of' – of *politike* (1094b7–8). It would follow from all of this, that Heidegger's view of the political is founded upon speech, *logos*, based on this detailed reading of Aristotle's *Rhetoric*. To live with one another in the *polis* is to be part of a speech community, to possess and be possessed by language.

> In the being of the human itself lies the fundamental possibility of being-in-the-*polis*. In being-in-the-*polis* Aristotle sees the proper [*eigentlichte*] life of humans. Concerning this indication, he shows that the being of the human is *logon ekhein*. In this determination lies summarised a whole peculiar [*eigentümliche*], fundamental manner of the being of humans, characterised as being-with-another [»*Miteinandersein*«], *koinonia*. This being, that speaks with the world, is such, that is in the being-with-others [*Sein-mit-anderen*]. (GA18, 46)

The term so central to *Being and Time*, being-in-the-world, *In-der-Welt-sein*, is here being-in-the-*polis*, *In-der*-polis-*sein*. It is notable that *Being and Time*, thought to be so apolitical, and indeed mentioning politics only rarely, carries forward so much of this analysis. But it does so without the obvious use of terms such as community or society – *Gemeinschaft* or *Gesellschaft* – both ways of rendering Aristotle's *koinonia*. (There is one key exception to this, as well as a revealing aside in a lecture course on this topic, which are discussed below.) Nor does Heidegger concern himself in *Being and Time* with the term *polis*, or the misleading translation of this as 'city' or 'state', or the combination 'city-state'.[38] Instead, the political aspects come through in the notions of *Mitsein*, being-with, *Mitdasein* and *Miteinandersein*, being-with-another.

Before we come to *Being and Time*, it is worth showing how Heidegger pursues this issue in this course devoted to the analysis of the *Rhetoric*. He does this by analysing the important passage from the *Politics* where Aristotle describes the humans as the *zoon politikon* (1253a7–18; GA18, 45–9). What distinguishes the human from other animals that associate, such as bees, is that humans have *logos*, speech, while animals only have *phone*, voice or sound. Whilst animals can use voice to express pain or pleasure, speech is able to signify what is useful and harmful or just and unjust as well. This indication [*Anzeige*] is important. While animals have perception, *aisthesis*, in relation to pain and pleasure, humans have *aisthesis* in relation to good and bad, just and unjust. Animals and humans share something, but it is the question of speech and this notion of a particular type of judgement that sets them apart. 'It is the sharing of a common view [*koinonia* – association, i.e. being-with-another] in *these* matters that makes an *oikia* [a household] and a *polis*' (1253a9–17). Heidegger's paraphrasing translation of this sentence is important: 'This being-with-another in that way (i.e. the way they are in the world, that they speak with you) forms the household and the *polis*' (GA18, 47).

This importance is for a number of reasons. First, that Heidegger blurs the actual distinction that Aristotle is making. For Aristotle it is not just the speech that is important, but the kinds of things that it can indicate – good and bad, just and unjust. For Heidegger the stress is on the indication itself. Equally, although Heidegger translates *agathon* and *kakon* as good and evil, *dikaion* and *adikon* become *das Gehörige und Ungehörige*, which we might render as the 'seemly' and the 'unseemly'. Politically this is important, as it is part of Heidegger's general suggestion that notions of justice are a Latinate invention.[39]

Perhaps most importantly, and central to understanding later developments, association or community is given a definite ontological status, rather than merely being a social phenomena.

Going beyond this one sentence, Heidegger stresses this *Miteinandersein* as a fundamental character of human Dasein, not 'in the sense of being-put-additionally-to-each-other [*Nebeneinandergestelltseins*], but in the sense of the being-speaking-with-another [*Miteinandersprechendseins*] in the manner of announcement, refutation and argument [*Mitteilung, Widerlegung, Auseinandersetzung* – the latter being literally a setting apart from another]' (GA18, 47). It is not a simple case of summing up an aggregate of humans, a mere addition (GA20, 329), but the binding that comes through their shared language exchange. Humans therefore do not solely exist, but constitute themselves through their speaking with others, and it is through this community of speaking and hearing that their being-with-another is constituted. As Heidegger exhorts his students to keep in mind, 'the Greeks see existence as existence in the *polis*' (GA19, 231; see GA18, 46, 56, 67, and so on). The *zoon politikon* is indeed the *zoon ekhon logon* (GA18, 50, 56, 63–4, 134–5, and so on).[40]

The question of *Mitsein* in *Being and Time* is extremely complicated, but crucial politically.[41] Being-with is a mode of connection to others, sometimes taking form as being-with objects or animals that do not share our mode of being – a theme to be explored in detail in Chapter Three – and sometimes as being-with other humans, *Mitdasein*.[42] More generally, this theme encompasses what we might call community or society, or indeed any form of association, and as we have seen the key is language. As Heidegger makes clear, while it is true to say that the human can be understood as the being that talks, 'this does not signify that the possibility of vocal utterance is peculiar to them, but rather that they are the being which is such as to discover the world and Dasein itself' (GA2, 165). We have seen how the notion of indication is important here.

In Chapter IV of Division I of *Being and Time*, Heidegger moves from the analysis of being-in-the-world and its relation to what is present-at-hand to two other structures which are 'equiprimordial' to being-in-the-world, *Mitsein* and *Mitdasein* (GA2, 114). Dasein is in each case mine, that is, it pertains to I myself. But just as we cannot understand our being as something separate from the world, thereby rather as being-in-the-world, so too can we not understand it without a relation to others (GA2, 116; see GA20, 327; GA64, 113). These others, it is stressed, are *Dasein* themselves in their being, and are therefore being-in-the-world in their exchange with us (GA2, 118). He puts this succinctly in the *The Concept of Time* lecture: 'Dasein is as this being-in-the-world, also *being-with-another*, being with others [Mit-einander-sein, *mit Anderen sein*]: having the same world there with others, encountering one another, being with-another in the mode of being-for-another [*Für-einander-seins*]' (GA64, 113; see GA2, 121). In this sense, the others are not something entirely separate from us, 'everyone else but me', but rather those from which we do *not* distinguish ourselves (GA2, 118). Discourse is both about something, and to someone. It is therefore both being-in-the-world and being-with (GA20, 362).

> By reason of this *like-with* [mithaften – literally 'sticking-with'] being-in-the-world, the world is always already the one that I share with others. The world of Daseins is a with-world [*Mitwelt*]. Being-in is *being-with* others. Their within-the-world being-in-themselves is *Mitdasein*. (GA2, 118)[43]

Heidegger insistently makes the point that we do not encounter others as person-things [*Persondinge*] present-at-hand, but in their being-in-the-world: 'the other is encountered in their *Mitdasein* in the world' (GA2, 120). Other humans [*Mitmenschen*] 'join with us in constituting the world' (GA24, 422). But it is important to recognise that *Mitsein* is not something that occurs only when others are present, for 'being-alone is a deficient mode of being-with' (GA2, 120–1; see GA20, 328–9; GA29/30, 300–1). It is only because *Mitsein* is an essential structure of Dasein that *Mitdasein* with others is possible (GA2, 121); 'being-with others belongs to the being of Dasein, which is an issue for it in its very being' (GA2, 123).

From this, the well-known concept of 'the one' is introduced, a fall from this ideal of being-together. Instead of each Dasein being itself, this is taken away, and not by any specific other, nor by a particular other, but by an entirely general, neuter, the one, or the they. 'They' do things in this way, or 'one' does it that way. Our own Dasein is entirely dissolved into this, as is that of the others themselves – we do things as one does them, we do things as they do them. This is everydayness, averageness – it leads to levelling down and distance (GA2, 126–7; see GA20, 335ff). Something similar happens when *Rede*, that essential characteristic of humans, the *logos*, becomes *Gerede*, idle talk or chatter, which is the proper mode of the being of 'the one' (GA2, 169; GA20, 373).[44] Such modes of being are inauthentic, or perhaps better, inappropriate [*Uneigentlich*] (GA2, 175–6).[45]

It is worth noting, however, that this does not mean that we could begin the analysis with others, rather than Dasein. It is, as Heidegger carefully explains in a lecture course a couple of years after *Being and Time*, only because of the implicit egoicity of Dasein that it can exist as another for and with another Dasein. This is not an ontic statement that suggests all humans act only in their own self-interest, but an ontological statement that makes possible any kind of being-with-others, be it selfless or selfish (GA26, 240). This course here offers some quite detailed discussion of this problem (see also GA27, especially 86–92, 137–48), perhaps in defence of criticisms of this approach.[46] What is worth remembering is that each other Dasein comes from the same starting point, but that it is only through abstracting from the particular and moving to the neutral abstract that such analysis is possible at all. Heidegger notes elsewhere that while his analysis inevitably presents such issues in sequence, they are not derived from each other, but are rather *co-original* [*miteinander gleichursprünglich*] (GA20, 332; see GA21, 223–4, 226; GA64, 24). Indeed, Heidegger suggests that 'the very fact that we can make the I–you relationship into a problem at all indicates that we are transcending each factual I and factual you and that we grasp the relation as a relation of Dasein as such, that is we grasp the relationship in its metaphysical neutrality and egoicity [*Egoität*]'. While this is, in itself, defensible, he acknowledges the problem that arises: 'there are sociological, theological, political, biological, and ethical problems which ascribe a prominence to the I–you relationship; yet the philosophical problems are thereby concealed' (GA26, 241). The issue is not some particular, individual I-ness but the essence of mineness and selfhood as such, which underlies not only each individual 'I', but which also constitutes the essence of the 'you' (GA26, 242–3).

From *Mitsein* to Community

The highpoint of Heidegger's work on Aristotle came in 1924. Although he would return to him many times in his career, there is never again the level of attention that we find in the *Basic Concepts* course, which I have barely scratched the surface of, with its deep excavation of Aristotle's works. There are long discussions of passages in the *Ethics* not treated elsewhere, of the *Metaphysics* and the *Physics*. Reading both the student transcripts and the extant manuscript, collected in different parts of GA18, gives a sense of what a dynamic lecturer Heidegger was, elaborating and improvising around prescripted themes. There is an obvious rhetorical component to Heidegger's pedagogy. Had this been further developed into the projected book on Aristotle, it would doubtless have been, as Kisiel suggests, a 'remarkable' study: 'From all indications, it would have been even more difficult than BT, in view of the staggering depth, detail, and density of this Greek–German dialogue with the original texts of the Aristotelian opus, in a frenetic intensity that must have overwhelmed the students of this course'.[47]

In terms of my own concentration here on the political elements in Heidegger's thought at this time, numerous issues arise which are worth noting an although these might appear minor in 1924 or 1927 – in the Aristotle course or in *Being and Time* itself – they seem to be initial hints of how Heidegger's politics would develop in the late 1920s, and until the decision of 1933. It is, however, crucial to be aware of the potential to over-interpret. Words such as *Volk*, *Führer* and *Entscheidung* – people, leader and decision – scream off the page to contemporary eyes, but were not so burdened with their later connotations at this time. On the other hand, there is much that is hidden. When Heidegger makes reference to the being that reads the newspapers, for instance, we need to think of what would have been in them in 1924 – the economic crisis, the occupation of the Ruhr, and Weimar politics generally. It is therefore important to read Heidegger contextually, looking forward while understanding the present moment.[48]

It is equally worth noting that Heidegger would have straight-forwardly denied the idea that these *ontological* analyses lead to any particular political outcome. But it is never as simple as that. In the *History of the Concept of Time* course, he offers a reason for why the structures of community are not outlined in detail: a lack of time, and a desire to concentrate on what is essential. Being-with-another is, Heidegger reminds us, founded upon the earlier analyses of being-in, that is, being-with-another is always *in a world* (GA20, 332–3).

> This is the basis upon which this being-with-another, which can be indifferent and unconscious to the individual, can develop the various possibilities of community [*Gemeinschaft*] as well as of society [*Geschellschaft*]. Naturally these higher structures and the ways they are founded cannot be pursued here in greater detail. (GA20, 333)

What is revealing is both that Heidegger does not follow this limita-tion, betraying particular political ideas through his ontological examination, and that the source on which he so explicitly draws – Aristotle – was far from unconcerned with such issues.

An example of the latter, in the *Basic Concepts* course, is the discussion of Aristotle's claim in the *Nicomachean Ethics* (1097b8ff) that self-sufficiency includes relations with 'parents, children and wife, friends and other citizens [*politais*], since the human is by nature of the *polis* [*phusei politikon o anthropos*]'. We have both a crucial determination of the human, and the particularity of its relations. But, counters Aristotle, this can go too far: 'a limit has to be established in these relationships, for if the list be extended to one's ancestors and descendents and to the friends of friends, it will go on for ever'. Heidegger asserts, therefore, that *Miteinandersein* has to be limited: 'Appropriate [*eigentliche*] being-with-another loses itself, if it is an undisciplined or unruly with-all-humans [*ein wildes Mit-allen-Menschen*]. It is only genuine [*echtes*] therefore if it has a determined border [*bestimmte Grenze*] around it' (GA18, 96–7).[49] What is important is that the limits drawn to a political community – both actual and figurative – are clearly related to speech, they are linguistically determined. Although anything but the most utopian cosmopolitanism requires an exclusion to make the inclusion viable, this is in no sense insignificant or neutral. As has been argued insistently, if not always entirely convincingly, and as will be evaluated in Chapter Two, Heidegger's nationalism was based much more on language than race.

Another example of a political intrusion can be found in paragraph 74 of *Being and Time*, which, as various commentators have noted, includes language close to conservative politics of the later Weimar era.[50] A striking passage is the following, which for Fritsche is 'as brilliant a summary of revolutionary rightist politics as one could wish for'.[51]

But if fateful [*schicksalhafte*] Dasein exists essentially as being-in-the-world in being-with with others [*im Mitsein mit Anderen*], its happening [*Geschehen*] is a co-happening [*Mitgeschehen*] and is determinate for it as a *destiny* [Geschick]. This is how we designate the occurrence [*Geschehen*] of the community, of the people [*der Gemeinschaft, des Volkes*]. Destiny is not something that puts itself together out of individual fates [*Schicksalen*], any more than being-with-another can be conceived as the occurring together of several subjects. Our fates have already been guided in advance, in our being-with-another in the same world and in our resoluteness [*Entschlossenheit*] for definite possibilities. Only in communicating [*Mitteilung*] and in struggling [*Kampf*] does the power of destiny

[*Geschickes*] become free. Dasein's fateful destiny [*schicksalhafte Geschick*] in and with its 'generation' goes to make up the full appropriate [*eigentliche*] historicizing of Dasein. (GA2, 384–5)

There is clearly lots to say about this. Immediately important is the well-known distinction that Heidegger draws between *Geschichte* and *Histoire* – history as it actually happens, and as it is written, historiography.[52] The advantage of *Geschichte*, for Heidegger, is that it is not dependent on Latinate roots, and links to a range of other related words: to happen, destiny and fate, for example. Heidegger is suggesting that Dasein exists as *Mitsein*, and that therefore its historical orientation is equally a shared one, a *Mitgeschehen*. Where an individual has a fate, *Schicksal*, the community has a destiny, a *Geschick*, the prefix *Ge-* acting as an intensifier, a collector. But this collective destiny is not a summation of lots of individual fates, just as the community cannot be understood as a mere addition of individuals. Communication is one of the ways that this collective destiny can be understood; the other is *Kampf*. Given that this collective is not merely the neutral sounding 'community' but also the *Volk*, in other words a community determined through the people, the struggle of the people sounds like a premonition of political rhetoric to come. While he does not yet use the term *Volksgemeinschaft*, this is not far away. And crucially, the full nature of Dasein seems to be fulfilled only in this generative move, something which will reach its consequence in later texts where Heidegger talks of the Dasein of a *Volk*, a Dasein of a collective.

The dangers of this move are already evident in the difficulties that come from the orientation of such a collective. Rather than a kind of self-direction, Heidegger talks of 'the appropriate retrieval of a possibility of existence that has been – the possibility that Dasein may choose its hero – is grounded existentially in anticipatory resoluteness' (GA2, 385). Just who or what this hero might be is not made clear. Equally, in the analysis of being-toward-death, Heidegger notes that while another can deputise or stand-in for, or represent someone in many instances, this is emphatically not the case in terms of death (GA2, 239–40).[53] Of course, one person can sacrifice themselves for another, but they cannot die their death for them (GA2, 240, see 253). My concern here is not with the idea of death, but with the very idea that 'one Dasein *can be represented* [Vertretbarkeit] by another' at all. Heidegger says this is 'one of its possibilities of being in being-with-another in the world', and that this is indisputable (GA2, 239). Indeed, when *Dasein* is subsumed into the one, 'any other can represent it' (GA2, 126). Related to the word used as 'representative' in political terms, such as *Volksvertreter* or *Abgeordnete*, political representation is also a mode of someone standing in for, replacing or deputising.[54] This raises the question of leadership.

This issue is broached in the 1924 course on Aristotle, when Heidegger makes a brief digression into Plato's *Gorgias*. In the passage under consideration, Gorgias suggests that rhetoric is 'a cause of freedom to humans in general, but also of dominion to people in their *polis*' (452d7–9). In response to a further prompt from Socrates, he defines this as the 'ability to convince by means of speech a jury in a court of justice, statesmen [*politikos*] in their Chamber, voters at a meeting of the Assembly, and any other gathering of citizens whatever it may be' (452e1–5). Socrates suggests that this means that 'rhetoric is productive of conviction'. The Greek for this phrase is *'peithous demiourgos estin he rhetorike'* (453a2–3). In a clarifying gloss Heidegger suggests that 'the rhetor is the one that has the proper power [*die eigentliche Macht*] over Dasein . . . Proficiency in speech [*Redenkönnen*] is that possibility to have proper rule [*eigentliche Herrschaft*] of the self over the convictions of the people [*der Menschen*], of how they are with-another [*miteinander*]' (GA18, 108). This over-valorisation of the speaker over those hearing is important in a political context. The hearing ability, the capacity to hear [*Hörenkonnen*], is continually stressed by Heidegger (see, for example, GA18, 104).

Concrete being-with-another therefore depends on the listener (GA18, 123), but there are more worrying political implications in this ideal of a to-and-fro exchange of listening and speaking. Listening is hearkening, that is, obeying, deriving from the Latin *oboedire*, which is to give ear, bearing more relation to *audire*, to hear, than *dicere*, to speak. In a sense, then, Heidegger's community of speakers is a community of listeners, with the speech reserved to a few, and the listeners in a position of obeisance. Similarly charged political possibilities emerge on re-reading *Being and Time* §34 in the light of this lecture course (GA2, 160–6).

> Hearing is constitutive for discourse [*Rede*]. And just as linguistic utterance is based on discourse, so is acoustic perception on hearing. Listening to . . . is Dasein's existential way of being-open as being-with for others [*Offensein des Daseins als Mitsein für den Anderen*]. Indeed, hearing constitutes the primary and proper way in which Dasein is open for its

ownmost potentiality-for-being [*eigenstes Seinkönnen*] – as in hearing the voice of the friend whom every Dasein carries with it. Dasein hears, because it understands. As an understanding being-in-the-world with others, Dasein is 'in thrall' to *Mitdasein* and to itself; and in this thraldom it 'belongs' to these. Being-with develops in listening-to-another [*Aufeinander-hören*] which can be done in several possible ways: following, going-along-with, and the privative modes of not-hearing, resisting, defying and turning away. (GA2, 163, the ellipsis is Heidegger's)[55]

There are some real issues here. In the first few sentences, Heidegger is rehearsing much of what is implied in the earlier reading of Aristotle. But hearing now takes on a role of constituting the possibility of each Dasein's being, and that this may come from 'the voice of the friend', who, like the hero, is undefined. But the most remarkable sentence follows this. In the above passage I have largely followed the translation by Macquarrie and Robinson and left it without any of the German. The German reads:

Als verstehendes In-der-Welt-sein mit den Anderen ist es dem Mitdasein und ihm selbst »hörig« und in dieser Hörigkeit zugehörig.

Hören, hearing, is the root of the words Heidegger is playing with here. Macquarrie and Robinson offer 'in thrall', 'thraldom' and 'belongs' for *hörig*, *Hörigkeit* and *zugehörig*; Stambaugh offers the far-too-neutral 'listens to', 'listening' and 'belongs'. Thrall is good, indeed quite possibly the best translation for general purposes, given the relation between it and enthral – literally to be held captive by, but now often used to describe the mood produced by a particularly riveting speech. A thrall is someone who is in bondage to another, a slave or a serf. Thraldom is the state of being in thrall. Implied in this passage is that Dasein is heavily embedded in *Mitdasein*, dependent, submissive, even – pushing the point to its limit – enslaved. It is also notable that the ways of listening that follow are first and foremost those of acquiescence and obedience – following a lead, or going-with, *Mitgehens* – and modes that might be characterised as part of an exchange – challenging, disagreeing, answering or responding – are instead the privative modes of 'not-hearing, resisting, defying and turning away'.

Although the key issues emerge from this passage in the light of the 1924 course, this passage of *Being and Time* is one of those carried forward almost word-for-word from the 1925 course, *History of the Concept of Time*. But there are some important differences.

> *Mitsein* is not being-present-at-hand also among other humans; as being-in-the-world it means at the same time being 'in thrall [*hörig*]' to others, that is 'heeding' and 'obeying' them, listening [*hören*] or not listening. *Mitsein* has the structure of *belonging* [*die Struktur der* Zu(ge)hörigkeit] to the other, and it is only by virtue of this primary belonging that there is something like separation, group formation, development of society, and the like [*Absonderung, Gruppenbildung, Ausbildung von Geschellschaft und der gleichen*] (GA20, 367).

Heidegger goes on to talk about modes of compliance and non-compliance, but what is particularly notable is threefold. First, 'that is "heeding" and "obeying" them' finds no parallel in the German, but is the translator Kisiel's editorial intrusion, a helpful gloss on the meaning.[56] Second, that *Zu(ge)hörigkeit* is a structure of *Mitsein*. Third, the suggestion that the presumably secondary characteristics of groups or society follow from this primary mode of connection. This is not said in *Being and Time*, and it is worth noting that the earlier discussion of secondary modes of community and society also comes from this lecture course (see above, and GA20, 333). Equally, in both the course and *Being and Time* itself, Heidegger claims that 'it is on the basis of such a capacity to hear [*Hörenkönnens*] . . . that there is something like *hearkening* [Horchen] (GA2, 164; see GA20, 367).[57]

Phronesis and Leadership

That the book on Aristotle was abandoned means that Heidegger left almost all of this work unpublished, and many of the passages in *Being and Time* are obscure without the supporting architecture of his interpretation of the Greeks. Crucial in the story of the abandonment is, as Kisiel has shown, the turn to the explicit theorising of time. *Basic Concepts of Aristotelian Philosophy* was delivered in the Summer Semester of 1924: on 25 July of that year, to the Marburg Theological Society, Heidegger delivered the lecture 'The Concept of Time' (GA64, 107–25). Instead of the projected book on Aristotle, we now have the beginning of the process that leads to *Being and Time* itself.

Being and Time, in its originally projected form of two parts and six divisions, was to contain one division on Aristotle, and Aristotle plays an important role within the book as actually published. The planned division was to treat 'Aristotle's essay on time, as providing a way of discriminating the phenomenal basis and the limits of ancient ontology' (GA2, 40). This question receives quite detailed treatment in

The Basic Problems of Phenomenology (GA24, 327–88). That said, it is not so much in the explicit material on Aristotle that the debt is felt in *Being and Time*, but that *Being and Time*, in the actually existing version of the first two divisions, owes much of its terminology to Aristotle. This much should be clear from the preceding analysis. What is even more remarkable, it seems to me, is that the very structure of *Being and Time* as published is grounded on an Aristotelian distinction.[58]

The key to understanding this can be found in the aforementioned *Plato's* Sophist course, delivered in 1924–25.[59] Originally, this was to have been a course devoted to two Platonic dialogues including the *Philebus*, although only the *Sophist* was actually considered in depth, in part because as a prelude Heidegger provides an extensive discussion of *Nicomachean Ethics*, Book VI (GA19, 21–188). This should not merely be seen as a continuation of the interest in Aristotle, but as part of the process of creating the architectonic of *Being and Time*. In the course, he makes a great deal of Aristotle's distinction between *poiesis* and *praxis*, making and doing, and the intellectual virtues that apply to them – *tekhne* and *phronesis*.[60] It is instructive to read *Being and Time* as concerned with the *tekhne* of *poiesis* in the first three chapters of Division I; and the remainder of this Division and Division II as concerned with the *phronesis* of *praxis*.[61] The analysis of *Zeug*, equipment such as hammers, in the first few chapters of *Being and Time* is of *Vorhandensein*, things occurring in the world, and their relation to each other which he terms *Mitvorhandensein*. But it is clear that these are 'beings whose kind of being is not of the character of Dasein' (GA2, 54, see 66–7, 114). Although Heidegger notes that the Greek term for 'thing', *pragma*, is that which pertains to *praxis* (GA2, 68), it is in relation to the second, the *phronesis* of *praxis*, that Heidegger suggests that the basic constitution of human Dasein, human existence, in its comportment to other beings which share its way of being, is speaking. It is in speaking *about* something, about something in the world, that it expresses *itself*. In other words, this is a distinction between our everyday dealing with equipment in the world, and insight into our actions. In the former we deal with things which do not share our way of being, objects, tools, and so on, in the *Umwelt*, the surrounding world or environment; in the latter we deal with beings that share our way of being, other humans, in the *Mitwelt*, the with-world or shared world (GA19, 386).[62]

In order to fully clarify the distinction between *tekhne* and *poiesis*, and *phronesis* and *praxis*, the remainder of this chapter deals with

Heidegger's detailed reading of the *Nicomachean Ethics*, Book VI, the book on the so-called intellectual virtues [*aretas dianoias*],[63] in order to demonstrate how the distinction functions in this course, to highlight how this distinction works in *Being and Time*, and to bring out some further explicitly political issues. The key one here, important in the issues arising from the discussion of *Mitsein* above, and here explicitly related to the crucial notion of *phronesis*, is the question of leadership.

Heidegger's aim in the reading of the *Ethics*, which is supplemented by discussion of other Aristotelian texts, notably *Metaphysics* and *Physics*, is to come to an understanding of *sophia* in order to read the *Sophist* dialogue. One of the key distinctions drawn in the *Nicomachean Ethics* is between *tekhne*, *episteme*, *phronesis*, *sophia* and *nous* – the five ways the mind arrives at truth [*aletheuein*] (1139b16–17). These would usually be translated as art or skill; scientific knowledge; practical wisdom or prudence; philosophic wisdom; and intellect. Whilst all these ways of leading to truth [*aletheia*] are connected to *logos*, with the exception of *nous* they are also *meta logou*, that is to say, they are with it, modes of it. *Dianoien* – literally '*noien* through', or the intellect as a process from/to – is the general term for these *aletheuein*, which means they are all also related to *nous*.

Aristotle first distinguishes these parts of the mind on the basis of their object – things that could be otherwise, or things that could not. Science, *episteme*, works on the invariable, it works without need for deliberation [*bouleuesthai*]; equally, there is a deliberative calculating part of the mind [*logistikon*] which works on what is variable (1139a10–15). *Episteme* has as its realm that which is necessary, which is without qualification, everlasting.

Next, Aristotle suggests that *praxis* does not equal *poiesis*: action or doing is different from production or making. They are so different that there is no overlap at all, neither is even part of the other. This leads him to a crucial distinction between *tekhne*, which is related to *poiesis* (and is concerned with things that can be otherwise), and *phronesis*, which is related to *praxis* (also concerned with things that can be otherwise). *Tekhne* is an intellectual virtue concerned with making. Indeed, *tekhne* can be defined as being identical with *logou alethous poietike* – a mode of *logos* aiming for truth concerned with production (1140a10–11). *Phronesis*, for its part, therefore involves deliberating well, to promote a good end, *telos*, but which is outside the ambit of skill, *tekhne*. Somebody who uses *phronesis* does not just act for good health or good strength, but for the good life as a whole.

Phronesis therefore does not equal *episteme* – otherwise there would be no need for deliberation – nor *tekhne*, because it is concerned with action rather than production, *praxis* not *poiesis* (1140a33–b3).

There is something crucial here: in making, in production, *poiesis*, the end, the *telos*, is other than the process, whereas for *praxis*, doing well, *eupraxia*, is itself the *telos*. *Phronesis* is therefore *alethe meta logou praktiken* – a quality of *logos* seeking truth, practical, and concerned with the good for humans (1140b5–6, 20–2). '*Phronesis* is therefore a *arete* [virtue] but not a *tekhne*', it is excellence of opinion, *doxa*, because 'both *doxa* and *phronesis* are concerned with what is variable'. But it is not purely contemplative, because of its decisive relation to *praxis* (1140b24–30). *Phronesis*, then, is linked to *logos*, *aletheia*, *praxis*, *agathon* and humans. Little wonder, therefore, that Heidegger found it so interesting.

Episteme, which is thinking about things which are universal and necessary, must work with principles, which have to be taught, and learned. But the first principle, the ground of what else is demon-strable, cannot be an object of *episteme*. First principles themselves are not demonstrable. But neither can they be an object of *tekhne* or *phronesis*, because a first principle cannot be otherwise, and both *tekhne* and *phronesis* are concerned with what can be otherwise. And nor can these first principles be the realm of *sophia*, as this uses demonstration. First principles, *arkhon*, are therefore the concern of *nous*, intellect (1139b31–3, 1140b31–1141a). Aristotle has therefore separated apart the five ways the mind arrives at truth – *tekhne*, *episteme*, *phronesis*, *sophia* and *nous*.

The distinction between *sophia* and *phronesis* is particularly im-portant for our purpose here, because of the way the tradition has tended to devalue *phronesis* in favour of *sophia* (see, for example, GA19, 60), and also because of the political interpretations of these terms. Aristotle suggests that the question of health or goodness will differ between men and fish, whereas the definition of what is white or straight will not. Therefore *sophia* is the same, whereas *phronesis* is different (1141a22–5). By this he means that *phronesis* is something particular, that is, particular to humans. It is concerned with human affairs, those things we can deliberate about (1141b9–10). It follows from this that *sophia* cannot be related to *politike*, because *sophia* is not supposed to be particular, and *politike* is particular to humans (1141a29–30). Therefore, whilst *sophia* is *episteme* coupled with *nous* (1141a19, b3–5), *phronesis* is something rather different and does have a crucial relation to *politike*. *Phronesis* is not merely concerned with universals, but also with particulars, because of its essential relation to *praxis* (1141b15–17). Now comes the crucial passage in Aristotle in relation to the role of *phronesis* and its political implications:

> And since *phronesis* is practical [*e de phronesis praktike*], one needs both kinds of knowledge [that is, the universal kind of *phronesis* and the particular kind], but especially the particular kind. Here too [that is, in relation to the particular kind of *phronesis*] there must be some architectonic, some master science [*eie d'an tis kai entautha arkhitektonike*], (1141b22–3)

Whilst Heidegger suggests that the above quotation from Aristotle is part of Chapter 8, most editions of the *Nicomachean Ethics* have it in Chapter 7, as the final lines of that chapter.[64] What is interesting is that the next passage that Heidegger cites from Aristotle is about halfway through Chapter 8, some twenty lines or so later. Before I carry on with Aristotle's text, providing a reading of what Heidegger skips over, I want to reflect on a few points from Heidegger's reading. What I have just said, though indebted to Heidegger, is largely straight Aristotle.

Tekhne, *episteme*, *phronesis*, *sophia* and *nous* – what we above called the five ways the mind arrives at truth (1139b16–17) – are for Heidegger the five ways human Dasein discloses being in affirmation or denial [*Zu- und Absprechen*]. He renders them as 'know-how (in taking care [*Besorgen*], manipulating, producing); science; circumspection (insight) [*Umsicht – Einsicht*]; understanding; and perceptual discernment' (GA19, 21; see GA22, 311–2). That there are four that are *meta logou* means that there could not be any *tekhne*, *episteme*, *phronesis* or *sophia* that would not also be a speaking [*Sprechen*] (GA19, 22). This does not mean that speech is arbitrary, an annex to these modes of *aletheuein* [truth-making], but that it lies at their very heart (GA19, 27).

Heidegger then works slowly and carefully through Aristotle's writing, almost line by line. He looks at the way that the initial split between *epistemonikon* and *logistikon*, and the latter's link to *bouleuesthai* (which he translates as *umsichtige Betrachten* [circumspective consideration] rather than just deliberation [*Überlungen*] (GA19, 28)) plays out in the book. He analyses the distinction between *poiesis* and *praxis*, and their relation to *tekhne* and *phronesis*. This is the distinction that will be elaborated in *Being and Time*. For Heidegger, following Aristotle, the *zoe*, that is the life, of the human is *praktike meta logou* (see 1098a3ff), that is, it is a form of action which is grounded upon speech. (We should note here that Heidegger regularly translates *zoe*, life or animality, as Dasein. As he suggests most explicitly later, 'the object of *phronesis* is *praxis*, the *zoe* of the human, human Dasein itself' [GA19, 143, see 626, Supplement 25].) Equally, human *zoe* is *praxis kai aletheia* (see 1139a18), characterised by *praxis* and *aletheia*, action and 'the uncoveredness of Dasein itself as well as of the beings to which Dasein relates in its actions . . . *Every* comportment of Dasein is thus determined as *praxis kai aletheia*' (GA19, 39).[65]

We noted above that in making, in production, *poiesis*, the end, the *telos*, is other than the process. The object of *tekhne* is the *poieton*, the *ergon* – a finished product. It is for the sake of something, for someone, other than the process itself. Heidegger's illustration is strikingly simple. A shoe is made for wearing by some person. While it is being fabricated the product is the object of the *tekhne*, but when finished it is something separate from it, it escapes the dominion of the *tekhne*, because it becomes an object for its proper use. The cobbler delivers up the shoes, and their *telos* is separated from the process; *tekhne* is orientated toward beings only as they are in the process of becoming (1140a10; GA19, 41–2; see GA2, 70). Crucially, the *telos* escapes *tekhne*, so the *telos* is *peras*, beyond *tekhne* (*Metaphysics*, 1022a4). Even the *arkhe* is in a certain sense *peras* (1022a12), so *telos* and *arkhe* are, for *tekhne*, *peras* – a fundamental deficiency in the *aletheuein* which characterises *tekhne* (GA19, 44).

Heidegger's reading of *phronesis* is particularly important and through its decisive relation to *praxis*, far more than *mere* theory, or *just* knowledge. Indeed, this separation of *phronesis* from *episteme* and *sophia* – through the notion of *praxis* – is crucial. For Heidegger,

> In the delimitation against *episteme*, *phronesis* emerges as *doxa*, and in the delimitation against *tekhne*, as *arete*. That constitutes the tight cohesion of Chapter 5 of Book VI of the *Nicomachean Ethics*, where Aristotle carries out the analysis of *phronesis*. (GA19, 48)

We should remember that Heidegger translates *phronesis* as *Umsicht* or *Einsicht*, circumspection or insight, or indeed as *die umsichtige Einsicht*, circumspective insight – a clear stress on the visual, the seeing (GA19, 47). As noted above, he uses *umsichtige Betrachten* [circumspective consideration] to translate *bouleuesthai* (GA19, 28).

It is regrettable that the notion of 'theory', itself so tied to the Greek *theorein*, a kind of seeing, has become so polluted and used up (GA19, 62–3). It is also essential to recognise that, in Heidegger's reading, *phronesis* is directly related to Dasein. This is because Dasein is both the *arkhe* of the deliberation of *phronesis*, and its *telos*. The *telos* is not something outside and beyond Dasein, as it is with *tekhne*, rather it is the human itself, *anthropos*. This is because in *poiesis*, the aim is to produce something, whereas this is not the case with *praxis* (GA19, 51).

It is worth saying a bit more about this analysis of *telos*. Whilst the object of *tekhne* is the *ergon*, a finished product, a for the sake of something for someone, other than the process itself, this is not the case with *phronesis*. In *phronesis*, the *telos* is the deliberation as it relates to the deliberator themselves. 'The *aletheuein* of *phronesis* therefore contains a referential direction to the *aletheuon* themselves'. As we noted above in reading Aristotle, this is not merely for the sake of health or strength, but with regard to well-being as a whole – in Heidegger's language, not a particular regard of Dasein, but the being of Dasein as a whole, *eu zen*, the right and proper way to be Dasein (GA19, 48–9).

> The *telos* of *phronesis* is hence not *para*, over and against the being of the deliberation itself, as is the case with the *ergon* of *tekhne*. Rather in the case of *phronesis*, the object of the deliberation is *zoe itself*; the *telos* has the same ontological character as *phronesis* . . . 'In the case of *poiesis*, the *telos* is something other; but this does not hold for *praxis*: *eupraxia* is itself the *telos*' [1140b6ff]. In the case of *phronesis*, the *prakton is of the same character of being as the aletheuein itself*. And here, presumably, the *telos* is in fact disclosed and preserved; for it is the being of the deliberator themselves (GA19, 49).

Phronesis is therefore the intellectual vision that discerns *praxis*, seeing both its *telos* and *arkhe* (1143b10–14). The *telos* in *phronesis* is the *anthropos* itself; the *arkhe* of *phronesis* is Dasein itself. What *phronesis* deliberates about is not what brings *praxis* to an end, the result or consequence is not what constitutes a being of an action, but the *eu*, the how [*das Wie*], the good constitutes the being of an action. This is the *eu* of the *eupraxia* (GA19, 50–1). Somewhat later in the course, in an analysis of the *Metaphysics*, Heidegger adds a supplement to this. The notion of virtue, *agathon*, often misunderstood as 'value', is rather:

> A *determination of the being of beings*: it applies to those beings which are
> determined by a *telos*. Insofar as a being reaches its *telos* and is complete, it
> is as it is meant to be, *eu*. The *agathon* has at first no relation to *praxis* at
> all; instead, it is a determination of beings insofar as they are *finished*,
> *com-plete*. A being that always is does not at all first need to be produced;
> it is always already constantly there as finished . . . If we take the *agathon*
> as value [*Wert*], then this is all nonsense (GA19, 123–4).

In one of the very few references to the political in the Aristotle part of
the course in question, Heidegger suggests that

> *Phronesis* is supposed to render Dasein transparent in the accomplishment
> of those actions which lead man to the *eu zen* [the good life]. If, accord-
> ingly, *phronesis* is the gravest and most decisive knowledge [*Erkenntnis*],
> then that science which moves within the field of *phronesis* will be the
> highest. And insofar as no man is alone, insofar as people are together
> [*miteinander*], *politike* (*Nic. Eth.* VI, 7, 1141a21) is the *highest science*
> [*Wissenschaft*]. Accordingly, *politike episteme* is proper [*eigentliche*]
> *sophia*, and the *politikos* is the true *philosophos*; that is the conception
> of Plato. (GA19, 135–6)

Importantly, though, Heidegger contests this progression precisely
at the point where *phronesis* is collapsed into *sophia*, or where
Erkenntnis becomes *Wissenschaft*, knowledge science (GA19, 136).
As we noted above, Aristotle suggests that *sophia* cannot be related to
politike, because *sophia* is too general to just apply to humans, and
politike is particular to humans (1141a29–30). What is revealing is
that Heidegger is using Aristotle to challenge the ideas of Plato
concerning the relation between politics and philosophy. This theme
will be picked up in Chapter Two. Arendt notes in this context that
'Aristotle, with the great example of Plato still vividly in view, has
already strongly advised philosophers against dreaming of the philo-
sopher-king who would rule *ta ton anthropon pragmata*, the realm of
human affairs'.[66]
We should note here that before the Platonic shift that he contests,
Heidegger introduces the term *miteinander*: 'And insofar as no man
is alone, insofar as people are with-another [*miteinander*], *politike*
(*Nic. Eth.* VI, 7, 1141a21) is the *highest science* [*Wissenschaft*]'
(GA19, 135–6). This is crucial because, as we shall see, this notion
of being-together broadens the sense of *phronesis* to encompass
politike, although Heidegger does not make this explicit. The closest
he comes is in a remark in the draft introduction to the book on

Aristotle, where he translates *phronesis* as '*fürsorgende Umsicht*' (PIA, 45/129). This is ambiguous and problematic. We are clearly looking here at a kind of circumspection that is *concerned*, and in a literal sense *concerned for*. However, *fürsorgende* can also mean thoughtful, and this ambiguity may be important to Heidegger's intention.[67] Whilst *die Fürsorge* usually means welfare or social security, the translators of *Being and Time* chose 'solicitude' (GA2, 121–2).[68] Although this is not made obvious here, it would appear that it is concerned with both personal and interpersonal well-being, and that *phronesis* is insight into this.

To return to the main thrust of the argument, it is because *phronesis* is connected to *praxis* – and not just as some kind of addition, but essentially and at every stage – that it is a different form of *aletheuein* to *sophia* (GA19, 138). Crucially,

> *Phronesis* is not a *exis meta logou monon* (*Nic. Eth.*, VI, 5, 1140b28), it is not a mere discussing [*Durchsprechen*] that proceeds for its own sake, but instead, already in every word, in every saying it utters, it speaks of the *prakton* and for the sake of the *prakton* . . . '*Phronesis* must have both': *aletheuein* and *praxis*, 'or, rather, the latter still more' [1141b21–2]. Phronesis *dwells in* praxis *still more than in* logos. What is decisive in *phronesis* is *praxis*. In *phronesis*, the *praxis* is *arkhe* and *telos*. In foresight [*Vorblick*] toward a determinate action, *phronesis* is carried out, and in the action itself comes to its end. (GA19, 139)

All of this insight and the political implications that follow from it can, I believe, be focused in one particular passage, a gloss on lines 1141b22–3 of the *Nicomachean Ethics*, which reads: *eie d'an tis kai entautha arkhitektonike*. A standard English translation is 'there must be some master science', although, preserving the difficulty of the key term, I prefer 'there must be some architectonic'. Heidegger's commentary on this passage is both extremely elliptic and politically very revealing. It is revealing in part because it must stand in, in his interpretation, for the twenty lines he skips over. While the reading of the *Rhetoric* in the previous semester illuminates some of it, there are a number of issues which require careful unpacking and detailed exegesis.

> And also here within the *praktike* there may exist a certain order of connection [*ein gewisser Ordnungszusammenhang*], a leading and a guiding [*eine Führung und Leitung*]. Insofar as the *anthropos* is the *zoon politikon*, *praxis* is to be understood as being as being-with-another [*als*

Sein im Miteinandersein]; and insofar as this is the *telos*, *phronesis* is of the character [*von der Art*] of the *politike*.

    Praxis is thus decisive [*das Entscheidende*] for *phronesis*. This gives rise to an essential distinction between *phronesis* and *episteme*, one which concerns the *genesis* of *phronesis* and *episteme*. Aristotle shows this in Chapter 9. (GA19, 140)

As the editor notes, 'Heidegger did not elaborate further' (GA19, 140, n. 4).

Following the careful distinctions elaborated in Heidegger's reading of the earlier parts of Book VI, some of these formulations can become clear. Here, and then later in this chapter, I offer a reading of the passage line by line.

> And also here within the *praktike* there may exist a certain order of connection [*ein gewisser Ordnungszusammenhang*], a leading and a guiding [*eine Führung und Leitung*].

This is Heidegger's paraphrasing translation of the line from the *Ethics* (1141b22–3). *Praktike* here is the practical form of *phronesis*, and the problematic term *arkhitektonike* is translated as *Ordnungszusammenhang*, an order of connection. This is glossed with 'a leading and a guiding', which is unclear.

> Insofar as the *anthropos* is the *zoon politikon* . . .

Zoon politikon has to be understood in a more fundamental sense than merely 'political animal'. It is more rightly understood as the being of humans in the *polis* (GA19, 577), but it is also clear that this needs to be understood in the light of the suggestion that the *anthropos* is also the *zoon ekhon logon*. What distinguishes the human from animals is *logos*. And, of course, this means that speech, and not reason, is crucial. The human is not the *animal rationale*, but a being that has language, a being-in-the-world which addresses and discusses its world, through its *praxis*. Therefore

> . . . *praxis* is to be understood as being as being-with-another [*als Sein im Miteinandersein*] . . .

Praxis, action or doing, is always an orientation towards others. Humans do not solely exist, but constitute themselves through their speaking with others. This is the crucial distinction between *poiesis* and *praxis*, and their relation to *tekhne* and *phronesis*; our everyday dealing with equipment in the world, and insight into our actions. In the former we deal with things which do not share our way of being, objects, tools, and so on, in the *Umwelt*, the environment; in the latter we deal with beings that share our way of being, other humans, in the *Mitwelt*, the with-world. What characterises the former is concern, *Besorgen* (Heidegger's translation of *tekhne* at GA19, 21); the latter is *Fürsorge* (see GA2, 121).

> . . . and insofar as this is the *telos*, *phronesis* is of the character [*von der Art*] of the *politike* . . .

We should note that *telos*, for both *praxis* and *phronesis*, is not separate from the process. In making, in production, *poiesis*, the *telos*, is other than the process, whereas for *praxis* doing well, *eupraxia*, is *itself* the *telos* (see *Politics*, 1325b14–20; and GA27, 274–5). Indeed, the *telos* for *phronesis* is the human Dasein, the *zen* itself. *Phronesis*, unlike *sophia*, is particular to humans, and therefore, because the *anthropos* is the *zoon politikon*, *phronesis* is related to *politike*.

> *Praxis* is thus decisive [*das Entscheidende*] for *phronesis*. This gives rise to an essential distinction between *phronesis* and *episteme*, one which concerns the *genesis* of *phronesis* and *episteme*. Aristotle shows this in Chapter 9.

This is now the most straightforward part of the passage. The distinction between *phronesis* and *episteme* is the crucial point of much of Heidegger's discussion, and is based on the importance of the notion of *praxis*. *Praxis*, in opposition to *tekhne*, is oriented toward other Dasein, rather than equipment. It is action rather than production. While both *praxis* and *tekhne* are concerned with things that can be otherwise, *episteme* is concerned with the invariable. To a certain extent, then, we would be justified in saying that it was not that Heidegger 'did not elaborate further', but that he was summarising what had come before. That said, there is something significant missing in his reading, which is revealing in terms of his political action.[69]

The line of Aristotle that Heidegger is summarising is 'here too there must be some architectonic'. This architectonic, this master science, is what Heidegger suggests is 'an order of connection, a leading and guiding'. But this architectonic is clearly *politike* – both because, as Rackham suggests, it is the next thing considered,[70] and also because right at the start of the *Ethics* Aristotle discusses the architectonic, and explicitly states that it is *politike* (1094a14–15, 28–9). In 1926, Heidegger examines the discussion of the architectonic in the *Metaphysics* (1013a10–14) and suggests that it can be understood as moving what is moved, changing what is changed, that is, as 'leading, guiding, directing, ruling over [*Führung, Leitung, Direktion, Herrschaft über*]'. This is both for 'kings and tyrants, and also for some sciences in rank [*Wissenschaften im Rang*] over others' (GA22, 34). We are equally told that the whole study of the *Ethics* is of *politike* (1094a11–12).[71]

At the point where Heidegger skips over the first lines of Chapter 8, Aristotle introduces some crucial distinctions. Here is the passage Heidegger is in effect summarising:

> *Politike* and *phronesis* are in practice the same quality, though the words do not mean the same. There are two sides to *phronesis* as regards the *polis*, the directing kind [*arkhitektonike*] is legislative [*nomothetike*], while that concerned with particulars is *politike*, which properly belongs to both. That concerned with particulars is *praktike* and deliberative, since a decree is to be acted on, as the last thing reached in deliberation. This is why it is only people exhibiting this kind of *phronesis* who are said to participate in politics: they are the only ones who practice politics in the way that craftsmen work [*kheirotekhnia*]. *Phronesis* is also thought of especially in terms of that form concerned with oneself, the individual, it has the name *phronesis*, which properly is common to the various kinds, namely household management [*oikonomia*], legislation [*nomosthesia*] and *politike*, the latter being divided into deliberative and judicial arts [*bouleutike e de dikastike*] (1141b24–34).

There are therefore a number of subdivisions proposed. Whilst *phronesis* and *tekhne* are opposed – because of the opposition between *praxis* and *poiesis* – to practice politics is like the work of the craftsman [*kheirotekhnia*]. There is clearly an opposition suggested here between *kheirotekhnia* and *arkhitektonike* – the former is the practical side, the latter the directing abstractive. Although Aristotle makes it clear that both sides of this in relation to politics are *politike*, it is common for only the former to be seen as politics. *Politike* is therefore identical with *e peri polin phronesis*, the *phronesis* that concerns the *polis*. But the relation of *phronesis* to the *polis* must be understood in two ways – the *arkhitektonike*, which is *nomosthesia*, and the one that is akin to *kheirotekhnia* which is *politike* in the narrow sense. *Politike* also has a narrow sense and a wider sense. *Politike* is both the *arkhitektonike*, which is *nomothetike*, concerned with laws, and concerned with particulars [*politike*]. This narrow sense of *politike* is further divided into deliberative arts [*bouleutike*] and judicial arts [*dikastike*], concerned with justice. This can be schematised as:

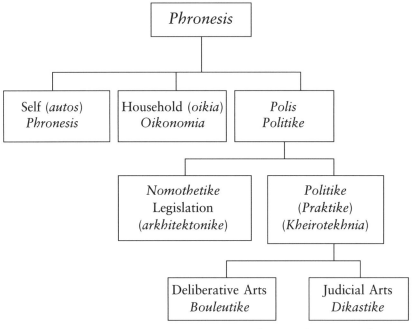

Nicomachean Ethics, 1141b24–34

Phronesis is not simply concerned with the self [*autos*], but with the *oikia* and the *polis* too. *Phronesis* is the name common to all three, but also to the narrow sense. *Phronesis*, *oikonomia* and *politike* are three kinds of *phronesis* in this wider sense.[72] Whilst concern for the self is one form of *phronesis*, it is very different from other kinds, and there is, unsurprisingly, a resistance to *phronesis* being used over others. But, and this seems crucial, personal well-being is not possible without *oikonomia* and *politeia*, that is, without household management and a constitution (1142a9–10). Ultimately, of course, because the *anthropos* is a *zoon politikon*, and as the *Eudemian Ethics* also makes clear a *oikonomikon zoon* (1242a23–4), these forms of *phronesis* are superior, in that the narrow form is only possible with the others. The human, as Aristotle suggests, is not a solitary but a communal animal [*koinonikon anthropos zoon*] (1242a24–6).

However, Heidegger narrows his interest in *phronesis* to simply the concern for the self, something which is shown by the way he sometimes translates *phronesis*. In a recollection of these lectures, Gadamer talks of how Heidegger was able to liberate Aristotle 'so profoundly and strikingly from the sedimentations of the scholastic tradition and from the lamentably distorted image of Aristotle contained in the criticism of the time'. Gadamer particularly recalls the analysis of *phronesis*, the distinction of this concept from knowledge [*Wissen*] and *doxa*, belief, and the discussion of the concluding lines of Chapter 5 of Book VI: '*lethe men tes toiautes hexeos estin, phroneseos d'ouk estin*' (1140b29). This is usually translated as something along the lines of 'but *phronesis* is not something which can be forgotten'. Gadamer remembers: 'We were unsure of this sentence and completely unfamiliar with the Greek concepts; as we groped for an interpretation, he declared brusquely, "That is the conscience! [*Gewissen*]"'.[73]

This phrase in question proves, for Aristotle, that *phronesis* is not a purely intellectual quality, but has a decisive relation to action, *praxis*. Purely intellectual qualities can be forgotten, but *phronesis* cannot. Heidegger underscores this by noting the Greek words involved. What I experience, notice or have learned can be forgotten – in other words, *aletheuein* is subject to *lethe*: 'what is disclosed can sink back into concealment'. (As Heidegger continually insists, the alpha in *aletheuein* is an alpha-privative – see, for example, GA19, 15.) Now, because the 'ability to become forgotten is a specific possibility of the *aletheuein* which has the character of *theorein*', *aletheuein* in this sense has the proper [*eigentümlichen*] character of fallenness [*Verfallens*]. But, whilst we can experience or notice or learn things a second time, this is not the case with *phronesis*, which is 'in each case new'. 'Hence there is no *lethe* in relation to *phronesis* . . . there is no possibility of falling into forgetting [*nicht die Verfallensmöglichkeit des Vergessens*]' (GA19, 55–6). Here, then, is the passage Gadamer is remembering:

> Certainly the explication which Aristotle gives here is very meagre. But it is nevertheless clear from the context that we would not be going too far in our interpretation by saying that Aristotle has here come across the *phenomenon of conscience* [*Phänomen des Gewissens*]. *Phronesis* is nothing other than conscience set into motion [*Bewegung*], making an action transparent. Conscience cannot be forgotten. But it is quite possible

that what is disclosed by conscience can be distorted and allowed to be ineffective through *hedoun* and *lupe*, through the passions [*Leidenschaften*]. Conscience always announces itself. Hence because *phronesis* does not possess the possibility of *lethe*, it is not a mode of *aletheuein* which one could call theoretical knowledge. (GA19, 56)

This is an astonishing passage, ripe with future potential and revealing not just in terms of this course, but also for *Being and Time*. This is because the term *phronesis* – seemingly so important – does not appear anywhere in *Being and Time*.[74] Sometimes it is rendered as the understanding of circumspection [*Umsicht*] (see, for example, GA2, 73–6, 79–83, 102–8, 351–64), but it is also behind the notion of the conscience [*Gewissen*].[75] It first appears in the introduction to the second division, where we are told that conscience demands 'a genuinely existential interpretation', which 'leads to the insight [*Einsicht*] that a proper potentiality-for-being [*eigentliches Seinkönnen*] of Dasein lies in *wanting-to have-a-conscience* [Gewissen-haben-wollen]' (GA2, 234, see 270).[76]

This insight is developed at length in the second chapter of this division, which looks especially at this potentiality-for-being, and the notion of resoluteness [*Entschlossenheit*]. It talks about the retrieval of being-one's-self from being lost in the one, something it must find, and the 'voice of conscience [*Stimme des Gewissens*] is an indication of this (GA2, 268). The analysis here, for Heidegger, is not about describing or classifying experiences of conscience, nor putting forward a biological explanation, but an ontological analysis. Conscience in this sense is understood as a call [*Ruf*], a mode of discourse; the call of conscience [*Gewissenruf*] is an appeal [*Anrufs*], an appeal to its potentiality-for-being-its-self. Crucially, in relation to the exchange of speaking and listening, call and response, analysed earlier in the chapter, 'to the call of conscience there corresponds a possible hearing' (GA2, 269, see 271–2). The reason the conscience is important is that its call 'reaches the one-self [*Man-selbst* – i.e. the alienated form] of concernful *Mitsein* with others' (GA2, 272), but because the appeal is only to the self, one's own self, 'the one collapses' (GA2, 273); 'conscience summons Dasein's self from its lostness in the one' (GA2, 274).

It is easy to misunderstand this, thinking that the call is from another, and that it is somehow external. Although the call does not come from someone else, it comes both '*from* me and yet *from beyond me*', and so rather than assigning a definite pronoun to the call, *es ruft*, 'it calls' (GA2, 276), in the sense of *es gibt, il y a*, 'there is', like the idea that 'it is raining'. Difficult though this undoubtedly is, and it becomes more so when the notion of guilt is introduced, there are a couple of points worth drawing from it. First, that 'the call of conscience – that is, conscience itself – has its ontological possibility in the fact that Dasein, in the very basis of its being, is care' (GA2, 277–8). Second, that the conscience is in each case mine, and therefore not the voice of the one, or a public, shared, conscience (GA2, 278).

Heidegger, therefore, is concerned with *phronesis* simply in relation to the self, in terms of its practical side, and this *arkhitektonike* is therefore neglected, except for the brief passage I am concerned with here. In a later course on Aristotle's *Metaphysics*, Heidegger notes that 'besides ethical-practical behaviour, *phronesis* also signifies the self-sensing of human beings' (GA33, 126–7/107–8; see GA28, 360), and it is clear this is what really interests him. Heidegger, because of his intent of rescuing a particular sense of *phronesis*, neglects its crucial political, that is communal, and as we shall see, ethical dimensions, in favour of a personal and ontological approach. What realm, then, does the person using *phronesis*, the *phronimos*, speak to? It cannot be merely the individual Dasein, the area of conscience, but in these lectures at least, it is unclear how this might speak to the wider realms of *oikia* or the *polis*. And yet, as Heidegger later notes, the opening up of such issues is absolutely crucial.

Heidegger continues, talking about how Aristotle argues that *phronesis* is not something like mathematics, which can be learned by the young, but which requires experience, *khronos*, time (1142a10–16). The knowledge of particulars, rather than just the universal, requires experience rather than just abstract thinking. Mathematics is an abstraction, and *phronesis* is not like *episteme*. *Phronesis* therefore corresponds to *nous*, because neither are ascertainable through *episteme*, the one being concerned with particulars, the other with first principles (1142a16–23; GA19, 140–1).

But again Heidegger neglects some of the crucial points. Aristotle links the notion of deliberation [*bouleuesthai*], and particularly good deliberation [*euboulias*], to *phronesis*. Like *phronesis*, *euboulias* is not *episteme* because it involves deliberation over what is variable; it is not mere guesswork because it involves *logos* and *khronos*; nor is it merely *doxa* (1142a32–b7). Deliberative excellence is that which leads to the desired *telos* – either a general or specific *telos* (1142b30–2). 'It is characteristic of man with *phronesis* to deliberate well, and deliberative excellence is correctness with regard to the *telos*, of which *phronesis* is the true conception [*alethes hupolepsis*]' (1142b33–5). In the final chapters of this book, Aristotle pursues this line. '*Phronesis* is concerned with acts which are just [*dikaia*], noble [*kala*] and good [*agatha*] for humans, but these are characteristic of the good person, and we are no more able to do them through knowing about them, since the virtues are permanent qualities' (1143b22–4, see 1099a24–31). It follows from this that 'one cannot have *phronesis* without being good' (1144b36–7). Socrates was therefore wrong to think that all virtues were *phronesis*, but correct that they all involve it (1144b17–21). In summary, then, 'we cannot be really good without *phronesis*, or have *phronesis* without virtue of character [*ethikes aretes*]' (1144b31–4); *phronesis* and *aretes* are both required for the *telos* (1145a5–7).

Heidegger does makes it clear that he recognises the importance of the good, the *eu* (for example, GA19, 148–9), and recognises the moral dimension:

> Only someone who is already *agathos* can be *phronimos*. The possibility of the *aletheuein* of *phronesis* is bound up with the proviso that the one who carries it out is himself, in his being, *already agathos*. Thus there appears, from this side as well, a peculiar appurtenance of *phronimos* to *praxis*. There pertains to *praxis* not only, as we have seen in the point of departure of our reflection, a certain orientation and leading [*Orientierung und Führung*]; it is not enough for *praxis* to be guided by circumspection [*geleitet durch die Umsicht*], the sight of *phronesis*. For it is clear that this sight, the anticipation of the *agathon*, as the mode of carrying out the disclosure, is only possible in an *agathos*. *Phronesis* is nothing if it is not carried out in *praxis*, and *praxis* as such is determined by *arete*, by the *prakton* as *agathon*. Merely possessing the *telos* of an action, merely having *phronesis* at our disposal, does not yet make us *praktikoteroi*; we are not therefore led to act morally [*sittlich*] if we are not already good . . . The mere having of the orientation and guidance [*Orientierung und Leitung*] does not place us on the level of being which properly corresponds to the meaning of *aletheuein*. Insofar as *phronesis*, with regard to the possibility of its correct execution, depends on being carried out by an *agathos*, it is not itself autonomous [*eigenständig*]. Thereby the *priority of phronesis is shaken*, although *phronesis* does indeed relate to human Dasein. (GA19, 166–7)

But although this moral dimension is allowed to surface, it is quite quickly buried again. Heidegger insists that the discussion is at a purely ontological level (GA19, 168). The problem is how can *phronesis* be both inferior to *sophia*, and the guiding principle to human behaviour, ruling and giving orders? (1144b33–7). 'Phronesis guides and leads [*leitet und führt*] all human acting, but it is still dependent on something else, namely the action itself' (GA19, 170). This is not the case with *sophia*, which does not have a goal in the same sense. Heidegger examines Aristotle's example to make this clear: using *phronesis* is like using medicine or medical knowledge to cure, to restore a state of health; but *sophia* is akin to health itself, it does not have a goal because it is itself the state (GA19, 171; see 1144a3–6; *Rhetoric* 1355b15–17). This is accordingly the highest state, to be what one always already is.

This discussion is useful, because it gives us insight into the importance of the ordering, leading and guiding that Heidegger mentions in the key passage under consideration, which until this point has remained obscure. We found these terms in the first line of the passage.

> And also here within the *praktike* there may exist a certain order of connection [*ein gewisser Ordnungszusammenhang*], a leading and a guiding [*eine Führung und Leitung*].

The *arkhitektonike* is the *Ordnungszusammenhang*, and as an *arkhitektonike* this is *eine Führung und Leitung*, a leading and guiding. But, as the discussion has made clear, *praxis* is guided and led by *phronesis*, because *phronesis* grasps the *telos* from the very outset. However, and this is the point that I believe Heidegger is largely glossing over, it is not enough for *praxis* to be guided by the insight of *phronesis* if one is not already *agathos*. That is, *phronesis* is nothing if it is not carried out in *praxis*, and *praxis* as such is determined by *arete*, by the *prakton* as *agathon*. In other words, it is not just that *phronesis* is decisive for *praxis*, but that *praxis* is decisive for *phronesis*.

> Insofar as the *anthropos* is the *zoon politikon*, *praxis* is to be understood as being as being-with-another; and insofar as this is the *telos*, *phronesis* is of the character of the *politike*.

But, as I have suggested, Heidegger narrows his interest in *phronesis* – at least in this course's reading of the *Ethics* – to simply the concern for the individual Dasein, what can be understood as conscience. He is content to look at *phronesis* in terms of its practical side, rather than the universal, and therefore this *arkhitektonike* is largely neglected.

Heidegger's analysis of the *Nicomachean Ethics* has taken until page 188 of the German text, 129 of the English translation. It is, as

Kisiel notes, the most thoroughgoing exegesis of *Nicomachean Ethics*, Book VI, we can ever expect from Heidegger, because it 'is virtually exhaustive'.[77] Virtually, but not quite; because the ethical dimensions, and the political issues that do not fit, are to an extent excluded, or covered over. Heidegger essentially neglects the crucial political, communal and ethical aspects of *phronesis* in favour of a personal and ontological approach.[78] But the ways in which he opens up Aristotle's text is enormously productive both for our understanding of Aristotle and Heidegger's *Being and Time*, and indeed for the role of Aristotle in *Being and Time*.[79]

Despite the interest in Heidegger's politics, the *early* Heidegger, the Heidegger that predates *Being and Time*, is still often seen as apolitical, uninvolved, uncommitted.[80] The stripping of the ethical from the analysis of *phronesis*, however, seems to be a major issue in the politics of the early Heidegger, and is at the very heart of his later political action. Although he contests the Platonic understanding he would later embrace, arguably he lays himself open to the problem he later encountered. Without some ethical element, on what basis do we distinguish guiding from leading? The question of the *phronimos* is the question of leading, what leads. As he wrote as early as 1921, philosophy should not concern itself with 'propheticism and the allure of a leader [*Führeralluren*]', although it is clear that 'people today are writing about the leader-problem! [*Führerproblem*]' (GA61, 70). While the later resonance of the term *Führer* is not yet present, the concern with leadership is certainly notable, though here Heidegger clearly distances himself from later developments.

This is the reason, given the stress the later Heidegger gives to language as, most fundamentally, the 'house of being', that understanding the source of Heidegger's meditation on language is important. Heidegger's reading of *logos* as speech helps us to understand Aristotle's parallel definitions of the human as the *zoon ekhon logon* and the *zoon politikon*, as well as the rhetorical politics of Heidegger himself. Heidegger opens up, but fails to adequately treat, the question of being-together politically. Chapters Two and Three will show what are, in effect, two different answers to this fundamental problem. When read with a view of the political as founded upon speech, *logos*, *Rede*, the Rectorial Address he gave in 1933, the *Rektoratsrede*, can be seen in a new light. His reading of Aristotle in the early 1920s, therefore, shows both the hermeneutic skill he brought to bear on ancient texts, but in the lacunae and glosses we see initial hints of his fateful political decision.

Notes

1. See the discussion of this in the Edward Robinson and John Macquarrie translation of *Being and Time*, Oxford: Blackwell, 1962, p. 58, n. 1.
2. For a discussion, see Thomas Sheehan, '*Hermeneia* and *Apophansis*: The Early Heidegger on Aristotle', in Franco Volpi (ed.), *Heidegger et l'idée de la phénoménologie,* Phaenomenologica Series, No 108, Dordrecht: Kluwer, 1987, http://www.stanford.edu/dept/relstud/faculty/sheehan/pdf/Hermenei.pdf
3. Indeed, the privileged role he gives the Greek *logos* is summed up in the later suggestion that 'the Greek language [*Sprache*], and it alone, is *logos*' (Martin Heidegger, *What is Philosophy?/Was ist das – die Philosophie?*, English–German edition, translated by William Kluback and Jean T. Wilde, London: Vision Press, 1963, pp. 44/45). Heidegger often suggests that German is the next most privileged language, because of its supposed relation to Greek.
4. On the *Habilitationsschrift*, see John Caputo, 'Phenomenology, Mysticism and the "*Grammatica Speculativa*": A Study of Heidegger's *Habilitationsschrift*', *Journal of the British Society for Phenomenology*, Vol. 5 No. 2, May 1974, pp. 101–17; and his *Heidegger and Aquinas: An Essay on Overcoming Metaphysics*, New York: Fordham University Press, 1982.
5. On the Heidegger/Lask relation, see Theodore Kisiel, 'Why Students of Heidegger Will Have to Read Emil Lask', in Theodore Kisiel, *Heidegger's Way of Thought*, edited by Alfred Denker and Marion Heinz, London: Continuum, 2002, pp. 101–36; and see also GA56/57, 123–4, 180.
6. See Immanuel Kant, *Lectures on Logic*, translated and edited by J. Michael Young, Cambridge: Cambridge University Press, 1992.
7. It is worth noting that sometimes '*Logik*' applies to the work of that name, and sometimes to the project, just as '*die Phänomenologie des Geistes*' sometimes refers to Hegel's book and sometimes to the movement of thinking. See Parvis Emad and Kenneth Maly, 'Translators' Foreword', in *Hegel's Phenomenology of Spirit* (GA32, xiii).
8. On Hegel's *Logic*, see GA2, 2, 3, 10, 22, and for the most extensive discussion, 432–3, n. 1, on time and the relation to Aristotle. See also 'Hegel and the Greeks', GA9, 427–44/323–36;

and the brief discussion of Hegel in relation to Heraclitus in GA7, 241–2. Heidegger did not discuss Hegel in his lectures in the same detail as other important thinkers (though, in relation to logic, see GA21, 14–15; GA28, 195–232; GA32, 2–3, 8–10; GA36/37, 69–77; GA68), but gave several seminars on this work. He gave a seminar on the *Logic* in 1925–26, and one on logic in Aristotle and Hegel in 1927; the work in the book *Identity and Difference* is based on seminar courses on the *Logic* in the winter semesters of 1955–56 and 1956–57 (see ID, especially 113–14/47–8; GA79, 81–176). This information is taken from Appendix B of Theodore Kisiel, *The Genesis of Heidegger's Being and Time*, Berkeley: University of California Press, 1993, pp. 461–76; and the Appendix of William J. Richardson, *Heidegger: Through Phenomenology to Thought*, The Hague: Martinus Nijhoff, Third Edition, 1974, pp. 663–71. The seminar 'On Time and Being' apparently discussed the relation between Heidegger and Hegel at some length. See ZSD, 28–9/26–7, 51–4/47–50. The neglect of Hegel's *Logics* – that is, both the *Science of Logic* and the *Encyclopedia Logic* – is surprising, given the discussion there of the notions of quantity, number and measure, and the relation this has to topics considered here in Chapter Three. See *Hegel's Logic*, translated by William Wallace, Oxford: Clarendon Press, 1975, §§99–111; *Hegel's Science of Logic*, translated by A. V. Miller, Amherst: Humanity Books, 1969, Book One, Sections Two and Three.

9. See the comments in GA40, 92–3, where Heidegger suggests that Leibniz, Kant and Hegel – 'three of the greatest German thinkers' – have made 'the decisive efforts in overcoming traditional logic', and that the term 'logic' in Hegel means metaphysics, with his 'Science of Logic' having nothing in common with 'the usual textbook on logic' (see also GA40, 143).
10. See, for example, GA2, 10–11, 28; GA20, 110; GA26, 1–7.
11. See also Daniel O. Dahlstrom, *Heidegger's Concept of Truth*, Cambridge: Cambridge University Press, 2001, Chapter One.
12. See Kisiel, *The Genesis of Heidegger's Being and Time*, p. 398.
13. See also Heidegger's reflection late in life in ZSD, 86/78: 'The clearer it became to me that the increasing familiarity with phenomenological seeing was fruitful for the interpretation of Aristotle's writing, the less I could separate myself from Aristotle and the other Greek thinkers. Of course, I could not immediately see what decisive consequences my renewed occupation with Aristotle was to have'.

14. Walter Bröcker and Käte Bröcker-Oltmanns, 'Nachwort der Herausgeber', GA61, 201.
15. See also Bröcker and Bröcker-Oltmanns, 'Nachwort der Herausgeber', GA61, 201.
16. On this, see Kisiel, *The Genesis of Heidegger's* Being and Time, pp. 238–48.
17. The source for all this course information is Appendix B of Kisiel, *The Genesis of Heidegger's* Being and Time, pp. 461–76; see also John van Buren, *The Young Heidegger: Rumor of the Hidden King*, Bloomington: Indiana University Press, 1994, pp. 220–2; Richardson, *Heidegger*, pp. 663–71.
18. We should note here the opening line of the *Metaphysics* (980a22), usually translated as 'all men naturally desire knowledge'. In Summer Semester 1922 (that is, the future GA62), Heidegger renders this as 'the urge to live in seeing, the absorption in the visible, is constitutive of how the human being is'. This means *phusis* is translated as 'how being' and *eidenai* by 'seeing'. Quoted in Kisiel, *The Genesis of Heidegger's* Being and Time, p. 239.
19. This is a move that Heidegger makes regularly. See, for example, GA19, 8; GA20, 110–22; GA2, 34–5.
20. See Käte Bröcker-Oltmanns, 'Nachwort der Herausgeberin', GA63, 113; and John van Buren, 'Endnote on the Translation', *Ontology: The Hermeneutic of Facticity*, pp. 101–2, n. 1.
21. See Dahlstrom, *Heidegger's Concept of Truth*, p. 181. See GA21, 135; GA2, 226; GA19, 182, 188, 617. In this, as in so much else, Heidegger is indebted to Franz Bretano, *Von der mannigfachen Bedeutung des Seienden nach Aristoteles*, Freiburg: Herder, 1862.
22. Lawrence J. Hatab, *Ethics and Finitude: Heideggerian Contributions to Moral Philosophy*, Lanham: Rowman & Littlefield, 2000, p. 113, n. 5. For an analysis of 'have', see GA59, 53–4.
23. For a lengthy discussion of hearing, see *De Anima*, 419b4–421a7.
24. See also GA2, 33, 37, where *logos* is discussed as *Kundgebung and Auslegung*: demonstration and interpretation
25. For a longer discussion of man in the biblical tradition, see GA63, 22–5
26. Kisiel, *The Genesis of Heidegger's* Being and Time; *Heidegger's Way of Thought*.
27. On this course, see Allen Scult, 'Aristotle's *Rhetoric* as Ontology:

A Heideggerian Reading', *Philosophy and Rhetoric*, Vol. 32 No. 2, 1999, pp. 146–59; Allen Scult, 'The Hermeneutics of Heidegger's Speech: A Rhetorical Phenomenology', *Journal of the British Society for Phenomenology*, Vol. 29 No. 2, May 1998, pp. 162–73; Theodore Kisiel, 'Situating Rhetorical Politics in Heidegger's Protopractical Ontology (1923–1925: The French Occupy the Ruhr)', *Existentia*, Vol. IX, 1999, pp. 11–30; Kisiel, *The Genesis of Heidegger's* Being and Time, pp. 286–301; P. Christopher Smith, 'The Uses of Abuses of Aristotle's *Rhetoric* in Heidegger's Fundamental Ontology: The Lecture Course, Summer, 1924', in Babette E. Babich (ed.), *From Phenomenology to Thought, Errancy and Desire*, Dordrecht: Kluwer, 1999, pp. 315–33; Laurence Paul Hemming, *Devaluing God: Postmodernity's Transcending*, Ashgate: SCM Press, forthcoming, Chapter Two. See also Allen Scult, *Being Jewish/Reading Heidegger*, New York: Fordham University Press, 2004.

28. Letter of 19 March 1924, reported in Kisiel, *The Genesis of Heidegger's* Being and Time, pp. 282, 540, n. 2.

29. For an early hint of how this will become the discussion of *Gerede*, idle talk, in *Being and Time*, see GA19, 306–7. See also Dahlstrom, *Heidegger's Concept of Truth*, p. 283. For a very valuable discussion of *logos* in Plato, see John Sallis, *Being and Logos: Reading the Platonic Dialogues*, Bloomington: Indiana University Press, Third Edition, 1996.

30. For other references to the *Rhetoric* in this course, see GA19, 219, 350–1. A similar reference is made in GA29/30, 439, where Aristotle is given credit both for his analysis of the structure of the propositional statement, and, in the *Rhetoric*, for the 'mighty task of submitting the forms and formations of non-thetic discourse to interpretation'.

31. Scult, 'Aristotle's *Rhetoric* as Ontology', p. 146.

32. For a brief textual comparison of GA20 with *Being and Time* on this point, see Kisiel, *Heidegger's Way of Thought*, p. 62. On the *Rhetoric*, see Alan G. Gross and Arthur E. Walzer (eds), *Rereading Aristotle's* Rhetoric, Carbondale: Southern Illinois University Press, 2000; Ronald Beiner, *Political Judgment*, London: Methuen, 1983, Chapter Five; Larry Arnhart, *Aristotle on Political Reasoning: A Commentary on the* 'Rhetoric', DeKalb: Northern Illinois University Press, 1981; and Eugene Garver, *Aristotle's* Rhetoric: *An Art of Character*, Chicago: University of Chicago Press, 1994.

33. Scult, 'Aristotle's *Rhetoric* as Ontology', p. 156.
34. Kisiel, *The Genesis of Heidegger's* Being and Time, p. 293.
35. On Heidegger on language, old but still helpful are Joseph J. Kockelmans (ed.), *On Heidegger and Language*, Evanston: Northwestern University Press, 1972; and Robert Bernasconi, *The Question of Language in Heidegger's History of Being*, Atlantic Highlands: Humanities Press, 1985.
36. See Scult, 'Aristotle's *Rhetoric* as Ontology', p. 150.
37. Kisiel, 'Situating Rhetorical Politics in Heidegger's Protopractical Ontology', pp. 18–19; and see his 'Rhetoric, Politics, Romance: Arendt and Heidegger 1924–26', in James E. Swearingen and Joanne Cutting-Gray (eds), *Extreme Beauty: Aesthetics, Politics, Death*, London: Continuum, 2000, pp. 94–109, pp. 105–6.
38. This point will be returned to in Chapters Two and Three. See also Stuart Elden, 'Rethinking the *Polis*: Implications of Heidegger's Questioning the Political', *Political Geography*, Vol. 19 No. 4, May 2000, pp. 407–22; and *Mapping the Present: Heidegger, Foucault and the Project of a Spatial History*, London: Continuum, 2001, pp. 67–75.
39. See in particular the reading of Anaximander in GA5, 321–73/242–81, and GA51, 94–123.
40. See Kisiel, 'Situating Rhetorical Politics in Heidegger's Protopractical Ontology', p. 16; Kisiel, *The Genesis of Heidegger's Being and Time*, pp. 294–5. We should note that in some later courses, such as GA33, 121/103, Heidegger translates *logos* as *Kundschaft*, conversance; and in GA45, 8 as *Aussage*, assertion. This, therefore, directly challenges Etienne Balibar's claim that Heidegger never equates these two fundamental definitions, therefore meaning that 'Heidegger will not even suspect *the originary unity of ontology, politics and anthropology*'. See his 'Subjection and Subjectivation', in Joan Copjec (ed.), *Supposing the Subject*, London: Verso, 1994, pp. 1–15, pp. 7–8.
41. Frederick A. Olafson, *Heidegger and the Ground of Ethics: A Study of* Mitsein, Cambridge: Cambridge University Press, 1998, unfortunately does not give a single substantive reference to Aristotle in his discussion, thereby neglecting the whole context from which this issue emerges. A similar situation is found in Peg E. Birmingham, '*Logos* and the Place of the Other', *Research in Phenomenology*, Vol. XX, 1990, pp. 34–54. See, however, Karl Löwith, *Das Individuum in der Rolle des Mitmenschen*, Darmstadt: Wissenschaftliches Buchges, 1969 [1928]; Hans-Georg

Gadamer, 'Ich and Du (K. Löwith)', in *Gesammelte Werke*, Tübingen: Mohr, 1985ff, Vol. IV, pp. 234–9; and for a valuable discussion, Axel Honneth, 'On the Destructive Power of the Third: Gadamer and Heidegger's Doctrine of Intersubjectivity', *Philosophy and Social Criticism*, Vol. 29 No. 1, pp. 5–21. Also useful is Michael Theunissen, *The Other: Studies in the Social Ontology of Husserl, Heidegger, Sartre, and Buber*, translated by Christopher Macann, Cambridge, MA: MIT Press, 1984. Despite complaints by the likes of Jean-Luc Nancy that Heidegger has little to say on the notion of *Mitsein*, in, for example, *Être singulier pluriel*, Paris: Galilée, 1996, it seems to me more a problem with what Heidegger did say. The fifth chapter of this work does, however, provide a very interesting brief discussion of the problem of measure.

42. In GA20, 326, he further hyphenates this to *Mit-da-sein* – being-there-with.
43. See GA20, 333, where he corrects the delineation of with-world and self-world that is found in earlier courses, such as GA58, 33–4, 43–6, 62–4; GA59, 59; GA64, 25, 31.
44. The formulation in the English translation of GA20 is not found in the German edition, being dependent on Simon Moser's transcript of the course, p. 367: '*Das Man hat im Gerede seine eigentliche Seinsform*' (personal correspondence with Theodore Kisiel, 15 September 2004).
45. For a justification, see GA9, 332/253 n. b.
46. Many years later Lévinas would make a related criticism, which only tangentially relates to the claims made later in this chapter. See Emmanuel Lévinas, *Totalité et infini: Essai sur l'extériorité*, The Hague: Martinus Nijhoff, 1961; *Autrement qu'être ou au-delà de l'essence*, The Hague: Martinus Nijhoff, 1974; and for a valuable discussion, David Boothroyd, 'Responding to Lévinas', in *The Provocation of Lévinas: Rethinking the Other*, edited by Robert Bernasconi and David Wood, London: Routledge, 1988, pp. 15–31.
47. Kisiel, *The Genesis of Heidegger's* Being and Time, p. 292.
48. Seemingly out of nowhere, for example, in 1920, Heidegger makes a passing reference to the Kapp *Putsch* (GA59, 72).
49. See also the discussion of *koinonia* in relation to Plato in GA19, 512–17.
50. See Johannes Fritsche, *Historical Destiny and National Socialism in Heidegger's* Being and Time, Berkeley: University of California

Press, 1999; Charles Bambach, *Heidegger's Roots: Nietzsche, National Socialism, and the Greeks*, Ithaca: Cornell University Press, 2003.

51. Fritsche, *Historical Destiny and National Socialism*, p. xii, more generally, see his Chapter 3.
52. For a discussion, see Elden, *Mapping the Present*, pp. 8–15.
53. See Françoise Dastur, *La Mort, Essai sur la finitude*, Paris: Hatier, 1994, especially Chapters 3 and 4.
54. For some interesting notes toward a discussion of representation [*Repräsentation*] in a more explicitly political sense, see GA90, 165ff.
55. See GA20, 366–7: 'there is phonetic speaking only because there is the possibility of discourse, just as there is acoustical hearing [*Hören*] only because being-with-another is characterised originally as *Mitsein* in the sense of listening-to-another [*Aufeinanderhörens*]'. See Jacques Derrida, 'Heidegger's Ear: Philopolemology (*Geschlecht* IV)', in John Sallis (ed.), *Reading Heidegger: Commemorations*, Bloomington: Indiana University Press, 1993, pp. 163–218.
56. Personal correspondence with Theodore Kisiel, 19 August 2004.
57. Much later, the same ideas appear in *The Principle of Reason*. See, for example, GA10, 137/92.
58. It is notable that several studies miss the embedded role of Aristotle. As well as Olafson, *Heidegger and the Ground of Ethics*, see, for example, Gerald Prauss, *Knowing and Doing in Heidegger's* Being and Time, translated by Gary Steiner and Jeffrey S. Turner, Amherst, NY: Humanity Books, 1999, which only mentions Aristotle to refer to the notion of *theoria*, when the reading of Aristotle in these lecture courses is crucial to the formulation of the entire terminology Heidegger is concerned with. More useful are Jacques Taminiaux, *Heidegger and the Project of Fundamental Ontology*, Albany: State University of New York Press, 1991, especially Chapter 3; Franco Volpi, 'Dasein as *praxis*: The Heideggerian Assimilation and the Radicalism of the Practical Philosophy of Aristotle', in Christopher Macann (ed.), *Critical Heidegger*, London: Routledge, 1996, pp. 27–66; John van Buren, 'The Young Heidegger, Aristotle, Ethics', in Arleen B. Dallery and Charles E. Scott, with P. Holley Roberts (eds), *Ethics and Danger: Essays on Heidegger and Continental Thought*, Albany: State University of New York Press, 1992, pp. 169–87; Ted Sadler, *Heidegger and Aristotle:*

The Question of Being, London: Athlone, 1996; Reiner Schürmann, *Heidegger on Being and Acting: From Principles
to Anarchy*, translated by Christine-Marie Gros and Reiner
Schürmann, Bloomington: Indiana University Press, 1987,
pp. 254–7.

59. See Richard Polt, 'Heidegger's Topical Hermeneutics: The *Soph-
ist* Lectures', in *Journal of the British Society for Phenomenology*,
Vol. 27 No. 1, January 1996, pp. 53–76; Ingeborg Schüssler, 'Le
Sophiste de Platon dans l'interprétation de M. Heidegger', in Ada
Neschke-Hentschke (ed.), *Images de Platon et lectures de ses
uvres: Les interprétations de Platon à travers les siècles*, Louvain:
Bibliothèque Philosophique de Louvain, 1997, pp. 395–415. On
related questions more generally, see Catherine H. Zuckert,
*Postmodern Platos: Nietzsche, Heidegger, Gadamer, Strauss,
Derrida*, Chicago: University of Chicago Press, 1996; and William McNeill, *The Glance of the Eye: Heidegger, Aristotle and
the Ends of Theory*, Albany: State University of New York Press,
1999.

60. For a thorough discussion, see Joseph Dunne, 'Aristotle After
Gadamer: An Analysis of the Distinction Between the Concepts
of Phronesis and Techne', *Irish Philosophical Journal*, Vol. 2,
1985, pp. 105–23; and *Back to the Rough Ground: Practical
Judgment and the Lure of Technique*, Notre Dame: University of
Notre Dame Press, 1993.

61. Such a division plays a fundamental role in Hannah Arendt, *The
Human Condition*, Chicago: University of Chicago Press, 1958.
Indeed, she states as much: 'The book had its origin in my first
Marburg days and in every way owes just about everything to
you' (letter to Heidegger, 28 October 1960, in Hannah Arendt
and Martin Heidegger, *Briefe 1925–1975 und andere Zeugnisse*,
Frankfurt am Main: Vittorio Klostermann, 1999).

62. On this, see Theodore Kisiel, 'The Genetic Difference in Reading
Being and Time', *American Catholic Philosophical Quarterly*,
Vol. LXIX No. 2, Spring 1995, pp. 171–87.

63. For mainstream readings of this book, see David Bostock, *Aristotle's Ethics*, Oxford: Oxford University Press, 2000, Chapter
Four, 'Virtues of Intellect'; J. O. Urmson, *Aristotle's Ethics*,
Oxford: Blackwell, 1988; and Anthony Kenny, *Aristotle's Theory of the Will*, London: Duckworth, 1979.

64. This is the case in Crisp's translation, Rackham's, that of David
Ross (revised by J. L. Ackrill and J. O. Urmson, Oxford: Oxford

University Press, 1980), and also Greenwood's bi-lingual edition. But the translation by Hippocrates G. Apostle, Dordrecht: D. Reidel, 1975, divides these chapters fifteen lines later, so that the passage cited is indeed in Chapter 8. Ultimately, though, the upshot is the same: Heidegger skims twenty lines of the text.

65. Heidegger often makes an opposition between *zoe* and *bios* that would problematise this, suggesting that *zoe* is life of humans in the presence of plants and animals, but *bios* is life in the sense of existence [*Existenz*], a leading of life [*Lebensführung*] determined by *telos*, 'a *telos* functioning for the *bios* itself as an object of *praxis*' (GA19, 244; see GA22, 312–13). Plants and animals have *zoe* but not *bios*, which is understood as 'life in the sense of a life-history; that is, they do not have the possibility of a freely chosen and formed Dasein that holds itself in what we call composure' (GA33, 123/105; see GA21, 34–5). In GA22, 312–13, he suggests 'such a Dasein is a proper [*eigene*] possibility of humans: *bios politikos* (see Nicomachen Ethics I, 5, 1095b18), "living in a community"'. On this, see Giorgio Agamben, *Homo Sacer: Sovereign Power and Bare Life*, translated by Daniel Heller-Roazen, Stanford: Stanford University Press, 1998; and *The Open: Man and Animal*, translated by Kevin Attell, Stanford: Stanford University Press, 2004.

66. Hannah Arendt, 'Martin Heidegger at Eighty', in Michael Murray (ed.), *Heidegger and Modern Philosophy: Critical Essays*, New Haven: Yale University Press, 1978, pp. 293–303, p. 300.

67. The French translation renders it as '*la circonspection prévoyante*', far-sighted circumspection. See *Interprétations Phénoménologiques d'Aristote*, French–German edition, translated by J.-F. Courtine, Mauvezin: Trans-Europ-Repress, 1992, p. 37.

68. For a discussion, see Olafson, *Heidegger and the Ground of Ethics*, p. 44. Bourdieu, *The Political Ontology of Martin Heidegger*, p. 76, suggests that this is Heidegger's tactic of wresting the word from its normal social connotations. The term *Fürsorge* is utilised in GA21 (222–4) in the context of a discussion of teaching and learning, through the process of communicating to a listener, of *Mitsein* as *Mitsorge* or *Fürsorge*, but in the sense of substitution it has connotations of leading and following. See Kisiel, *The Genesis of Heidegger's* Being and Time, p. 386.

69. It is, of course, conceivable that he missed out the twenty lines for external reasons, and there is a potential textual explanation. As

the editor Ingeborg Schüßler notes, the section of the course that this passage appears in is part of 'five unlabelled sheets . . . with notes on the interpretation of *Nicomachean Ethics* VI, Chapters 7 (second part)–9'. Most of the other sections of the course are on numbered pages. Further, this is in the first part of the course, which does not have the Moser transcript authorised by Heidegger himself. It is therefore part of the course assembled from the manuscript and student notes alone. (See 'Nachwort des Herausgeberin', GA19, 656–8). But I sense there is something more to it than that.

70. Rackham, *The Nicomachean Ethics*, p. 346, n. b.
71. We should note here, though parenthetically, that in the *Metaphysics sophia* is described as the architectonic (982b7). For a discussion, see Schürmann, *Heidegger on Being and Acting*, p. 254.
72. See Greenwood, 'Introduction', in *Nicomachean Ethics*, p. 60.
73. Hans-Georg Gadamer, *Neuere Philosophie 1: Hegel, Husserl, Heidegger, Gesammelte Werke Band 3*, Tübingen: J. C. B. Mohr, 1987, pp. 199–200; *Philosophical Hermeneutics*, translated and edited by David E. Linge, Berkeley: University of California Press, 1976, pp. 201–2. See also *Philosophische Lehrjahre: Eine Rüchschau*, Frankfurt am Main: Vittorio Klostermann, 1977, pp. 210–21; *Heideggers Wege*, Tübingen: J. C. B. Mohr, 1983, p. 118. On Heidegger as a teacher more generally, see Arendt, 'Martin Heidegger at Eighty'. See also Volpi, 'Dasein as *praxis*', pp. 118–19.
74. In fact, *phronesis* is rarely mentioned after this period. See, though, notably, GA54, 178, where *phronesis* and philosophy itself are equated. For a suggestion that this reading of *phronesis* anticipates that of 'en-owning', which is becoming an all-too-regular translation of *Ereignis*, see Frank Schalow, 'Questioning the Search for Genesis: A Look at Heidegger's Early Freiburg and Marburg Lectures', *Heidegger Studies*, Vol. 16, 2000, pp. 167–86, pp. 170–1.
75. For a discussion of the role of conscience in 'The Concept of Time' (GA64), see Thomas Sheehan, 'The Original Form of *Sein und Zeit*: Heidegger's *Der Begriff der Zeit* (1924)', *Journal of the British Society for Phenomenology*, Vol. 10 No. 2, May 1979, pp. 78–83.
76. See also GA20, 319, where, according to student transcripts, but not the course as published, Heidegger used the word *phronesis*

in his analysis of concern. See Thomas Sheehan, 'Caveat Lector: The New Heidegger', *New York Review of Books*, Vol. 27 No. 19, 4 December 1980, www.nybooks.com/articles/7216.

77. Kisiel, *The Genesis of Heidegger's* Being and Time, p. 301.

78. As Lawrence J. Hatab, *Ethics and Finitude: Heideggerian Contributions to Moral Philosophy*, Lanham: Rowman & Littlefield, 2000, p. 103, suggests: 'In a discussion of Book VI of the *Nicomachean Ethics*, Heidegger specifically brackets Aristotle's (ontical) ethical problematic in order to draw out its ontological implications'.

79. Richard Wolin, *Heidegger's Children: Hannah Arendt, Karl Löwith, Hans Jonas, and Herbert Marcuse*, Princeton: Princeton University Press, 2001, merely hints at the philosophical impact of Heidegger's lectures. More useful is a single footnote by Schürmann, *Heidegger on Being and Acting*, p. 328, n. 30, which suggests the impact it had on Gadamer and Arendt.

80. See, for example, Dominique Janicaud, *L'ombre de cette pensée: Heidegger et la question politique*, Grenoble: Jérôme Millon, 1990.

Two – Against: Polemical Politics

'The Inner Truth . . .'

The issues that arise from the reading of Aristotle outlined in the previous chapter play out in a number of ways. On the one hand there is a continuity, where Heidegger stresses the idea of the human as the being with the *logos*, with language (for example, GA29/30, 442–3; GA31, 54; GA32, 91; GA33, 125/106; GA34, 198), and discusses the fallen sense of modern logic (such as GA32, 109, 149–50; GA36/37, 69–77, 103; GA40, 142). On the other, we find a continual effort to rethink and problematise earlier discussions, such as the argument that because *legein* means *lesen*, to glean, 'to harvest or gather [*zusammenlesen, sammeln*], to add one to the other, to include and connect [*mitrechnen*] one with the other', the primary meaning of *logos* is 'relation [*Beziehung*]' or 'relationship [*Verhältnis*]' rather than discourse (GA33, 5/2–3, 121/103; see GA34, 198; GA40, 95). This is both a partial rejection of the claim in *Being and Time* that *Verhältnis* is a misleading translation of *logos* (GA2, 32), but also builds into the claim that *logos* is rule or law, 'the ruling structure, the gathering of those beings related among themselves' (GA33, 121/103).

This is an important hint of the link between the mode of connection of humans in community, through language, and the calculative politics – through the notion of *mitrechnen* – to be discussed in Chapter Three. For if one thing is clear from the early discussions of these topics, it is that the failure to think through what being-together politically might mean leaves a substantial void at the heart of Heidegger's thinking. If political community is understood not as an exchange of equals but as one where leaders and rhetors hold sway, then a critique of democracy cannot be far behind;[1] if the bounds of that community are not set by geographical constraint but through linguistic determination, then an exclusionary internal politics and/or expansive foreign policy is not likely to be opposed. While it is instructive to see these issues in the political activism of Heidegger, it is ultimately more illuminating – and indeed damning – to see them at the very heart of his thought.

The end of the 1920s will be taken here as a decisive political and philosophical moment. I am cautious about the danger of too strongly emphasising changes in Heidegger's work, and wish to banish entirely the idea of a *Kehre* in his thought, which has exercised many commentators. Nonetheless, it does seem that the period around 1929–30 is important.[2] This is certainly not to say that there are no continuities: in terms of the lecture courses, for example, there is certainly one with studies of Aristotle (GA33), Kant (GA31) and Hegel (GA32). Equally, in the extensive course *The Fundamental Concepts of Metaphysics*, delivered over the Winter Semester of 1929–30, there is a detailed reading of Aristotle's work on the propositional statement (GA29/30, 441ff), which makes use of several earlier insights in a detailed codification of his ideas. But in this course there are also issues that should alert us to changes going on in Heidegger's thinking – both a sustained attempt at rethinking the problem of world (a theme more generally discussed in Chapter Three), and, in the analysis of the fundamental attunement of boredom, a deep sense of cultural and political malaise: 'everywhere there are upheavals [*Erschütterungen*], crises, catastrophes, emergencies: today's social misery, political chaos, the impotence of science, the hollowing out [*Aushöhlung*] of art, the groundlessness [*Bodenlosigkeit*] of philosophy, the weakness [*Unkraft*] of religion. Certainly there are emergencies everywhere' (GA29/30, 243).

If there is a political sense that emerges around this time, it seems important to recognise that one of the crucial elements in this story is not merely Heidegger's references to people like Oswald Spengler, Ludwig Klages and Leopold Ziegler, but his relation to Plato, rather than Aristotle.[3] Although Plato is treated in detail in of some of his early lecture courses – most obviously *Plato's* Sophist – Aristotle continually outweighs him. Not only was Aristotle the focus of much more work, including the prospect of a book on him, but *Being and Time* is a much more Aristotelian work. In addition, as Chapter One has discussed, the political pronouncements of the mid-1920s come in the context of a detailed engagement with the *Nicomachean Ethics*, the *Politics*, and, most especially, the *Rhetoric*. Nevertheless, Heidegger's explicit political career can be much more obviously understood through Plato, and this is most clearly philosophical in a recurrent theme that begins to be asserted in a new form again and again: the essence of truth.

Heidegger gave a lecture with this title as early as 24 May 1926, but it seems this was very close to material in the 1925–26 course on logic in Kant (GA21), which has an only initial sense of this material, and indications suggest that the first recognisable form of the lecture was given on 14 July 1930 in Karlsruhe; in Bremen in October; and in Marburg and Freiburg in December. 'The Essence of Truth' became an essay, reworked throughout the 1930s, including a 1932 lecture in Dresden, and which was finally published in 1943 (GA9, 177–202/ 136–54).[4] The essay 'Plato's Doctrine of Truth' (GA9, 203–38/155–82) also dates from this period and shares a number of themes. These essays and occasional lectures draw extensively on two lecture courses: *The Essence of Human Freedom* from the summer of 1930 (GA31), and *The Essence of Truth* from the winter semester 1931–32 (GA34). *The Essence of Human Freedom* shares common themes with other courses, particularly on Kant, although here the treatment is both of the *Critique of Pure Reason* and the second critique, the *Critique of Practical Reason*. But it is in *The Essence of Truth*, repeated in the winter of 1933–34 in a much more explicitly political form, that some crucial themes emerge. For here, above all, we find Heidegger engaging with Plato's *Republic*.

Heidegger's concern with truth is long-standing, and, as Chapter One demonstrated, runs through his engagement with Aristotle. Truth is the subject of the crucial section 44 in *Being and Time*, which concludes the first division (GA2, 212–31), but this is a discussion that does not engage with Plato. Even the course on ancient philosophy discusses Plato only briefly in relation to truth (GA22, 102–6). But what is crucial about this discussion is that it treats the myth of the cave in the *Republic*, which becomes the central focus of his discussions over some following courses (for example, GA24, 402–5; GA28, 347–61). Heidegger is making the claim that there is an important distinction between the truth of a being, that is its unconcealment, and the truth of an assertion about a being, the second being dependent on the first (GA27, 104; see GA2, 261). It is in the 1929 course *Einführung in das Akademische Studium* [Introduction to Academic Studies] that Heidegger provides the first sustained reading of the myth, although only a partial transcript is published (GA28, 351–61). The myth of the cave, and more broadly this question of truth, is a crucial issue for Heidegger, both philosophically and politically.

Philosophically it is important, because Heidegger suggests that the incomplete nature of the project of *Being and Time* could be understood through his inability to reverse the move of the genitive implied in the title 'The Essence of Truth', to allow an examination of the question of the truth of essence. There was intended to be a lecture with that second title, and the failure of that was, Heidegger suggests, outlined in the 'Letter on Humanism' (GA9, 201/154, 327–8/250). It is in this period, then, that *Being and Time* moves from being a work he still hoped to finish to being one that he realised was going to remain incomplete, as he turned to more historical work again (see GA66, 422). In Chapter Three there will be intensive discussion of the manuscript that has been hailed as his second major work, *Contributions to Philosophy*, the *Beiträge zur Philosophie*. There are conflicting reports here. According to another manuscript, *Besinnung*, plans for the *Beiträge* were underway by early 1932, that is, *before* the Rectorship (GA66, 424),[5] possibly developed during Heidegger's sabbatical semester of 1932–33.[6] But Heidegger's letter to Elisabeth Blochmann of 18 September 1932, concerning the non-appearance of the other divisions of *Being and Time*, tells her that 'I am no longer writing a book at all'.[7]

The political element is equally important, because the end of the 1920s is the time when the Nazi Party made its crucial electoral breakthrough. In the elections of May 1928 they received 2.6% of the vote; in September 1930 18.3%, becoming the second-largest party in the *Reichstag*.[8] One of the key reasons behind this was the Wall Street Crash of 29 October 1929, and the Great Depression which followed. Unemployment across the world but particularly in Germany soared – 8.5% in 1929; 14% in 1930; 21.9% in 1931; and 29.9% in 1932 – and there was a return to the economic crises of the early 1920s. But even in this period Heidegger rarely makes explicitly political comments. Two indications are important here. First, there is a story about how the Karlsruhe lecture of 14 July 1930 equated truth and *Bodenständigkeit*, autochthony or rootedness in the earth, which played to an audience 'purportedly receptive to "Blubo" talk'.[9] *Blut und Boden* – blood and soil – is, as Bambach has shown, important in Heidegger's work.[10] Second, there is a parenthetical comment from the 1931–32 course (to be discussed below), which the editor suggests was probably never delivered, where Heidegger notes that *aletheia* can become history for us, only through a sustained and serious engagement with the essence of truth.

> Only by us awakening such a historical occurrence [*Geschehen*] – without imagining that we can reverse history [*Geschichte*] overnight; without the childish idea that the proof of success or failure of this task (which is not of today) is perhaps the removal of unemployment or the like. At bottom, whoever thinks in this way effectively thinks that the essence and spirit of man is something one gets at the pharmacist. (GA34, 123, n. 1)

In this passage we see both the recognition of a current political crisis – unemployment – which is being talked of in need of a solution, and also a suggestion that dealing with these issues is insufficient and unequal to the greater task at hand. This task is tied into the fateful language around historical destiny. Such aspiration and naïveté will be found throughout Heidegger's career.

Even so, these kinds of pronouncements are unlikely to fully explain what happened in early 1933 when he took over as Rector of Freiburg (21 April), joining the Nazi party shortly afterwards at the beginning of May.[11] As we noted in Chapter One, Heidegger contests the idea that *sophia* can help in the realm of *politike*, recognising that it is rather *phronesis*. Heidegger, through Aristotle, is explicitly ruling out exactly the Platonic notion of philosopher-kings, found in the *Republic*, the *Politeia*. And yet, in 1932 he effectively offers his services to the state as *philosophos*, something which he puts into practice in 1933. What then happens philosophically to effect this political move?

The reading here will concentrate on the *The Essence of Truth* course from 1931–32, comparing it to a 1933–34 course of the same title (GA36/37). Second time around, the discussion is much more explicitly politically orientated.[12] Between these two courses Heidegger delivers his Rectorial address on 'The Self-Assertion of the German University', in which Plato plays a muted but important role.[13]

As is well known, Heidegger wants to move discussion of truth beyond merely a concern with correspondence, whereby it is the truth to say that X is Y. These are particular truths, they utter something 'true', they concern correctness [*Richtigkeit*] (GA34, 2). But truth can be other than this, when for example we use it to describe a thing – 'true gold' or 'a true friend'. To get beyond this, it is necessary, contends Heidegger, to move beyond a sense of 'essence' as the universal, concerned with what-being, the question of what truth is (GA34, 4). This leads Heidegger to rehearse a sketch of what he calls 'the history of the concept of truth'. From the Middle Ages, truth has been understood in terms of *commensuratio*, thinking the commensurable, 'measuring up to [*An-messung*], or the measuring against [*Sich-messen*], something'. Essence was conceived as '*quidditas*, as what-ness, the what-being of a thing – its genus: the universality of the genus' (GA34, 8). At least, this is what appears on first glance. Heidegger's discussion then follows his well-known path: the Greek word for truth is *aletheia*, which should be understood as *a-letheia*, that is a negation of *lethe*. Various authorities such as Aristotle and Heraclitus are drawn upon to illustrate such claims. But all this is preparatory for the opening up of the reading of Plato's *Politeia*, which Heidegger suggests 'we miscomprehendingly translate into German as "Der Staat"', that is literally *The State* (GA34, 18), or, in the standard English version, *The Republic*.

Heidegger's discussion of Plato's *Republic* is centred around the allegory of the cave, where bound people are watching the shadows of the outside world thrown by a fire onto the wall of a cave, and take them for the world itself (514a–518b). An individual is able to escape from the cave, first to see the fire itself, and then to see the world outside, illuminated not by the fire but by the sun. Although initially disorientated by the new source of light and taking a while to understand this new world revealed, the escapee would eventually have an understanding beyond even the most valued occupants of the cave. That is, they would have sight of the forms. Though they return to the cave to attempt to free those left imprisoned and to show them the illusion of their perception, they undoubtedly receive a hostile response. For one thing, the recognition of the shadows would now be difficult for them, because their eyes were no longer accustomed to darkness, and therefore what they recognised as important would be unvalued. Plato's presentation is of the parallels between the world of everyday concern and the life of the philosopher, who has removed themselves from the things usually available to sight and gained access to a higher realm of thought.

Heidegger uses his interpretation to claim that 'truth as correctness is grounded in truth as unconcealedness [*Die Wahrheit als Richtigkeit gründet in der Wahrheit als Unverborgenheit*]' (GA34, 34) – that is, the person who has been led from the cave can perceive and make correct judgements because they have had things unconcealed, that is revealed, to them. This person 'understands the *being* of beings; in perceiving the idea he therefore knows what belongs to a being and to its unconcealedness . . . with his view of essence he can now see what happens in the cave for what it is' (GA34, 89). Heidegger translates *aletheia* as the unconcealed or the unhidden, removed from its previous state. He finds a similar proposition in Plato's *Seventh Letter* (344b3), freely translating as 'only then is the perceiving of essence [*Wesenblick*] unfolded, the perceiving that stretches as far as possible, namely as far as the innermost capacity of human being reaches' (GA34, 112). The cave allegory, then, for Heidegger, is 'about the liberation and awakening of the innermost power of the essence of man' (GA34, 112). This is the case because the fundamental, primordial sense of truth, as unconcealed, does not apply to a property of a being, a proposition concerning it, but to the being itself. The propositional character of truth is a secondary aspect, it describes something that is already true, that is unconcealed (GA34, 118–19). It is for this reason that Heidegger can argue that 'truth as correctness is grounded in truth as unconcealedness' (GA34, 34, see 146–7, see 105–6).

The closing lines of the course summarise the position Heidegger claims to have reached:

> We attempted to answer the question concerning the essence of truth by looking at a piece from the history [*Geschichte*] of the concept of truth [the myth of the cave], and at a piece from the history of the concept of untruth [the *Theaetetus*]. But perhaps we have learnt to understand that it is precisely *here*, and *only* here, in such *history*, that we experience the *presencing* of truth. We cannot bring anything to the appearance of its essence through sheer cleverness and empty pedantry. For this reason we can reach what truth is, and how it presences, only by *interrogating* it in respect of its own *occurrence* [*Geschehen*]; above all by asking after *what* remained *un*-happened in this history [*Geschichte* un*geschehen*] and which was closed off, so much closed off that ever since it has seemed as if in its primordiality it *never was* [gewesen]. (GA34, 322)

In the original published version of the 'Essence of Truth' essay, Heidegger suggests that 'the essence of truth is freedom'. In a later version, he suggests that 'the essence of truth, as the correctness of a statement, is freedom'. Although the previous sentence, which had suggested that 'the openness of comportment as the inner condition of the possibility of correctness is grounded in freedom' already makes that clarification, it is interesting to note that Heidegger felt it necessary to make it (GA9, 186/142). What this means is essentially the same as the suggestion that correctness is made possible by unconcealedness, that is, that correctness is a second order question. Indeed, a few lines on Heidegger suggests that 'freedom is the essence of truth itself' (GA9, 186/143).

For Plato, the role of education is to reorientate the human mind, to recognise a capacity it has, but which is being underused (518d). There are those who can use their capacity to educate, and work in the interest of the community, that is, those who turn back to the cave. Heidegger notes that their potential fate [*Schicksal*] is to be killed, 'the most radical ejection from human-historical community [*menschlich-geschichtlichen Gemeinschaft*]' (GA34, 81). They are the *philosophos*, 'the friend of being', the person who pursues philosophy not as an academic subject but as a way of existence, an understanding of being as a whole (GA34, 82). The liberated one has a role to play in the community, despite the likely reaction of the prisoners.

> In regard to the 'state' (as we somewhat inadequately translate *polis*) and the question of its inner possibility, Plato sets out his highest principle that the proper guardians of the being-with-another of humans, in the unity of the *polis*, should be those humans who philosophise. This does not mean that Professors of Philosophy should become chancellors of the Reich [*Reichkanzler*], but that philosophers must become *phulakes*, guardians. The ruling and rule-ordering [*Die Herrschaft und Herrschaftordung*] of the state should be guided through by philosophical humans who, on the basis of the deepest and widest, freely questioning knowledge, bring the measure and rule [*Maß und Regel*], and open the routes of decision [*Entscheidung*]. (GA34, 100)[14]

Although this runs counter to the arguments made about Aristotle discussed in Chapter One, Heidegger excuses this by suggesting that the prisoners are being freed from *aphrosune*, delusion, 'the counter-concept to *phronesis*, *sophrosune*'. He notes that *phronesis* here is different from how it appears in Aristotle, where it is narrowed down, and is, for Plato, 'the word for knowledge in general, that is for grasping the true, for circumspection *and* insight [*Umsicht* und *Einsicht*] in relation to world and self, the unity of both' (GA34, 36). The prisoner is not released when freed from their shackles, but only when they come up to the light, and no longer fight what is revealed to them (GA34, 41).

'. . . and Greatness . . .'

The Essence of Truth was the penultimate course delivered before Heidegger took over as Rector. In the summer of 1932 he lectured on Anaximander and Parmenides – a course which will appear as GA35 – and he was on leave for the winter semester 1932–33, spending most of the time in his ski-hut (GA16, 652; HC, 92).[15] During this time, the Nazis secured 37.3% of the vote in July 1932, but slipped to 33.1% in November. Despite this, Hitler became Chancellor on 30 January 1933. When the Reichstag burned on 27 February, it was used as justification for the emergency *Verordnung des Reichspräsidenten zum Schutz von Volk und Staat* [Decree of the *Reich* President for the security of people and state] the following day. This suspended most of the human rights of the Weimar Constitution, including *habeas corpus*, freedom of speech, assembly and the press. The Reich Minister of Public Enlightenment and Propaganda was established by law on 13 March, followed by the first two *Gleichschaltung* laws coordinating the Federal *Länder* with the Reich as whole on 31 March and 7 April. Particularly important were the new elections on 3 March, which allowed the passing of the Enabling Act [*Ermächtigungsgesetz*], or, to give it its full title, the *Gesetz zur Behebung der Not von Volk und Reich* [Law to Remedy the Emergency of the People and the *Reich*] on 23 March 1933, effectively beginning the Nazi dictatorship, since it gave Hitler the power not only to make legislation but also to deviate from the constitution. Dachau opened the previous day.[16] Although Heidegger would later claim that it was only after the Night of the Long Knives of 30 June 1934 that potential University administrators 'could know clearly with whom one was bargaining' (GA16, 390), it seems enough was already clear. But on his return to Freiburg Heidegger took over the academic leadership of the University, on 21 April 1933, shortly before the start of the new semester. On 6 May, in an address for student registration, 'Zur Immatrikulation', Heidegger declares that

> The whole German people have found themselves under a great leadership [*einer großen Führung*]. This leadership creates the *Volk* coming into itself which grows into the nation [*In dieser Führung schafft das zu sich selbst gekommene Volk wächst hinauf zur Nation*]. The nation takes on the fate [*Schicksal*] of the *Volk*. The *Volk* achieve themselves this historical spiritual mission [*geschichtlichen geistigen Auftrag*] among *Volks* and creates its own history. (GA16, 95)

Heidegger's political rhetoric is particularly unforgiving in the formal address he gave on 27 May 1933, entitled 'The Self-Assertion of the German University', known as the Rectorial Address [*der Rektoratsrede*]. He again talks of the 'spiritual mission' which is the fate of the German *Volk*; but now speaks of his role in '*spiritually* leading [geistigen *Führung*]' the University as part of this larger fate, to educate and discipline the 'leaders and guardians [*die Führer und Hüter*] of the fate of the German *Volk*'; and of the Greek beginning which first cements a particular language and national-character [*Volkstum*] in the understanding of '*beings in total* [Seiende im Ganzen]' (GA16, 107–9; HC, 29–31). While a particular emphasis on thinking is to the fore, this is in the context of 'the glory and greatness [*die Herrlichkeit und die Größe*] of this new beginning' (GA16, 117; HC, 38). Elsewhere the national-character has a particular form in the Black Forest (GA16, 97), and the spiritual and political leadership are seen as a hyphenated whole (GA16, 95). The language of *Volk* appears on almost every page of the Address, as does that of decision, resoluteness and struggle. Terms Heidegger has previously largely avoided, including state and community, are used without caution. Indeed, Heidegger now employs the composite term *Volksgemeinschaft* to indicate the precise character of this community (GA16, 113; HC, 35; compare GA2, 384). He talks of 'the soil and blood [*erd- und bluthaften*] of a *Volk*' and the 'will to greatness [*Willen zur Größe*]' (GA16, 112; HC, 34); and he uses the term *Volksgenossen*, a Nazi term for fellow-traveller or comrade. The one explicit reference to Plato is the closing lines, an extremely idiosyncratic translation of a line from the *Politeia*: 'all that is great [*Große*] stands in the storm [*Sturm*]' (GA16, 117; HC, 39; see *Republic*, 497d9).[17]

The division of labour service, military service and knowledge service, while indebted to Ernst Jünger's work in the first two terms, highlights some valuable issues.[18] Labour service is to work for the *Volksgemeinschaft*; military service to work for the destiny of the nation [*Geschick der Nation*], but in amongst other *Völker*, other peoples. While these clearly relate to two central planks of Nazi policy, internal and foreign politics, the third shows a programme partially of Heidegger's own, the 'spiritual mission of the German *Volk*', which he links to the question of being (GA16, 113; HC, 35). The inaugural lecture of 1929, 'What is Metaphysics?', had already talked about the possibility of the way the 'position of service in research and theory evolves in such a way as to become the ground of the possibility of a proper though limited leadership in the whole of human existence [*Existenz*]' (GA9, 104–5/83).[19] Now, of course, this is not nearly so limited. While these and many other examples can be given of how saturated Heidegger's language is with National Socialist vocabulary, what is ultimately more revealing is how his own earlier language is employed. Much is obvious here, but note in particular that Heidegger uses *Schicksal* to relate to the collective *Volk* rather than *Geschick*, which is now reserved for the nation; and that Dasein now applies to the German *Volk* as a whole (GA16, 111; HC, 33). Does this mean that the *Volk* effectively functions as a single entity?

An indication of this comes in a discussion of freedom under the new system. 'Freedom [*Freiheit*] is not being-free [*Freisein*] *of . . .* commitment, order and law [*Bindung und Ordnung und Gesetz*]. Freedom is being-free *for . . .* resolution [*Entschlossenheit*] towards shared spiritual dedication [*gemeinsamem geistigen Einsatz*] for German fate' (GA16, 96, ellipses Heidegger's).[20] Being part of this collective destiny allows new kinds of freedom, namely the kinds of service outlined above, and not a false kind of 'academic freedom' (GA16, 112–3; HC, 34–5). Registering for a course of study in the new Reich 'signifies a change of allegiance [*Übertritt*] into a *struggle-and education-community* [Kampf- und Erziehungsgemeinschaft] of which the first and last is the spiritual mission [*Sendung*] of the German *Volk*' (GA16, 96; see GA16, 125–6; HC, 42–3). Heidegger also gave addresses to those attending the labour service programmes designed to solve unemployment (GA16, 232–9; HC, 53–60).

Heidegger offers speeches in honour of the Freiburg student Albert Leo Schlageter, executed in 1923 for sabotage against the French (GA16, 759–60; HC, 40–2; see GA16, 97); lends support in several speeches to Hitler's plebiscite on the withdrawal from the League of Nations, but which also acted as a referendum on Nazi policy as a whole (GA16, 184–5, 188–93; HC, 46–52); and had the Horst-Wessel-Lied sung at University ceremonies (see, for example GA16, 196). He talks about the sacrifice paid by comrades dying an early death in the Great War, 'the greatest death because it dared to be the highest sacrifice for the fate of the *Volk*' (GA16, 279).

> The Great War is *only now* coming upon us. The awakening of our dead, the two million dead from the endless graves, the graves that extend themselves like a secret wreath around the borders of the Reich and of German Austria [*Deutsch-Österreichs* – literally the Eastern German Reich], is only now beginning. The Great War is only today becoming for us Germans – and for us first among all *Volk* – a historical reality of our Dasein, for history is not what has been, nor what is present. History is, rather, the futural and our mandate for this. (GA16, 280)[21]

Heidegger concerned himself with the *Gleichschaltung* principle in the University, sending a telegram to Hitler to this effect on 20 May 1933

(GA16, 105; see GA16, 112; HC, 34) and did implement various racial laws against Jews. But his Rectorial Address, 'The *Self*-Assertion of the German University', is anything but a straightforward assertion of the homogenising principle.[22] However, in one of the plebiscite-supporting speeches Heidegger utters the famous words that 'the National Socialist revolution is bringing about the total transformation of our German Dasein', and 'the Führer alone *is* the present and future German reality and its law' (GA16, 184–5; HC, 46–7). On 1 October 1933 he became officially the *Führer-Rektor*.[23] Ugly stuff, shocking, and likely not yet the whole picture.

Philosophically, much of this is uninteresting, and yet Heidegger clearly did not disassociate his work from his thought. In a brief biographical note from early 1934 – that is, just before he resigned – he lists seven publications: his doctoral and *Habilitation* theses, *Being and Time*, 'What is Metaphysics?', 'The Essence of Ground', *Kant and the Problem of Metaphysics*, and the Rectorial Address (GA16, 247). The date of the resignation is not straightforward. Heidegger claims that he asked to resign in February, but he only officially wrote to that effect on 23 April 1934, and was formally released by the Minister on 27 April (GA16, 274, 826), shortly before giving another course on logic (GA38).[24] Before we turn to this course, I want to provide a brief reading of the two courses delivered while Heidegger was Rector, collected in the double volume GA36/37. The first course in GA36/37 treats *Die Grundfrage der Philosophie* [The Basic Questions of Philosophy]; the second is the new version of *The Essence of Truth*.

For our concerns here, *Die Grundfrage der Philosophie* is of interest because of some remarks on mathematics, to be noted in Chapter Three. But the course, which is largely concerned with issues around metaphysics in Kant, Hegel, Descartes and Baumgarten, is bracketed by some fiery political language about the historical moment, the destiny of the German *Volk*, the necessity of leadership and spiritual missions: Heidegger later puts the insufficient nature of the course down to the demands of being Rector (GA66, 422). Heidegger equates will and breeding or discipline [*die Zucht*] with education, and the call to 'spiritual-political leadership' is related to the future of the *Volk* and the state in the world of peoples. Heidegger sees 'essential leadership' as coming from the 'power of a great determination, in its ground hidden [*aus der Macht einer großen, im Grunde verborgenen Bestimmung*]' (GA36/37, 3). Learning in this context is the requirement of the German *Volk*, and philosophy 'is the question of the law and construction [*dem Gesetz und Gefüge*] of our being' (GA36/37, 4).

Heidegger stresses the affinity between the questioning of the Greeks and that of the Germans (GA36/37, 6, 268; see GA39, 134, 205), and declares that philosophy is unique to a people. Philosophy, on this account is the passion for inquiry, 'the uninterrupted inquiring *Kampf* into the essence and being of beings'. Such inquiry can create new Dasein, setting forth humans in their world and the possibility of greatness [*Größe*] (GA36/37, 8). His final words of the course continue this theme. The German *Volk* are not like those people who have lost their metaphysics, but rather cannot lose it, because they have not yet found it. This means that the Germans are a *Volk*, but one that has to win its metaphysic, and will win it, because it has a fate (GA36/37, 80).

If this course is less polemical than his political rhetoric of the same time, it is still remarkable just how much Heidegger allows the political to intrude into the thought. And though he would make bold claims about the spiritual destiny, it is notable just how much ontic mud is found in these ontological waters. And yet, the main body of the course appears to be largely untouched by such concerns.

The same cannot be said of the second course collected in this volume. Superficially, this course is very similar to the one delivered two years before, treating the myth of the cave and the *Theaetetus* as two halves of a complementary analysis. But the opening pages raise some charged ideas – decision and sacrifice (GA36/37, 84), fate and courage (GA36/37, 86–7), and the question of essence is used to inquire into the essence of the *Volk*, the state, work, the world and human Dasein (GA36/37, 86). Heidegger begins this course with an analysis of one of the fragments of Heraclitus, which says that '*polemos panton men pater esti, panton de basileus, kai tous men theous edeixe tous de anthropos, tous men doulous epoiese tous de eleutherous*' – '*polemos* is the father of all, the king of all: some it shows as gods and some as men; some it makes slaves and others free'.[25] The key word is *polemos*, which Heidegger here renders as '*Krieg, Kampf*', 'war, struggle' (GA36/37, 90).

Heidegger stresses that this is not *agon*, the matching of two friendly adversaries [*freundliche Gegner*], but *polemos*, war. It is severe struggle, where the opponent is not a partner, but an enemy [*Feind*]; this is an *Auseinandersetzung*, an argument or confrontation, literally a setting-apart-from-another (GA36/37, 90). What is particularly important is that the enemy can be seen as injurious to the Dasein of a *Volk* (GA36/37, 91). In sum, 'the essence of being is *Kampf*; each being goes through decision, victory and defeat [*Entscheidung, Sieg und Niederlage*] throughout' (GA36/37, 94). This is significant for two obvious reasons – first, the obvious equation of human life with struggle, *Kampf*; and second, the stress on the enemy, in Greek the *polemios*. If the first is obviously using language closely associated with Hitler, and in particular his *Mein Kampf*, the second is reminiscent of Carl Schmitt's *The Concept of the Political*, originally published in 1932.[26] Heidegger received a copy of the book from Schmitt, and in an August 1933 letter of thanks declared that he was 'in the middle of *polemos* and all literary projects must take second place'.[27]

But the key contrast with Schmitt, and indeed, predominant strands of Nazi thought, is that the enemy is not named. Heidegger is not, seemingly, against anything in particular, but argues for a reading of politics as *polemos*. Unlike Schmitt, his *polemos* is not against a *polemios*, there is not *an* enemy. It is more a reading of politics as struggle, as *Auseinandersetzung*, as confrontation. Chapter Three argues that Heidegger can be seen as orientating his work – implicitly in the earlier part of his career, much more explicitly later on – against number, against calculative determinations of the world and the political. In a sense, then, this book's title needs to be understood both as a phrase and as three separate words: 'speaking against number', but also Speaking, Against, Number; *Reden, Auseinandersetzung, Zahl*; *Logos, Polemos, Arithmos*.

Heidegger later explicitly ties the use of *Kampf* in the Rectorial address – 'the *Kampfgemeinschaft* of teachers and students' and the *Kampf* between the leaders and followers (GA16, 116; HC, 37–8) – to Heraclitus, and this particular fragment. But in the explanation he tries to say that it really means 'strife [*Streit*]', attempting to distance himself from a warlike understanding (GA16, 379). Presumably there had been a philosophical interpretation in the 1932 course on the ancients (forthcoming as GA35, see the reference at GA16, 378) in order to substantiate this, otherwise the philosophical would seem to come after the political interpretation. It is surely demanding too much of his listeners in 1933 to understand *Kampf* as a reading of Heraclitus, and a particular reading at that. He was still translating *polemos* as *Kampf* in 1934–35, although he does there explicitly relate it to the Greek *eris*, that is *Streit*, strife (GA39, 125). The following semester he renders *polemos* as *Auseinandersetzung*, underlining that *polemos* as *Kampf*, as *Streit*, is 'not war in the human sense' (GA40, 47, see 87, 101, 110; compare GA66, 16, 84). But in the Hölderlin course he also uses the term *Feindseligkeit*, which has a meaning close to enmity or animosity (GA39, 222).

The next part of the 1933–34 course rehearses a number of positions around language and *logos*, familiar from earlier discussions. In its transition to the question of truth Heidegger remarks in passing about the problems of liberalism, but that an over-eager proclamation of the death of liberalism can lead to the substitute of a liberal National Socialism, oozing 'harmlessness, respectability and the Youth Movement' [*von Harmlosigkeit und Biederkeit und Jugendbewegtheit*] (GA36/37, 119). Coming after these kinds of pronouncements, it is now impossible to read the interpretation of Plato neutrally. Heidegger talks of the notion of *Herrschaft*, power or rule, and now seems to accept *Staat* as a translation of *Politeia*, implying that he is allowing the transition from Ancient Greece to modern Germany, which at other times he was inclined to disallow (GA36/37, 124).

Most of the discussion is very similar to that of two years before, but of course Heidegger is now the holder of a political post, and Germany is now ruled by the Nazi party. Heidegger allies himself to the Nietzschean struggle on three fronts: against humanism; rootless [*bodenlosen*] Christianity; and the Enlightenment. According to Heidegger, 'he has the arms [*Waffen*] to fight the emergency [*Notlage*]' (GA36/37, 147). Ridding German society of these problems is therefore a war, and this is an immense moment in that struggle, prepared for and urged by National Socialism, preparing for a 'new spirit of the earth' (GA36/37, 148). Heidegger stresses the threefold determination of humans as seeing, hearing and speaking, before again directly equating the *zoon ekhon logon* with the *zoon politikon*. The human is, he declares, 'a creature [*Lebewesen*], which by birth belongs as a *with-another in the state* [*das von Haus aus zugehörig ist einem Miteinander im Staat*]' (GA36/37, 158). All caution in moving from *Mitsein* to community seems to have gone.

This being with-another needs to be understood not simply in that there are many people who need to be kept in order [*Ordnung*], but 'belonging with-another in the State [*als miteinander zugehörig dem Staate*], as existing out of the state; and in fact carrying out and forming this existence through discourse, the *logos*'. The 1924 interpretation of Aristotle is introduced forcefully into the 1932 interpretation of Plato, made explicit by the following sentence: 'The science that is concerned with the capacity to speak [*Redenkönnen*], the *Rhetoric*, is the fundamental science of humans [*die Grundwissenschaft vom Menschen*], the *political* science' (GA36/37, 158).[28]

We are now at the end of 1933, and after the Christmas break

Heidegger returns, via a short digression into the *Sophist*, to the implications of Plato's myth of the cave (GA36/37, 173ff). Bear in mind this is now shortly before his resignation, and indeed that in 1945 he suggests that it was over the break that he made the decision to resign and to cease duties at the end of the semester (GA16, 400; HC, 63). Heidegger quotes the *Sophist*: 'the philosopher, always devoting himself through reason to the idea of being as such, is very difficult to see on account of the brilliant light of the place he stands; for the eyes of the soul of the multitude are not strong enough to endure the sight of the divine' (254a8–b1, see GA36/37, 181; GA34, 82). The philosopher risks death in their work, which Heidegger notes for Plato is naturally equated with Socrates (GA36/37, 182); but is there a biographical issue here? In the earlier version of the course Heidegger had spoken of just such a rejection of the philosopher's role, a symbolic death, of marginalisation or where popularity and experiences reminiscent of the one and idle talk take over (GA34, 83–4). Reading similar lines here (GA36/37, 182–3) has a rather different implication.

Nonetheless, Heidegger suggests that the philosopher, who has walked from the cave, is obligated to return, to show and guide the others. He is the *Befrier*, the liberator (GA36/37, 186). 'The individual man [*der Mensch*], insofar as he exists, *is* in the truth. It appears however, that the person exists as historical *Volk* in the community [*geschichtliches Volk in der Gemeinschaft*]' (GA36/37, 184). The movement from the individual to the collective, with the problematic allusion to a *Volksgemeinschaft*, that politically charged idea of a community of the (German) people, shows that the political implications are still a concern for Heidegger. 'Standing in the truth is a confrontation [*Auseinandesetzung*], a struggle. Pausing in untruth is a let up in the struggle' (GA36/37, 185). Heidegger notes that such a struggle requires the 'appropriate governing powers of Dasein to *lighten* and carry the reality of a *Volk* in history', of their 'spirit and spiritual world' (GA36/37, 185). Such a project is not to be thought able to be accomplished quickly, 'not by 1934 or 1935, but maybe by 1960' (GA36/37, 185).

His exhortations of the importance of philosophy become increasingly shrill:

This philosophising is not any old replaceable speculation [*abgelöste Spekulation*] over any old things, but philosophy and philosophising is the *actual process* [eigentliche Prozeß] of the history of a person and a *Volk*. (GA36/37, 188)

Heidegger then repeats what philosophers must do (see GA34, 100), but with some important inflections. The *polis*, the state, needs a form of '*rule* of the being-with-another [*die* Herrschaft *des Miteinander-seins*] of humans in the state, essentially determined through a determined kind of ruler and a determined form of rule'. In a popular interpretation, he suggests, this is that the philosopher should rule the state (GA36/37, 194).

> This naturally does not mean that philosophy professors should be *Reichkanzler*, that was from the start a disaster. But it does mean that the humans that carry the rule of the state in itself must be philosophical humans. Philosophers, as philosophical humans, have the duty and the service [*die Aufgabe und die Leistung*] of *phulakes*, guardians [*Wächter*]. They have to watch over [*darüber zu wachen*] the ruling and rule-ordering of the state, ensuring that it is philosophical, but not as a system, rather as a knowledge [*Wissen*], which is the deepest and widest knowledge of the human and of human being [*vom Menschen und menschlichen Sein*].
>
> Out of this knowledge is set the standard and rule [*Maßstab und Regel*], within which each appropriate decision and measure setting [*Maßsetzung*] is carried out. In a state-system [*Staatswesen*], says Plato, there can be only a few such guardians. (GA36/37, 194)

It is worth noting that the essays 'The Essence of Truth' and 'Plato's Doctrine of Truth', first published in 1943 and 1947 respectively, with the latter apparently composed in 1940 (GA9, 483/380), and which draw so much on these courses, are almost entirely apolitical. Or, perhaps more accurately, they have their potentially political implications obscured or muted. See, for example, the discussion of the return to the cave of the liberator, where the possibility of death is dealt with only in terms of an actual death with Socrates as the example (GA9, 222–3/171). And the discussion of the role of the philosopher in the *polis* or the state is entirely absent.[29]

On 15 February 1934, Heidegger takes it upon himself to interpret the words of Hitler, suggesting that when he speaks of a 're-education [*Umerziehung*] to the National Socialist *Weltanschauung*, world-view' this is not mere slogans, but 'a *total change* [Gesamtwandel], a *world-plan* [Weltentwurf], at base an education of the whole *Volk*. National Socialism is not any old theory, but a fundamental change for the German, and we believe, the European world' (GA36/37, 225). It is clear that even by the end of the course, at the end of February, Heidegger still sees the questions that concern him in explicitly political terms. 'The essence of truth is a *struggle* with un-truth'

(GA36/37, 262). Heidegger continues to speak about the will of a *Volk*, and its strength to face the difficult and severe tasks ahead of it (GA36/37, 263).

> Therefore the *will to knowledge and spirit* are that by which we stand and fall. Today there is much speech about *blood and soil* as much-called for forces [Blut und Boden *als vielberufener Kräfte*]. Already the literati, [such] that there is still today, have authorised this. Blood and soil are powerful and necessary, to be sure, but are not a sufficient condition for the Dasein of a *Volk*.
>
> Other conditions are knowledge and spirit, not as a supplements alongside another [*Nebeneinander*], but because only knowledge brings the flowing of the blood into a direction and a path, only it brings the soil into the pregnancy or fertility [*Trächtigkeit*], to bear [*tragen*] what it is able to. Knowledge provides nobility to the soil of resolution [*Austrag*], to bear what it is able to. (GA36/37, 263)

In terms of the themes discussed so far in this chapter, this is a further twist. Heidegger is concerned with the Dasein of a *Volk*, but accepts the importance of the rhetoric of *Blut und Boden*, while pointing toward their inadequacy alone. But this is clearly not a criticism, rather a modification, a redirection or pointing toward a particular path or direction. The knowledge service and the spiritual leadership offered in the Rectorial Address still clearly have a role. But what is emerging is also a dalliance with a key term, the notion of the will. Several of these terms – blood and its biological implications; soil and its association with homeland; the will and its linkage to power – exercise Heidegger over the next few years. Before we turn to the first few lecture courses after the resignation, where the first signs of a critical distance begin to appear, the final lines of the course are worth noting. These immediately follow those quoted above.

> Whether we are capable to take on this whole in the same origin and equally strongly, lies in the decision. If we are capable of giving our Dasein a real seriousness and a real weight [*eine wirkliche Schwere und ein wirkliches Gewicht*]; only if we succeed in that, do we create the possibility of *greatness* [Größe] for us.
>
> Obviously only great [*großen*] humans and great *Volk* become great things. Small humans take the small for the enormous. The *true* is for us to achieve, the decision concerning our mission. Only through the decision of this struggle do we create ourselves the possibility of a *fate*. Fate is only there where the human in free decision itself abandons the danger of its Dasein. (GA36/37, 264)

While the language of decision and struggle has been remarked upon throughout this chapter, the recurrent theme of greatness, stressed particularly here, has not. *Groß* can mean big or of large size, or other indicators of measure, but also grand, great or major, signs of value. The same range of meanings is true of the noun *der Größe*, size or greatness. Although this term plays an important role in a number of the claims being made by Heidegger in this period, such as the 'will to greatness [*Willen zur Größe*]' (GA16, 112; HC, 34) and the greatness of the *Volk*, their fate and their Führer (for example, GA16, 95, 104; GA36/37, 3, 8), the sense of the term does not seem to be fully investigated. This will not always be the case.

'. . . of National Socialism'

By the beginning of the summer semester 1934, Heidegger was back as an ordinary professor in the philosophy department. In his later letters, interviews and statements, Heidegger would give three specific references for his confrontation [*Auseinandersetzung*] and spiritual resistance [*geistigen Widerstand*] to National Socialism following his resignation: a 1934 course on *Logic*, the first course on Hölderlin, and the Nietzsche lectures given from 1936–40 (GA16, 402, 404, 664; HC, 65, 66, 101). The lectures on Nietzsche, delivered at the same time that the *Beiträge* was being composed, will be discussed in Chapter Three. This section discusses the *Logic* course in detail, and supplements it with some remarks on the Hölderlin lectures[30] and the *Introduction to Metaphysics* course, important perhaps by its omission from Heidegger's reference.

Logik als die Frage nach dem Wesen der Sprache [Logic as the Question of the Essence of Language] (GA38), was his first course given after the resignation. But the course catalogue shows that this was not the originally projected title, which was rather *Der Staat und die Wissenschaft* [State and Science]. Apparently, when Heidegger declared in the opening lecture that the course was on logic, this was to the 'surprise and annoyance of the NS-functionaries' attending,[31] and only those interested in his philosophy attended the second lecture.[32] Given the concerns around the subject of logic for a number of years, it might appear an unremarkable topic, perhaps a safe option, a return to earlier concerns. The idea of the human as that being that has the *logos* has, however, acted as a determination of a particular concept of the political, and the course delivered is no exception to this deep vein of political questioning. In fact, after its initial opening, it is as explicitly a political course as he ever gave, concerned with the *Volk*, human community, the nature of the 'we' and, in passing, with biological determinations of race in Nazi discourse.

It has generally been supposed, even by many of his sternest critics, that Heidegger was critical of this area of Nazi thought.[33] The place most often turned to is his important 1929–30 lectures *The Fundamental Concepts of Metaphysics* (GA29/30), which, as well as providing a detailed analysis of the mood of boredom, also discuss the animal and the human in terms of their encounter with world. In this course, Heidegger discusses some work on biology, and insists that there is something much more fundamental than this as a determination of the human. The *Nietzsche* lectures are also looked at as a challenge to a biological reading of Nietzsche. However, the work on *Volk*, particularly in the 1934 course, is not as straightforward as Heidegger would have us believe, something the indications from previous courses already alerts us to.

Heidegger certainly thought this course was important. Although there is some discussion of issues concerning race, community and the 'we' in the *Beiträge*, Heidegger there refers us back to this lecture course (GA65, 48). Equally, in the well-known 1966 interview with *Der Spiegel* he mentions these lectures, and suggests that here, along with the first course on Hölderlin and the *Nietzsche* lectures there is 'a confrontation with National Socialism' (GA16, 664; HC, 101).[34] Much later he would see this course as the first where he properly dealt with the question of language (GA12, 89/8; GA8, 158/154). In his 1945 letter to the Rector of Freiburg in defence of his political behaviour he is more explicit:

> During the first semester that followed my resignation I conducted a course on 'logic' and under that title, the doctrine of *logos* as the essence of language. I sought to show that language was not the biological-racial essence of man, but conversely, that the essence of man was based on language as a basic reality of *spirit*. All intelligent students understood this lecture as well as its basic intention. It was equally understood by the observers and informers who then gave reports of my activities to [Ernst] Krieck in Heidelberg, to [Alfred] Bäumler in Berlin, and to [Alfred] Rosenberg, the head of National Socialist scientific services. (GA16, 401–2; HC, 64)[35]

Earlier in this interview Heidegger had suggested that this was in part a continuation of his previous views, and even claims that the suggestion in the Rectorial Address that 'a spiritual world alone guarantees the greatness of a *Volk*' (GA16, 112; HC, 34) is a direct challenge to Rosenberg's position that spirit is 'merely an "expression" and emanation of racial facts and the physical constitution of man' (GA16, 398–9; HC, 62). The remarks at the end of the second course on *The Essence of Truth* about blood and soil being necessary but not sufficient conditions for the Dasein of a *Volk* show that this is not nearly as clear-cut.

Indeed, Heidegger explicitly frames his decision to resign, taken over the Christmas break 1933–34, as a realisation 'that it was a mistake to believe that, from the basic spiritual position that was the result of my long years of philosophical work, I could *immediately* influence the transformation of the bases – spiritual or non-spiritual – of the National Socialist movement' (GA16, 400; HC, 63). The stress on 'immediately', found in the German original, is surely not insignificant – recall the suggestion that 1960 is a more realistic target than this year or the next (GA36/37, 185). In retrospect, Heidegger considers that it was obvious that in his teaching his 'opposition to the principles of the National Socialist world-view would only grow'. He continues to suggest 'that there was little need for me to resort to specific attacks; it sufficed for me to express my fundamental philosophical positions on language in contrast to the dogmatism and primitivism of Rosenberg's biologism'. Pushing these contentious claims even further, he rather desperately suggests that just to philosophise in a climate of unthinking was 'itself a sufficient expression of opposition or resistance [*Widerstand*]' (GA16, 401; HC, 64).

In the course itself, Heidegger repeats his earlier formulation that 'logic is the science of *logos*, of speech [*Rede*], strictly speaking of language [*Sprache*]' (GA38, 13). The question of logic is therefore one of language, but here relates to the crucial questions 'What is the human?', and 'Who are we?' (GA38, 29–30; 34, and so on; see GA65, §19; GA69, 7). Unsurprisingly in the contemporary climate, this leads Heidegger to the question of the *Volk*, which is the notion of the human writ large [*im Großen*] (GA38, 67). In order to interrogate this, Heidegger gives a number of politically charged examples of the use of the term *Volk*.

> We hear folk-songs and see folk-dances, visit a folk-festival. We participate in the delivering of the lists to the houses for the purpose of the census [*Volkszählung* – literally *Volk*-counting]. Measures [*Maßnahmen*] for the improvement [*Hebung*] and protection of the *Volk*'s health [*Volksgesundheit*] are met. The ethnic movement [*völkische Bewegung*] wants to bring back the people to the purity of the tribal-type [*Stammesart*].

Friedrich the Great calls the *Volk* an animal with many tongues and few eyes. On the 12th November 1933 the *Volk* are asked the question [the referendum on the withdrawal from the League of Nations and on Hitler's rule]. A police-colonel commands: 'break up the *Volk* with truncheons!' On August 1 1914 the *Volk* stood in arms. 18 million of the German *Volk* dwell [*wohnen*] outside the borders of the state [*Staatsgrenzen*]. Karl Marx calls the '*Volk*' the totality of the workers in distinction from the loafers and the exploiters. The spirit of the *Volk* [*Volksgeist*] is the root or ground [*der Wurzelgrund*] for belief, poetry and philosophy in romanticism. Religion is the opium of the *Volk*. (GA38, 61)[36]

The question, for Heidegger, is what is meant by '*Volk*' in these instances? Is the *Volk* broken up by the police the same as the *Volk* in the referendum [*Volksbefragung*]? Do any of these definitions get us close to what the *Volk* really is? In the referendum only the voters are counted, those under age are not included. Does this mean they are not part of the *Volk*? Heidegger continues with a number of questions: 'during a census we count the *Volk* [*Volkszählung das Volk gezählt*], but what do we hear in a folk-song? Or are the *Volk* of folk-art not countable, so that we count the population [*Bevölkerung*] only in the first case?' (GA38, 61).

Understanding a group of humans, the 'we' is not through a mere addition of I and you and you, a counting, in terms of belonging [*zugehörig*] (GA38, 40–1). Heidegger gives the example of a lecture as belonging-together [*Zusammengehörigkeit*], as a hearing-with [*Mithören*], of the inclusion of the individual into the listening-group [*Hörerschaft*]. The you plural [*Ihr*] of the listeners is made up of separate you singulars [*Du*], 'out of such a relationship as being spoken to' (GA38, 41). Again this is politically charged, as Heidegger gives the examples of 'you, my *Volk*-comrade [*Ihr, meine Volksgenosse*]' and 'you, my *Volk*' [*Du, mein Volk*]. 'There is a particular explanation for the transformation of the singular into the plural', and the you plural cannot be understood simply as a number [*Anzahl*], nor 'mere numbers [*bloßen Nummern*]' (GA38, 42). Heidegger's example in the summary he provided at the start of the next lecture is of a company-commander at the front counting out volunteers for a dangerous reconnaissance mission, bare numbers [*bloßen Nummern*] (GA38, 47). But it is not any group, a 'nameless crowd . . . a rebellious mass . . . a bowling club . . . a gang of thieves'. A simple over-valorisation of the 'we', which alone means nothing, can even allow a 'drift into criminality' (GA38, 51; see GA29/30, 244).

There is a problem with a calculative understanding of the *Volk* as a population [*Bevölkerung*] or 'the inhabitants of a country [*die Einwohnerschaft eines Landes*]', as, just with the census, only a certain part of the *Volk* is considered, that is, those within the borders of the state, with 'Germans abroad not counted [*Auslandsdeutschen sind nich mitgezählte*]', and therefore appearing to not be part of the *Volk*. 'A census [*Volkszählung*] is therefore only a counting of inhabitants [*Einwohnerzählung*]' (GA38, 65). What comes through here is not only a resistance to calculation, but much more explicitly a denial of the idea that the German *Volk* can be contained by the borders of the state, redrawn of course in 1919 at Versailles.

One of the problems of a calculative understanding is that it is a mere summation, a total of atomised individuals. Heidegger discusses Descartes' formulations of the individual subject as crucial to this. His work has a number of consequences, including the break from the Christian church and the authority of dogmas, and the separation of the human from a connection with nature, a living-measure [*lebensmäßig*] of the human. Following this, 'nature becomes reinterpreted into the mechanical, and the [human] body [*der Leib*] becomes a mere machine, which the spirit prevails over' (GA38, 143). This clearly anticipates later comments about an instrumental way of viewing nature and the understanding of modern technology. But it is the third consequence which is most important here,

> The separation of humans from the community, of the original order [*von der Gemeinschaft, von den ursprünglichen Ordnungen*]. This transition is not in the direction of chaos; rather humans become even more consciously individual as the outcome and element of the new order [*der Neuordnung*], which has the character of a society, that is an association [*der Gesellschaft, d. h. eines Verbandes*]. This is the origin of the new concept of the state (state-treaty) [*Staatsbegriffs (Staatsvertrag)*]. (GA38, 143)

The last term is ambiguous here, usually meaning international treaty. It is interesting to note that the treaty most commonly associated with the beginning both of modern state politics and international relations is the Peace of Westphalia, finally signed in 1648, seven years after Descartes' *Meditations* which is Heidegger's reference here. This is significant because of the way that attacks on the Treaties of Westphalia, which effectively broke up the first German Reich, that is the Holy Roman Empire, was often a surrogate for attacks on the Treaty of Versailles.[37] Equally, a little way on, Heidegger suggests that liberalism has its roots in the Cartesian view of the humans as individual subjects (GA38, 149). Heidegger clearly wants to avoid either a straightforward split between the *Geist* and the body, or the individuation of the thinking subject.

That said, the *Volk* cannot simply be reduced to a biological, that is a racial, determination. Both the biological and the census determinations are merely the accumulation of individual humans (GA38, 63). Heidegger declares that this is part of a wider problem: 'the thought of race, that is calculating with race emerges from in the experience of being as subjectivity and is not (itself) a political issue . . . Race-cultivation [*Rassen-pflege*] is a measure for keeping hold of power [*ein machtmäßige Maßnahme*]' (GA69, 70; see 223). Indeed, 'the metaphysical ground of race-thinking is not biologism', but rather those metaphysical determinations of the thinking subjectivity of the being of beings (GA69, 71). The idea of a body – and Heidegger plays with the different meanings inherent in the two German terms of *der Körper*, the physical body, and the living body, *der Leib* – is inadequate, because the notion of the *Volk* has associations with spirit and soul. But, for Heidegger, race is something which is associated with the body, and though therefore his notion of the *Volk* is not based on crude, biological understandings (see GA38, 61, 65–6), he is not entirely separating race from the *Volk*.

> We also use the word '*Volk*' in the sense of 'race [*Rasse*]' (for example in the expression 'ethnic movement [*völkische Bewegung*]'). What we call 'race' has a link with the bodily [*leiblichen*], blood-measured [*blutmäßigen*] connection of the members of the *Volk* [*Volksglieder*], their generation [*Geschlechter*]. The word and the concept 'race' is no less ambiguous than '*Volk*'. That is no coincidence, because they are connected. (GA38, 65)[38]

Heidegger continues to exploit the ambiguity in the word *Rasse*, which can also mean 'pedigree', or, in more colloquial terms, can be used to describe someone in positive terms as having courage or even spirit, rather like the idea of 'mettle'. Heidegger stresses, therefore, that *Rasse* need not mean 'racial [*Rassisches*]', in the sense of an inheritance, hereditary blood-connection or the like. While he is clearly trying to show how the notion of the *Volk* is determined, here, first, as body, he is opening up other possibilities and ambiguities in the phrase. Boys, at least, he suggests, might talk of a sporty car [*rassiges Auto*], which shows it is not confined to living things, and though 'the racial [*das Rassige*]' implies a definite rank and rule [*Rang und Gesetze*] it is not always understood in a bodily way, as linked to the family and sex [*Geschlechter*] (GA38, 65).

If the first determination of the *Volk* as 'population, inhabitants, connection of the generations [*Zusammenhang der Geschlechter*]', of the *Volk* as the body of the people, is problematic, Heidegger turns to the idea of the *Volk* as the soul, and the spirit.[39] What this means is that though the *Volk* is crucially related to a notion of logos – language – race can be understood as a biological consequence, in a sense the reversal of Rosenberg rather than his rejection. Blood and bloodlines can be 'an essential measure [*wesenmäßig*] of the determination of human beings', but only if they themselves are determined [*bestimmt*] in turn by mood or attunement [*Stimmung*] (GA38, 153). Indeed, it is notable that the discussion of race in relation to the *Volk* is only in terms of the determination of *Volk* through the body, not in terms of soul or spirit (GA38, 65–70).[40]

In large part the spiritual determination comes through language, which Heidegger suggests 'is the management [*Walten*] of world-pictures and the preserving middle of the historical Dasein of the *Volk* [*geschichtlichen Daseins des Volkes*]'. In other words, language links the *Volk* to their historical existence. As Heidegger continues, 'only where temporality itself temporalises [*Zeitlichkeit zeitigt*], does language happen [*geschieht*]; only where language happens, does temporality temporalise' (GA38, 169). The key summary suggestion of this course is that 'the being of the *Volk* is neither the mere presence of a population [*Bevölkerung*] nor animal-like being [*tierhaftes Sein*], but determination [*Bestimmung*] as temporality and historicality' (GA38, 157). There is more to the people than a calculative understanding of population; the introduction of *logos*, time and history disassociate them from animals and the purely biological or bodily. This linking back to the language of *Being and Time* is crucial in understanding how he is philosophising politics rather than simply politicising his philosophy. But equally, it is behind a suggestion that certain 'humans and human groups [*Menschengruppen*] (Negros, such as Kaffirs)' lack a history, and thereby a future (GA38, 81, 83–4), and that only historical *Volk* are really a *Volk* (GA39, 284).[41] Although the claim that not all peoples have a history is not uncommon in the tradition,[42] it is perhaps more appalling here given that in the discussion of what history is Heidegger gives a particular political reading. History is tied to soil (GA38, 85), and he gives the example of the turning of an aeroplane's propeller. Nothing essential happens [*geschieht*] in this, but of course 'if the aeroplane brings the Führer from Munich to Mussolini in Venice then history happens [*geschieht Geschichte*]', and this makes it a historical event. It is not the operation of the machine that is historical, despite the fact that the flight can only happen because of it; Rather, it is what arises in the future. Of course, the machine may later end up in a museum (GA38, 83). This kind of contemporary example is regularly found in Heidegger's subsequent lecture courses.[43]

It is clear that the earlier structures of being-with-another and for-another are part of a larger picture, that of the *Volk* and indeed the state. These two notions are explicitly tied together: 'The state is the historical being of the *Volk*' (GA38, 165). Heidegger talks of the way in which liberty is not about being able to do or not-do without limit, but 'entering the inevitableness of being, the receiving of historical being into knowing will, the imprinting of the inevitability of being in the rule of a fitting structured order [*gefügten Ordnung*] of a *Volk*. Care [*Sorge*] for the freedom of a historical being is in itself author-isation of the power of the state as the essential structure [*Wesensge-füges*] of a historical mission' (GA38, 164). Earlier in the course he had noted that sociology as a discipline often tried to discuss the *Volk*, and in particular to differentiate between society, state and Reich. But he suggests that such discussion is fundamentally flawed, in that these terms must be understood historically, 'as in each case belonging to a historical being [*als einem jeweils geschichtlichen Sein zugehörig*]' (GA38, 68). The state is not simply the form of organisation of a society, but that which originates from the mission and assignment [*aus Sendung und Auftrag*] of a willed-rule [*Herrschaftswillens*] (GA38, 165). Perhaps the original aim of the course, under the title of *Der Staat und die Wissenschaft*, was not entirely abandoned.[44]

There is continual usage of another crucial term, 'decision' [*En-tscheidung*] (for example, GA38, 27, 56–60, 69–77), which Heidegger had used extensively himself in his explicitly political period. He continues to use the term *Volksgenossen* (GA38, 42, 43), *Volksge-meinschaft* (GA38, 26) and the language of *Kampf*, fate (GA38, 8) and *Arbeit* (GA38, 128, 153).[45] He talks of the role of students in 1933, including the SA and the faculty student body [*Fachschaft*] (GA38, 73), suggesting that the role of education is still seen as the 'strengthening and training of the internal ordering of the *Volk*' (GA38, 57). Indeed, this is stressed with the relation of the University to the state, and both as part of 'the willed-rule and rule-form [*der Herrschaftswille und die Herrschaftsform*] of the *Volk* over itself. As Dasein we fit in a proper manner [*eigener Weise*] into the belonging [*Zugehörigkeit*] of the *Volk*, we stand in the being of the *Volk*, we are the *Volk* ourselves' (GA38, 57). Heidegger talks of the decisional moment [*Augenblick*] of the assertion of the *Volk* (GA38, 59), and stresses the importance of the distinction between belonging to a state, effectively citizenship [*Staatsangehörigkeit*] and belonging to a *Volk* [*Volkszugehörigkeit*] (GA38, 60). This is the question of decision, a futural question. Although this is all a prelude to the discussion of what the *Volk* actually is, it is still clearly a discussion going on from within National Socialist discourse, rather than from a position external to it.

Equally, there is a dismissive reference to his concern with logic not being due to some 'arbitrary [*beliebigen*] *Gleichschaltung*' (GA38, 11; see also GA36/37, 161), but rather with a much more profound upheaval and transformation of thought, existence and destiny. There is also a suggestion that, while the Rector today appears in 'SA uniform rather than the traditional gown', this does not prove that anything about the University has changed (GA38, 74). There has been no real revolution or transformation in the German University (GA38, 76). The Rector, of course, is no longer Heidegger but rather his successor Eduard Kern, and this must have been delivered only shortly before the disbanding of the SA following the Night of the Long Knives.

This course – only available since 1998 and so previously not available to evaluate Heidegger's claims[46] – therefore goes some way toward indicating his position, but it is clearly not nearly as straightforward as Heidegger might have us believe. Whilst Heidegger might be critical of National Socialist understandings of race, this does not mean that he escapes what we might understand by the term 'racism'.[47] Bernasconi argues that one can be a racist without determining race biologically, and that many National Socialists did not sign up to this view.[48] Whilst Heidegger rejects the idea that the *Volk* can be reduced to biology, his own view of the *Volk* is deeply problematic. Although he recognises that *Volk* is itself an ambiguous term, he gets into some quite serious problems when he attempts to articulate an alternative. As Bernasconi suggests, 'the text of the 1934 lecture course thus supports Heidegger's subsequent claim that he opposed biological racism, but not that he proposed in its place an account of language framed in terms of *Geist*'.[49]

This ambiguous attitude or lack of critical distance, which can only generously be understood as a transitional phase, is found in other courses too, such as the following semester's course on Hölderlin. Here he oscillates between Hölderlin's calling to a greater spiritual fate that transcends contemporary politics (GA39, 172, 176, 178) and criticism of biologism (GA39, 26–7); and references to fatherland [*Vaterland*], homeland [*Heimat*] and *Volk* (for example, GA39, 90, 99, 104–5, 120, 121, 134, 137, 284),[50] criticism of liberalism (GA39, 99) and the same kind of valorisation of the great, community and listening that arguably led to his involvement in the first place (GA39, 146, 227; 71–3; 68–9, 200–3).[51] In the criticism, he dismisses the biological determination of poetry found in Kolbenheyer, is sceptical of the 'soul' model of Spengler or the racial or Volkish notions of Rosenberg (GA39, 26–7),[52] and derides the way studies of poetry have moved from an earlier concern with psychoanalytic work to 'now everything dripping with national-character, blood and soil [*Volkstum, Blut und Boden*]' (GA39, 254). The historical Dasein of a *Volk* is misunderstood if it simply means favouring *Volkstum* and creating more chairs in ethnology [*Volkskunde*] and prehistory' (GA39, 99).[53]

If many of the other references can be seen as an interpretation of Hölderlin, who for Heidegger rises above the particular context and sets out a spiritual destiny, some claims simply drag such a rationale down: 'The fatherland is beyng [*Seyn*] itself, which carries and adds the ground of the history of a *Volk* as its Dasein; the historicity of its history' (GA39, 121); 'this *Miteinandersein* of Dasein [of the *Volk*] is, measured by a fundamental character of Dasein, historical in itself, and accordingly to the powers of history, bound and added to it' (GA39, 143). Heidegger was clearly influenced by the work of Norbert von Hellingrath, an early twentieth-century editor of Hölderlin, who declared in a 1915 lecture on 'Hölderlin and the Germans' that 'language is the soul of a *Volk*, boundary of a *Volk*, the inner core of a *Volk*', and that this language is at the heart of what he called 'the secret Germany'.[54] In his reading of Hölderlin, Heidegger notoriously equates the role of a poet, a thinker and a state-founder [*Staatsschöpfer*] in the historical fate of a *Volk* (GA39, 143–4; see 51, 120; GA40, 36, 47).[55] Spirit or intellect, *Geist*, was the measure of political leadership in the Rectorship, which seems closer to the poet and thinker, but of course the culmination of spirit in history for Hegel was the state, just as Heidegger notes in this course (GA39, 133).[56]

The problematic claims can also be found in the famous 1936 *Origin of the Work of Art* lecture – 'world is the self-opening openness of the broad paths of simple and essential decisions in the destiny of a historical *Volk*' (GA5, 35/26) – and in the *Beiträge*, written between 1936 and 1938. Although treatment of this text will largely be confined to Chapter Three, in terms of the issues of *Volk* and race there are some important remarks. Heidegger characterises the people of today as fleeing into 'new' contents, and though their conceptions of the 'political' and the 'racial' were 'previously unknown', they are merely 'dressings for the old facade of School-Philosophy', that is, metaphysics (GA65, 18–19). He later claims that 'all biologisms and naturalisms . . . stay within the soil [*Boden*] of metaphysics' (GA65, 173). Although it is a common metaphor, the use of *Boden* is not insignificant. Clearly, central term within Nazi language, Heidegger is here turning it around, suggesting that being rooted in the soil shows the limited nature of these claims, that they remain within the problematic they seek to exceed. A similar claim is made later: 'all doctrines which focus on "values", "meaning", "ideas" and ideals; correspondingly, the doctrines which deny such, like positivism and biologism' still remain within Platonism (GA65, 218).[57] He similarly criticises the 'metaphysics' of Richard Wagner and Houston Stewart Chamberlain (GA65, 174).

The most important section here is number 15 (GA65, 42–3). The section heading reads 'Philosophy as "Philosophy of a *Volk*"'. Who could deny this is the case, Heidegger asks? We have Greek philosophy and German philosophy – this seems self-evident. But in truth, none of this comes close to what philosophy itself is – philosophy is not something like clothing or a style of cookery which can be understood as peculiar to a people. Almost as a throwaway, Heidegger declares that 'it is sheer nonsense to say that experimental research is Nordic-Germanic and rational research comes from *foreigners*! We would then have to already count [*zählen*] Newton and Leibniz among the "Jews"' (GA65, 163). Equally, such a claim to national philosophy rests upon a problematic term, *Volk*.[58] Heidegger suggests that the forgetting of being shows itself particularly in failing to note the ambiguity of what is deemed essential: his example is the question of the '*Volk*' and related terms such as 'community, the racial, the lower and higher, the national' (GA65, 117; see GA66, 167); but when he returns to these problematic terms five years later, he notes that all of them rest on a problematic notion of the individual and the I–you relationship (GA54, 204, 247).

Heidegger is clearly treading on dangerous ground when he discusses the notion of *Volk*. While these are important questions, even today, Heidegger is not doing what he later claims. He is not so much suggesting an alternative way of conceptualising race on the basis of spirit, as suggesting that biological racial thinking falls within the remit of metaphysics. Calculative understandings of population can be seen in the same way. This is, of course, to ignore that other forms of racism do not admit to the same understanding, such as cultural forms of, for example, anti-Semitism. Clearly, neither does Heidegger depart from the sense of a historical fate of the German people and the role of the state in this.

We might expect, given the stress Heidegger put on the 1934 lecture course, that it might have been one he chose to have published in his lifetime. If the critique was as clear as he implied, this would presumably have been an important intervention. He was certainly willing to publish some material from this time. The first course on Hölderlin was not published until after his death, but a book, *Erläuterungen zu Hölderlins Dichtung* [Elucidations of Hölderlin's Poetry] (GA4), did appear in various editions with a number of essays on the poet, trading extensively on lecture material, though largely forsaking the political aspects.[59] And the next set of lectures, *Introduction to Metaphysics*, and ones on Kant, Schelling and Nietzsche (GA40, GA41, GA42, GA43, GA44, GA47 and GA48) all appeared in some form during Heidegger's life. As the preceding analysis has shown, many of these texts show that Heidegger's coming to terms with the Nazi regime was far from one-sided or unequivocal. He is not advocating a notion of *Volk* free from race, but recognising how the two concepts are complicit, and precisely because of their determination within metaphysics (GA38, 65). This criticism is sufficiently convoluted for there to have been a real purpose in having a clear, officially authorised, account given after the war, which the original manuscripts would have muddied and complicated.[60] In other instances, such as the valorisation of the state, these courses would have shown a side Heidegger was at pains to leave unexposed.

A particular example of this textual detail and the contentious claims made in this period is found in the *Introduction to Metaphysics* course, from 1935. While the more interesting material is found in the comments on geopolitics, there is also a notorious phrase which has provided the section headings of this chapter.

What is being peddled about nowadays as the philosophy of National Socialism but which has nothing whatever to do with the inner truth and greatness [*der inneren Wahrheit und Größe*] of National

Socialism (namely the encounter between global technology and modern humans) – is fishing in the troubled waters of 'values' and 'totalities'. (GA40, 152)[61]

Although delivered in 1935, this was published in 1953, the first of Heidegger's lecture courses to appear as a publication. There is lots of debate over this phrase, in particular over the way in which an expression of faith is allowed to stand. If it were as simple as that, then we might at least accept an honesty in preserving the historical record. But the lecture course is not as it was in 1935, and in its opening note from Heidegger we find that 'matter in parentheses was written while I was reworking the text' (GA40, XI). In other words, the clarification of what the 'inner truth and greatness' was, 'namely the encounter between global technology and modern humans', is a later addition. Given that, as we shall see, Heidegger holds that it failed to think that relation, a significant shift of emphasis is implied by the phrase. For Otto Pöggeler, 'with this elucidation the "greatness" of National Socialism is defined in a thoroughly negative way'.[62] Later in life, when asked about the clause in parentheses, Heidegger claims that it was indeed present in the course manuscript in 1935, but was not delivered, because 'I was convinced that my audience were understanding me correctly'. He continues, excusing the remark as one playing to 'the stupid, the spies, and the snoopers', who would understand him otherwise (GA16, 668; HC, 104).[63] Given that the manuscript page in question is missing,[64] the testimony of Heidegger's assistant Harmut Buchner that the phrase was added,[65] and the countless other examples given above of political claims being made in lectures, we should be deeply sceptical about this claim.[66]

There is a further complication, which is less often remarked upon. In the translation provided above, Heidegger refers the 'inner truth and greatness' back explicitly to 'National Socialism', following Pöggeler's account of the manuscript, whereas in the actually published version it is 'of this movement'.[67] 'This movement' clearly relates back to National Socialism, but it perhaps makes the distinction between the philosophy and the inner truth and greatness more explicit. However, rather than simply noting that the manuscript and the version Heidegger authorised for publication differ, Pöggeler also notes that, according to one audient, Walter Bröcker, Heidegger said something slightly, but significantly, different: not 'of National Socialism', nor 'of this movement', but 'of the movement'. Pöggeler reports Bröcker as underlining this: 'The Nazis, and they alone, used "the movement" for National Socialism. Hence Heidegger's "the" was for me unforgettable'.[68]

This chapter has analysed the way Heidegger utilised the notion of truth and the idea of greatness in his writings leading up to this period, which shows that the phrase has a particular significance, rather than being merely an avowal. By 1935 his own political career and aspirations are in tatters, but another model, a spiritual model, the 'inner' essence, is clearly still believed in. And it is not clear that it was ever really abandoned, despite a definite turn toward criticism of at least some aspects of actually existing National Socialism. Take, for example, the following well-known passage.

> This Europe, in its unholy blindness always on the point of cutting its own throat, lies today in the great pincers [*der großen Zange*] between Russia on the one side and America on the other. Russia and America, seen metaphysically, are both the same: the same hopeless frenzy of unchained technology and of the rootless [*bodenlosen*] organization of the average man. When the farthest corner of the globe [*Erdballs*] has been conquered technologically and can be exploited economically; when any incident you like, in any place you like, becomes accessible as fast as you like; when you can simultaneously 'experience [*erleben*]' an assassination attempt against a king in France and a symphony concert in Tokyo; when time is nothing but rapidity, instantaneity and simultaneity [*Schnelligkeit, Augenblick-lichkeit und Gleichzeitigkeit*], and time as history has vanished from all Dasein of all *Volk*; when a boxer counts as the great man of a *Volk*; when the tallies of millions at mass meetings are a triumph [*Millionenzahlen von Massenversammlungen ein Triumph*], yes then, there still looms like a spectre over all this uproar the question: what for? – where to? – and what then? (GA40, 28–9)

The nationalist thrust of this is still deeply problematic. It is the German *Volk*, that is the 'metaphysical *Volk*', that lies 'in the pincers', 'in the centre [*Mitte*]', that is 'richest in neighbours and hence the most endangered *Volk*' (GA40, 29). The idea of Germany being squeezed by external forces was a commonplace of discussion of foreign policy at the time,[69] although Heidegger possibly means Germany to be understood in the middle in a temporal sense as well: between the Greek past and its own future.[70] In a revealing comment in the much later interview with *Der Spiegel*, Heidegger explains the potential he saw in the National Socialist revolution as the necessity to 'find a national, and above all a social, point of view, perhaps of the sort attempted by Friedrich Naumann' (GA16, 655; HC, 95). Naumann was the author of the notorious book *Mitteleuropa*, advocating a central European power as a balance between the West and Russia, inevitably dominated by the German-speaking people of Germany and Austria-Hungary.[71] In 1935, Heidegger offers a renewed sense of the *Bestimmung* of the *Schiksal* of the German *Volk*, declaring that 'if the great decision [*große Entscheidung*] regarding Europe is not to go down the path of annihilation – precisely then can this decision come about only through the development of new, historically *spiritual* forces from the centre [*neuer geschichtlich* geistiger *Kräfte aus der Mitte*]' (GA40, 29).

He continues to talk about decision, but here hyphenating to *Ent-scheidung*, to bring out the meaning of cutting in the 'cision', and in a later clarifying gloss says this is not the 'judgement and choice of human beings, but rather a cut' regarding being (GA40, 84). Heidegger declares that noting this spiritual decline is not *Kulturpessimisus*, but needs to be understood metaphysically as a decline in terms of the fate of being (GA40, 29). He equally notes that respect should be shown to (National Socialist) 'organisations for the purification of language and for defence against its progressive mutilation', while noting that they do not go far enough, suggesting that the relation of the *Volk* to being is through language (GA40, 39). This concern with language is also important in considering why Heidegger turns from a discussion of Nietzsche's suggestion that being is a vapour and a fallacy to contemporary concerns with geopolitics.[72] It is because the question that must be asked is whether being is merely a word, 'its meaning a vapour, or is it the spiritual fate of the Western world [*Abendlandes*]?' (GA40, 29; see 32). Equally, and making explicit the way in which hearing was understood in the 1924 Aristotle lectures and later in *Being and Time*, Heidegger suggests that 'genuine being-obedient [*Hörig-sein*, that is, hearkening] is opposed to mere hearing and keeping one's ears open' (GA40, 99). The first step in the reform of Universities must be 'a real revolution in the prevailing view to language', and for this 'we need to revolutionise the teachers' and effect a transformation of the University (GA40, 41).[73]

All that said, there is something that goes beyond this here. Perhaps most obviously, there is the sarcastic reference to the Triumph that can be tallied through numbers at *mass* meetings. Is it necessary to note that Leni Riefenstahl's contemporary film of the Nuremberg rallies, *The Triumph of the Will,* had been released the year of Heidegger's lectures? Then there is the advent of a mechanised and technological 'globalisation', a process where the earth is but a ball, conceived as a whole, conquered and exploited. The later notion of machination is anticipated here, but without a full development. Heidegger's point about rapidity, instantaneity and simultaneity is more nuanced than a simple translation can capture. *Schnell* is the word for speed, and so this captures something of the transitory, accelerated nature of time; *Augenblick* is the 'moment'; and *Gleichzeitigkeit* implies each moment of time [*Zeit*] being made the same [*Gleich*]. The mournful references to 'the darkening of the world, the flight of the gods, the destruction of the earth, and the reduction of human beings to a mass [*die Vermassung des Menschen*]', that is a levelling down, which follow (GA40 29), are both embedded in Heidegger's political strategies up to this moment, and anticipate themes from his *Beiträge*. But, in the idea of a *Vermassung*, they look beyond the political ideas presented so far.

> The prevailing dimension became that of extension and number [*Ausdehnung und der Zahl*] . . . In America and Russia, then, this all intensified until it turned into the measureless [*maßlose*] etcetera of the ever-identical and the indifferent [*Immergleichen und Gleichgültigen*], until finally this quantitative temper [*dieser Quantitative*] became a quality of its own, (GA40, 35)

Heidegger's politics, as we have seen, was a spiritual mission. His complaint here is in part how the spiritual has been devalued and misinterpreted. When *Geist* is rendered as mere *Intelligenz*, it is simply reduced to calculating and examining [*Berechnung und Betrachtung*]. It leads to 'mass distribution [*massenhafter Verteilung*]' and the possibility of organisation, both alien to spirit. What is interesting is that this way of thinking, of *Geist* as intelligence as a tool [*Werkzeug*], is seen in action in three potential realms – 'the regulation and domination [*die Regelung und Beherrschung*] of the material conditions of production'; 'the intelligent ordering [*Ordnung und Erklärung*] of everything that is present and already posited at any time'; and as 'applied to the organisational regulation [*der organisatorischen Lenkung*] of the vital resources and race of a *Volk* [*der Lebensmasse und Rasse eines Volkes*]'. Heidegger notes that the first is found in Marxism, the second in positivism, by which he surely means its American form. He does not name the third, but this is clearly a reference to the contemporary situation (GA40, 35–6).[74] As Kisiel notes, too strongly but on the right track, 'thus the practice of German National Socialism is, already in 1935, "metaphysically the same" as that of Americanism and Russian Communism'.[75]

In order to fully comprehend what is being hinted at here, and which will reoccur again and again, particularly in Heidegger's next course on Kant and the thing and the *Beiträge*, some backtracking is required. The key questions will be what is meant by the notion of measure, the issues of extension and number, the problem of calculation and the quantitative temper. As Heidegger declares, following some illuminating remarks about how he sees philosophy in 1935, 'philosophizing always remains a kind of knowing that not only does not allow itself to be made timely [*zeitgemäß*, that is, in measure with the times] but, on the contrary, imposes its measure on the times [*die Zeit unter sein Maß stellt*]' (GA40, 6).[76] Metaphysics did not contribute to the Revolution, so should it be thrown away? Not at all, declares Heidegger. Philosophy can never directly supply the impetus to lead to [*heraufführen*] a historical state of affairs, because it is the preserve of the few. Philosophy is 'a thoughtful opening of the avenue and vistas of a measure- and rank-establishing knowing [*maß- und rangsetzenden Wissens*], a knowing in which and from which a *Volk* conceives its Dasein in the historical-spiritual world and brings it to fulfilment' (GA40, 8; see GA16, 483).[77] Heidegger is interested in the root of the term *Einführung*, introduction, a leading-into [*hineinführen*]. What does it mean to lead into? 'Leading [*Führen*] is a questioning going-ahead, a questioning-ahead [*Vor-fragen*, a preliminary question]. This is a leading that essentially has no following' (GA40, 15). How then are we to conceive of measure? Once again, the ideas are forged in the early lecture courses on Aristotle.

Notes

1. See, for example, GA43, 193; a passage removed from the 1961 publication of these lectures.
2. A similar justification is found in Otto Pöggeler, 'Heidegger's Political Self-Understanding', HC, p. 205; and Jürgen Habermas, 'Work and *Weltanschauung*: The Heidegger Controversy from a German Perspective', in Hubert L. Dreyfus and Harrison Hall (eds), *Heidegger: A Critical Reader*, Oxford: Basil Blackwell, 1992, pp. 186–208, pp 191–2.
3. See, for instance, GA29/30, 103–7. Spengler had previously been discussed in 1920–21, in a course on religion. See GA60, 42–50.
4. On the chronology, see GA9, 483/380; John Sallis, 'Deformatives: Essentially Other Than Truth', in John Sallis (ed.), *Reading Heidegger: Commemorations*, Bloomington: Indiana University

Press, 1993, pp. 29–46; and Theodore Kisiel, *The Genesis of Heidegger's* Being and Time, Berkeley: University of California Press, 1993, pp. 473, 475–6.

5. See also Friedrich-Wilhelm von Herrmann, *Wege ins Ereignis: Zu Heideggers 'Beiträge zur Philosophie'*, Frankfurt am Main: Vittorio Klostermann, 1994, p. 1.

6. See Heidegger to Jaspers, 1 July 1935, in *Correspondance avec Karl Jaspers*, texte établi par Walter Biemel et Hans Saner, traduite de l'allemand par Claude-Nicolas Grimbert, suivi de *Correspondance avec Elisabeth Blochmann*, traduite de l'allemand par Pascal David, Paris: Gallimard, 1996, p. 143.

7. Heidegger to Blochmann, 18 September 1932, in *Correspondance*, p. 270.

8. See Thomas Childers, *The Nazi Voter: The Social Foundations of Fascism in Germany 1919–1933*, Chapel Hill: University of North Carolina Press, 1983; Richard Hamilton, *Who Voted for Hitler?*, Princeton: Princeton University Press, 1982.

9. Kisiel, *The Genesis of Heidegger's* Being and Time, p. 562, n. 40. His reference leads us to Guido Schneeberger, *Nachlese zu Heidegger: Dokumente zu seinem Leben und Denken*, Bern: Suhr, 1962, p. 12, and particularly the note to that page. See also Victor Farías, *Heidegger and Nazism*, translated by Paul Burrell and Gabriel R. Ricci, Philadelphia: Temple University Press, 1989, p. 72, suggesting this was Heidegger's response to a call to a chair in Berlin. Heidegger's 1934 radio address outlining his refusal to take another Berlin chair similarly talks of how 'the inner belonging [*Zugehörigkeit*] of my own work to the Black Forest and its people comes from a centuries-long and irreplaceable rootedness [*Bodenständigkeit*] in the Alemannian-Swabian soil' (GA13, 10–11). It is worth noting that this piece first appeared in a National Socialist journal: *Der Alemanne: Kampfblatt der Nationalsozialisten Oberbadens*.

10. Charles Bambach, *Heidegger's Roots: Nietzsche, National Socialism and the Greeks*, Ithaca: Cornell University Press, 2003.

11. There is dispute over the date. The official chronology suggests 3 May, backdated to 1 May (GA16, 826); others see it as significant that a labour holiday was chosen. See Hans Sluga, *Heidegger's Crisis: Philosophy and Politics in Nazi Germany*, Cambridge, MA: Harvard University Press, 1993, p. 3. See Theodore Kisiel, 'In the Middle of Heidegger's Three Concepts of the Political', in François Raffoul and David Pettigrew (eds),

Heidegger and Practical Philosophy, Albany: State University of New York Press, 2002, pp. 135–57, p. 134 on Heidegger's rejection (in a letter to Rudolf Bultmann) of the 'outhouse rumour' that he had joined the party in December 1932.

12. See the comments of the editor, Hartmut Tietjen, 'Nachwort des Herausgebers', in GA36/37, 300–1.

13. For a discussion, see Graeme Nicholson, 'The Politics of Heidegger's Rectoral Address', *Man and World*, Vol. 20 No. 2, 1987, pp. 171–87; and Bambach, *Heidegger's Roots*, pp. 103–7. On the question of truth in Heidegger more generally, see David Farrell Krell, *Intimations of Mortality: Time, Truth, and Finitude in Heidegger's Thinking of Being*, Pennsylvania: Pennsylvania State University Press, 1986; Sallis, 'Deformatives: Essentially Other Than Truth'; and Daniel O. Dahlstrom, *Heidegger's Concept of Truth*, Cambridge University Press: Cambridge, 2001.

14. Sadler's translation seriously waters down the political importance of this passage. For a discussion, see Stuart Elden, *Mapping the Present: Heidegger, Foucault and the Project of a Spatial History*, London/New York: Continuum, 2001, pp. 68–9.

15. Although some scholars, such as Thomas Sheehan, 'Reading a Life: Heidegger and Hard Times', in Charles Guignon (ed.), *The Cambridge Companion to Heidegger*, Cambridge: Cambridge University Press, 1993, pp. 70–96, suggest that Heidegger supported the Nazis from at the latest 1932, his son reports that in 1932 Heidegger was still voting for 'the small, politically insignificant party of Württemberg winegrowers'. See Frank H. W. Edler, 'Philosophy, Language, and Politics: Heidegger's Attempt to Steal the Language of the Revolution in 1933–34', *Social Research*, Vol. 57 No. 1, Spring 1990, http://commhum.mccneb.edu/PHILOS/stealing2.htm. However, Elisabeth Young-Bruehl, *Hannah Arendt: For the Love of the World*, New Haven: Yale University Press, 1982, p. 61, reports a story of Heidegger's wife inviting Günther Stern – a Jewish student who later married Arendt – to join the National Socialist youth group in Marburg in 1925. The letter to Bultmann, referenced in Kisiel ('In the Middle of Heidegger's Three Concepts of the Political', p. 134), as noted above (note 11), suggests the distinction was that Heidegger had voted for the 'movement' in November, while seeing himself as distinct from the 'party'.

16. Two concentration camps were operated between 1933 and 1935 at Heuberg, near Heidegger's hometown of Meßkirch. See Farías, *Heidegger and Nazism*, p. 83.

17. A more standard translation would be 'great things are always hazardous'.
18. See Elden, *Mapping the Present*, p. 69. For Heidegger on Jünger, see GA9, 385–426/291–322; GA90; and GA16, 375.
19. Heidegger quotes approvingly from this lecture on this topic – albeit not this same passage – in 1935 (GA40, 37). Later on this page he also cites the Rectorial Address on the spirit.
20. See the discussion of freedom in relation to Kant in GA31. Heidegger's initial discussion includes the distinction between negative and positive freedom, or freedom from and freedom to. Freedom from is freedom from world, nature and God, a relation of non-dependence.
21. See Bambach, *Heidegger's Roots*; Mark Neocleous, *The Monstrous and the Dead: Burke, Marx, Fascism*, Cardiff: University of Wales Press, 2005.
22. For valuable discussions of this issue, see Alan Milchman and Alan Rosenberg, 'Martin Heidegger and the University as the Site for the Transformation of Human Existence', *The Review of Politics*, Vol. 59 No. 1, Winter 1997, pp. 75–96; Iain Thomson, 'Heidegger and the Politics of the University', *Journal of the History of Philosophy*, Vol. 41 No. 4, 2003, pp. 515–42.
23. Hugo Ott, *Martin Heidegger: A Political Life*, translated by Allan Blunden, London: HarperCollins, 1993, p. 199.
24. This challenges the earlier story that the resignation was in effect *from* February. See Ott, *Martin Heidegger*, pp. 246ff.
25. This is fragment 53 in the Diels–Kranz numbering. See Hermann Diels, *Die Fragmente der Vorsokratiker: Griechisch und deutsch*, edited by Walther Kranz, Berlin: Weidmann, sixth edition, 1951–52, three volumes, Vol. I, p. 162. Note that the treatment of Heraclitus in GA22 does not look at this particular fragment, and the likely discussion in GA35 is not yet available. The most comprehensive discussions, from 1943 and 1944, are in GA55; and a joint seminar with Eugen Fink from 1966–67 in GA15. For a reading of Heraclitus inspired by Heidegger, see Kostas Axelos, *Héraclite et la philosophie: la première saisie de l'être en devenir de la totalité*, Paris: Éditions de Minuit, 1962.
26. Adolf Hitler, *Mein Kampf: Unexpurgated Edition Two Volumes in One*, London: Hurst and Blackett Ltd, 1939; Carl Schmitt, *Der Begriff des Politischen*, Berlin: Duncker & Humblot, 1932; translated by George Schwab as *The Concept of the Political*, Chicago: The University of Chicago Press, 1996.

27. Martin Heidegger to Carl Schmitt, 22 August 1933, English/ German version, in *Telos*, No 72, 1987, p. 132. In a similar vein, in 1945 he reflects that at the time he 'renounced the proper vocation [*eigensten Beruf*] of thinking in order to be effective in an official capacity' (GA16, 390). According to Joseph W. Bendersky, *Carl Schmitt: Theorist for the Reich*, Princeton: Princeton University Press, 1983, p. 203, citing a letter from Heidegger to Schmitt, 22 April 1933, it was Heidegger who invited Schmitt to join the Nazi party. On the relation, see also Gopal Balakrishnan, *The Enemy: An Intellectual Portrait of Carl Schmitt*, London: Verso, 2000. It should, of course, be noted that Schmitt, for all his problems, is much more interesting than the generally reductive reading of his work – by friends and enemies alike – would suggest.

28. See GA16, 656; HC, 95 for a note on the sense of 'political science' at the time.

29. See also GA65, §233. In chronologies such as GA66, 107, the 1933–34 course gets cut out of the development of the story.

30. On these lectures, see Elden, *Mapping the Present*, Chapter 2.

31. Günter Seubold, 'Nachwort des Herausgebers', GA38, 172. In a retrospective on this period, Heidegger talks of a 'well attended seminar on "*Volk* and Science"' (GA16, 373), but this does not appear in listings of his courses, nor does it appear in prospectuses for the *Gesamtausgabe*. For a discussion and paraphrase of an unpublished 1933–34 seminar 'On the Essence and Concept of Nature, History and the State', see Kisiel, 'In the Middle of Heidegger's Three Concepts of the Political'. See also two lectures on 'Die deutsche Universität' delivered in August 1934 (GA16, 285–307).

32. Rüdiger Safranski, *Martin Heidegger: Between Good and Evil*, translated by Ewald Osers, Cambridge, MA: Harvard University Press, 1998, pp. 281–2.

33. See, for example, Thomas Sheehan, ' "Everyone has to Tell the Truth": Heidegger and the Jews', *Continuum*, Vol. I No. 1, Autumn 1990, pp. 30–44; Ott, *Martin Heidegger*, p. 187; Dominique Janicaud, *L'ombre de cette pensée: Heidegger et la question politique*, Grenoble: Jérôme Millon, 1990.

34. For a valuable account of Heidegger's work on the Nietzsche archival project in the years 1936 to 1942, see Marion Heinz and Theodore Kisiel, 'Heidegger's Beziehungen zum Nietzsche-Archiv im Dritten Reich', in Helmut Schäfer (ed.), *Annäherungen an*

Martin Heidegger, Frankfurt am Main: Campus Verlag, 1996, pp. 103–36.

35. For a full discussion of the relationship of Heidegger to Krieck, see Frank H. W. Edler, 'Heidegger and Ernst Krieck: To What Extent Did They Collaborate?', http://commhum.mccneb.edu/philos/krieck.htm. On the Bäumler question, see the series of articles by Edler, 'Alfred Baeumler on Hölderlin and the Greeks: Reflections on the Heidegger–Baeumler Relationship', *Janus Head*, Vol. 1 No. 3, Spring 1999, pp. 205–24; Vol. 2 No. 2, Fall 1999, pp. 157–84; Vol. 3 No. 2, Fall 2000, pp. 322–42.

36. The 18 million Germans were also a theme in a February 1934 address to workers, although here they were outside the Reich (GA16, 233; HC, 56). See also GA67, 47, where there is a reference to Nietzsche's claim in the Prologue to *Beyond Good and Evil* that Christianity is Platonism for the people.

37. See, for example, Friedrich Kopp and Eduard Schulte, *Der Westfälische Frieden*, München: Hoheneichen, 1940, which includes a 'Geleitwort' by Alfred Bäumler. As Heidegger remarks many years later, 'the second half of the seventeenth century after the 1648 Peace of Westphalia was not a time of peace. To the desolation and disaster that followed the great war, came new wars and threats, hunger and misery [*Elend*]. Enemy forces strafed the land. The plague devastated Vienna. The Turks were at the walls of the city' (GA16, 599). The reference to the 'great war' perhaps makes obvious the parallels between the seventeenth and twentieth centuries.

38. On the issue of *Geschlecht*, see Derrida's essays on this theme, the first two of which are collected in Jacques Derrida, *Heidegger et la question: De l'esprit et autres essais*, Paris: Flammarion, 1990; the fourth can be found as 'Heidegger's Ear: Philopolemology (*Geschlecht* IV)', in John Sallis (ed.), *Reading Heidegger: Commemorations*, Bloomington: Indiana University Press, 1993, pp. 163–218. The third essay is unpublished.

39. It is worth noting that spirit, soul and flesh [*pneuma, psuche, sarx*; *Geist, Seele, Fleisch*] are discussed as the attributes of the self in Paul in the 1920–21 course on religion. See GA60, 118–21.

40. For an excellent discussion, see Robert Bernasconi, 'Heidegger's Alleged Challenge to the Nazi Concepts of Race', in James E. Faulconer and M. A. Wrathall (eds), *Appropriating Heidegger*, Cambridge: Cambridge University Press, 2000, pp. 50–67, especially pp. 53–4.

41. See Bernasconi, 'Heidegger's Alleged Challenge', p. 51.
42. See, for example, Immanuel Kant, *Anthropology from a Pragmatic Point of View*, translated by Mary J. Gregor, The Hague: Nijhoff, 1974; G. W. F. Hegel, *The Philosophy of History*, translated by J. Silbree, New York: Dover, 1956, p. 91, which declares that Africa is 'lying beyond the day of self-conscious history'; and even Karl Marx, *Surveys from Exile: Political Writings Vol. 2*, edited by David Fernbach, Harmondsworth: Penguin, 1973, p. 320, which suggests that 'Indian society has no history at all, at least no known history'. For a discussion, see Robert Bernasconi, 'Will the Real Kant Please Stand Up: The Challenge of Enlightenment Racism to the Study of the History of Philosophy', *Radical Philosophy*, No 117, January/February 2003, pp. 13–22; and, more generally, his 'Philosophy's Paradoxical Parochialism: The Reinvention of Philosophy as Greek', in Keith Ansell Pearson, Benita Parry and Judith Squires (eds), *Cultural Readings of Imperialism: Edward Said and the Gravity of History*, London: Lawrence & Wishart, 1997, pp. 212–26.
43. In the Schelling course, Mussolini and Hitler are mentioned as initiating 'a counter movement to nihilism', inspired by Nietzsche, but not reaching his level of force (GA42, 40–1). These lines were not in the original German edition of this course, nor in the English translation. For a discussion, see Carl Ulmer, *Der Spiegel*, 2 May 1977, p. 10. For other examples, see the reference to the state-police, the Reich-ministry, and a discussion between the Führer and the English foreign minister in an interrogation of the being of the state (GA40, 27).
44. Heidegger also gave a lower-level seminar on the state in Hegel in 1934–35, along with Erik Wolf, an expert on legal history, appointed Dean of the Faculty of Law and Political Science at Freiburg under Heidegger. See William J. Richardson, *Heidegger: Through Phenomenology to Thought*, The Hague: Martinus Nijhoff, Third Edition, 1974, p. 668.
45. The most detailed analysis of the notion of *Arbeit*, in relation to Jünger, is found in GA90.
46. Their publication in the *Gesamtausgabe* in 1998 followed an edition put together by Victor Farías: *Lógica: «Lecciones de M. Heidegger (Semestre verano 1934) en el legado de Helene Weiss»*, bi-lingual German–Spanish edition, Barcelona: Anthropos, 1991.
47. Bernasconi, 'Heidegger's Alleged Challenge', p. 52.

48. Bernasconi, 'Heidegger's Alleged Challenge', p. 52. On the problem of *Geist*, see also Derrida, *Heidegger et la question*.

49. Bernasconi, 'Heidegger's Alleged Challenge', p. 54.

50. Though compare GA45, 126–7, where some distance is offered.

51. See also GA52, 88–93, for a discussion of the importance of fate in Hölderlin's poetry; and throughout this course for a discussion of hearing.

52. See also the discussion and critique of Kolbenheyer in GA36/37, 209–13.

53. See also the comments in the 1934 radio address refusing the chair in Berlin, GA13, 12.

54. Norbert von Hellingrath, *Hölderlin*, München: Hugo Bruckmann, 1921, pp. 16–17, 21. This is discussed in Edler, 'Philosophy, Language, and Politics'. Von Hellingrath died in the First World War, something which Heidegger adds to his dedication of the essay in 1936 (GA4, 33); and reminds his students of in 1942 (GA53, 2).

55. This is returned to in 1937, and again in 1944–45, but with only the thinker and the poet central to the history of a *Volk* (GA45, 2; GA50, 102). The published (1961) and delivered versions of the 1940 course on *European Nihilism* also differ on this: compare GA6.2, 228; N IV, 195; and GA48, 332. Only in the latter is the notion of *Staatsbildung*, state-formation, included along with 'politics, science, art, society'.

56. See G. W. F. Hegel, *Elements of the Philosophy of Right*, edited by Allen Wood, translated by H. B. Nisbet, Cambridge: Cambridge University Press, 1991.

57. Heidegger's view, throughout the *Nietzsche* lectures and elsewhere, is that that value-philosophy – putting a value on something – is another version of calculation, and remains within metaphysics.

58. See also '*Wege zur Aussprache*', GA13, 15–21.

59. See also the collection of previously unpublished writings in GA75.

60. This seems a more plausible reading that that of Dennis J. Schmitt, 'Strategies for a Possible Reading', in Charles E. Scott, Susan M. Schoenbohm, Daniela Vallega-Neu and Alejando Vallega (eds), *Companion to Heidegger's* Contributions to Philosophy, Bloomington: Indiana University Press, 2001, pp. 32–47, p. 40, who suggests that in the *Beiträge* 'the critique of Nazi racial policy is clear and unmistakable'.

61. By 1938 this has become the 'laborious fabrication of such absurd entities as "National Socialist philosophies"' (GA5, 100/75).
62. Pöggeler, 'Heidegger's Political Self-Understanding', HC, 220.
63. For a discussion, see Jürgen Habermas, 'Martin Heidegger: On the Publication of the Lectures of 1935', in HC, pp. 190–7; his 'Work and *Weltanschauung*', p. 200; and Janicaud, *L'ombre de cette pensée*, Chapter Four.
64. Petra Jaeger, 'Nachwort der Herausgeberin', GA40, 234.
65. Harmut Buchner, 'Fragmentarisches', in Günther Neske (ed.), *Erinnerung an Martin Heidegger*, Pfüllingen: Neske, 1977, p. 49, cited in Thomas Sheehan, 'Heidegger and the Nazis', *The New York Review of Books*, Vol. XXXV No. 10, 16 June 1988, pp. 38–47, p. 43.
66. It has even been alleged that Heidegger tried to have the phrase removed from the English translation in 1959. See Young-Bruehl, *Hannah Arendt*, pp. 443, p. 532, n. 10. This is regularly cited by Thomas Sheehan as fact, but Young-Bruehl provides no reference or corroboration for this, although she does suggest it was at the prompting of the German publisher. That said, it does not seem unlikely, and the translator, Ralph Manheim, did not take kindly to Heidegger. In his letter to Norbert Guterman of 9 May 1957, he remarks, 'incidentally I don't see why he is forgiven so easily for his Nazism. I understand forgiving musicians and chess players, but philosophers? Repulsive fellow anyway'. Judging from their extensive correspondence, archived in Columbia University library, Guterman, a long-running collaborator of Henri Lefebvre, had a large hand in the work.
67. See Otto Pöggeler, *Martin Heidegger's Path of Thinking*, Atlantic Heights: Humanities Press, 1987, pp. 277–8; Pöggeler, 'Heidegger's Political Self-Understanding', HC, p. 220; Rainer Martin, 'Ein rassistisches Konzept von Humanität', *Badische Zeitung*, 19–20 December 1987, p. 14, cited in Farías, *Heidegger and Nazism*, p. 227–8.
68. Pöggeler, 'Heidegger's Political Self-Understanding', HC, p. 241, n. 11. See also Petra Jaeger, 'Nachwort der Herausgeberin', GA40, 232–3, which cites some of Heidegger's letters on this issue; Thomas Sheehan, 'Heidegger and the Nazis', *The New York Review of Books*, Vol. XXXV No. 10, 16 June 1988, pp. 38–47; and Gregory Fried and Richard Polt, 'Translator's Introduction', in *Introduction to Metaphysics*, p. xvii.

69. See also the comments a year later on the situation of Schelling in 1809, that Napoleon 'oppressed and abused Germany' (GA42, 1/1). In 1936, this cannot fail to have a contemporary resonance: Hitler had sent troops into the demilitarised Rhineland in March of that year, and memories of the French occupation of the Ruhr in the 1920s were still strong.

70. I owe this point to Bambach, *Heidegger's Roots*, pp. 138–9. See also GA39, 290.

71. Friedrich Naumann, *Mitteleuropa*, Berlin: Georg Reimer, 1915. On Naumann, see H. C. Meyer, *Mitteleuropa in German Thought and Action 1815–1945*, Martinus Nijhoff: The Hague, 1955, particularly pp. 194–217; and more generally, Peter Stirk (ed.), *Mitteleuropa: History and Prospects*, Edinburgh: Edinburgh University Press, 1994.

72. Friedrich Nietzsche, *Götzendämmerung*, in *Samtliche Werke: Kritische Studienausgabe*, edited by Giorgio Colli and Mazzino Montinari, Berlin and München: W. de Gruyter and Deutscher Taschenbuch Verlag, fifteen volumes, 1980, Vol. VI, p. 76–8; translated by Walter Kaufmann as *The Twilight of the Idols*, in *The Portable Nietzsche*, Harmondsworth: Penguin, 1954, pp. 481–3.

73. See also the comments on the importance of revolution in GA45, 37, in distinction to the conservative outlook.

74. This is followed by an ambiguous passage about how Nazism can be seen as a response to Marxism, but that 'this ordering becomes untrue as soon as one grasps the essence of spirit in its truth' (GA40, 36). Selectively quoting this, and neglecting the 'if . . . then . . . but . . .' logic of the passage, allows Farías, *Heidegger and Nazism*, p. 220, to offer quite a different interpretation.

75. Theodore Kisiel, 'Heidegger's Philosophical Geopolitics in the Third Reich', in Richard Polt and Gregory Fried (eds), *A Companion to Heidegger's* Introduction to Metaphysics, New Haven: Yale University Press, pp. 226–49, p. 240.

76. This is undoubtedly a reference to Friedrich Nietzsche's *Unzeitgemäße Betrachtungen*, in *Samtliche Werke*, Vol. I, pp. 157–510; translated by R. J. Hollingdale as *Untimely Meditations*, Cambridge: Cambridge University Press, 1983, the second meditation of which was the subject of a seminar in 1938–39 (GA46). On this particular point, see particularly GA46, 105.

77. See also GA39, 205, where the Greeks are described in this way.

Three – Number: Calculative Politics

The Problem of World

> The essence of man has been decided long ago. Namely, man is an 'organism [or creature, *Lebewesen*]' and indeed an 'organism' that can invent, build and make use of machines, an organism that can *reckon* [rechnen] with things, an organism that can put *everything whatever* into its calculation and computation [*Rechnung und Berechnung*], into the *ratio*. Man is the organism with the gift of reason. Therefore, man can demand that everything in the world happen 'logically'. (GA51, 90–1; see GA54, 100–1)

Aristotle's definition of the human continues to exercise Heidegger throughout his career. In this example, from 1941, he makes clear a theme that has been developing in his thought for many years. Indeed, the discussion of this phrase back in the *Plato's* Sophist course, quoted as an epigraph to this book, had made the link between the 'rational animal' and the question of calculation: 'connected with this definition is that of man as the being which calculates [*rechnet*], *arithmein*. Calculating does not mean here counting [*zählen*] but to reckon something, to be designing [*berechnend sein*]; it is only on the basis of this original sense of calculating [*Rechnen*] that number [*Zahl*] developed' (GA19, 17–18). Many years later, in the winter of 1942–43 that saw the German army defeated at Stalingrad, Heidegger declares that 'man as *animal rationale* is the "animal" that calculates, plans, turns to beings as objects, represents what is objective and orders it' (GA54, 232; see GA7, 52).

It is therefore worth noting that if the first chapter of this study traced concerns across the period of about a decade, and the second narrowed its focus to a very short span of time, this final chapter ranges across Heidegger's entire thought, though with an emphasis on the period from 1936 to the end of the war. In a sense, this chapter's topic is Heidegger's mature political thought, a product undoubtedly of the thinking through of what had occurred between 1933 and 1934, but also of the sustained reflection his thought had brought to bear on a number of related issues. Chapters Two and Three, then, in part, show Heidegger offering two different responses to the key question Chapter One identified: the question of being-together politically, the wider realm to which *phronesis* is addressed. Chapter Two shows the immediate response in the face of the crisis; Chapter Three is the painful and painstaking rethinking of precisely this problem. The years 1933–34 are the time of crisis, in the Greek sense of *krisis* as a critical turning-point, a moment, one of decision, an *Augenblick*, a *kairos*. *Krisis* as a decision, related to *krino*, is a splitting apart, a separating, indeed an *Auseinandersetzung*. On reflection, across a longer stretch of time, a *khronos*, a more measured time that asks not only about the measure of time, other perspectives emerge. As Heidegger remarks early in his career, '*phronesis* requires *khronos*' (GA19, 140), '*bouleuesthai* needs *polun khronon*. As opposed to precipitous action, correct deliberation takes time' (GA19, 152). The key question is the extent to which the Heidegger of Chapter Three is only possible as a response to the Heidegger of Chapter Two.

The set of concerns that Heidegger mobilises to rethink this pro-blematic notably includes the move from *logos* to *ratio*; the mathe-maticisation of this notion; the relation between these words that share a stem in the notion of *rechnen*; and the subsequent ordering of the world. We begin with the last of these, because it enables us to return to Heidegger's early writings with a new emphasis. This is because, though the phenomena of world is important in Heidegger in numerous places, what is interesting politically is how 1924's notion of being-in-the-*polis* becomes being-in-the-world in *Being and Time*. Although it might be tempting to see this merely as an apolitical re-rendering of Aristotle, it is more complicated than that in two registers: the scope of being-in-the-world and the way in which this is put together.

Being-in-the-world, as a fundamental structure of Dasein, is largely concerned with the surrounding environment, the *Umwelt*. This is made up of material things, and the analyses of equipment come in this context. In terms of the structure of *Being and Time*, this is the first three chapters of the first division, before Heidegger broadens the inquiry to look at encounters with others, in the *Mitwelt*, as was discussed in Chapter One. This is the first complication: being-in-the-world is both an element of the *Mitwelt* and yet, in terms of the successive stages of Heidegger's argumentation, more limited, and therefore more circumscribed than the notion of being-in-the-*polis*. The second complication is that Heidegger wants to distance himself from many other understandings of what the world is. In part, this is about the mode of connection of the material world. We are not beings, who are in a world, but always already in a world in our being, being-in-the-world (GA2, 52–3). Similarly, the world is not constructed along mathematical, scientific lines, but encountered through experience and living.[1]

In *Being and Time*, Heidegger declares that 'in the ontology of the ancients, the beings we encounter within the world are taken as basic examples for the interpretation of being. *Noein* (or the *logos*, as the case may be) is accepted as a way of access to them' (GA2, 44). In his readings of the pre-Socratics, Heidegger uses Parmenides and Heraclitus to suggest that the world, the *kosmos*, is not 'present-at-hand beings as such [*vorhandene Seiende als solches*]', but rather a 'condition [*Zustand*]' or a 'mode of being [*Weise zu sein*']' (GA26, 219).[2] It is in that sense an ontological issue, concerned with how, rather than what, *is*, that is a question of the being of beings rather than beings themselves.

This stress on the ontological determination is important because, hinted at in *Being and Time*, and explored in much more detail elsewhere, is the fundamental question of the mode of connection. In a sense, this is a mathematical question, as we saw with issues concerning magnitude, calculation and measure in Chapter Two, and bears relation to understandings of arithmetic and geometry, numerical and spatial relations (GA22, 254; see GA56/57, 25–6). But Heidegger continually makes the point that the nature of mathematics is not itself a mathematical question; just as biology in itself is not biological and philology is not itself understandable through philology (see, for example, GA22, 5–6; see GA44, 117–18; N II, 111–12). The question of mathematics is not therefore one that can be reached by way of mathematics – that is, through proofs or concepts – but is a properly philosophical question. While the positive sciences can say something about beings, they cannot talk about *being* (GA22, 6–8). Their statements are exclusively about beings, which is why mathematics cannot be defined mathematically. 'The mathematician deals in numbers or spatial relations, but not in number as such, that is the being of numbers; he does not deal in space as such, the being of space, of what and how it is' (GA22, 8, see 293).

Heidegger certainly had some knowledge of mathematics that went beyond the merely philosophical. If our reading here is largely concerned with the ontological and political issues that arise from his discussions, this does not mean that only he knew this level. Between 1911 and 1913, as a graduate student, Heidegger took ten courses in geometry, calculus and algebra, alongside subjects in physics, chemistry and philosophy.[3] This was after he had left the theology faculty, and though his final dissertation was on judgement in psychologism (GA1, 59–188), and he later moved into philosophy, he used to examine mathematics PhD students, and continued to have an interest in mathematical issues.

For example, in a 1925 Kassel lecture on Dilthey (to appear in GA80) there is a discussion of the geometrical presuppositions of the theory of relativity, looking at elliptical and hyperbolic geometry.[4] On presenting his *Habilitationsschrift* to Freiburg in 1915, Heidegger offered three topics for the requisite trial lecture: 'The Concept of Time in History', 'The Logical Problem of the Question', and 'The Concept of Number'.[5] Only the first was delivered (GA1, 415–33), but it seems that the third was the original topic of the *Habilitationsschrift* itself, changed because of Heidegger's then desire to take up a chair in Catholic Philosophy.[6] Similarly, in the *History of the Concept of Time* course, he makes reference to the debate between Hilbert's formalism and Brouwer and Weyl's intuitionism. But, it has to be said, even here the aim is really to get to the question of foundations rather than to *do* mathematics (GA20, 4–5; see GA2, 9–10). It is also worth recalling the heritage of phenomenology: as Heidegger reminds his students, Husserl was 'originally a mathematician' (GA20, 28; see GA21, 31), and in a 1915 curriculum vitae Heidegger notes the importance of Husserl's *Philosophy of Arithmetic* (GA16, 38).[7]

There is not the space here to provide a detailed reading of Chapters II and III of the first division of *Being and Time*, which are entitled 'Being-in-the-World in General as the Basic State of Dasein', and 'The Worldhood of the World'.[8] A few remarks on one key issue are, however, necessary. This is the way Heidegger outlines four ways in which world is conceived. These are distinguished by two fundamental divisions – as ontic or ontological; and as including Dasein or separate from it. The first, ontic, exclusive understanding is 'the totality of those beings which can be present-at-hand within the world'; second, the ontological version of this, is the being of those beings. Third, ontic and inclusive, is an understanding of the 'wherein' each Dasein 'lives', either the *Mitwelt* of shared experience, or the domestic *Umwelt* particular to a Dasein. The fourth is the ontological understanding of this, worldhood, what makes the third kind possible. Heidegger reserves his use of the term world for the third kind, the kind found in the term being-in-the-world. What is interesting is that the first is the common understanding, and the second the ontological casting of this 'world' (Heidegger reserves single quotation marks for the world in this first sense) (GA2, 64–5; see GA26, 231–2). As Heidegger makes explicit slightly later, the key operation in an ontology of 'world' is found in Descartes understanding of *res extensa* (GA2, 66).

As Heidegger declares in early 1930, '*logos, ratio, Vernunft* [reason], *Geist* – all these titles are disguises for the problem of world' (GA29/30, 508). (It is worth noting that the last three are also 'translations' of the first (see GA2, 32, and the discussion in Chapter One)). These four terms, with their association with four great thinkers – Aristotle, Descartes, Kant and Hegel – are guiding themes in Heidegger's investigation into the ontological determination of the world. Aristotle, Descartes and Kant were, of course, the projected subjects of the three divisions of the second part; Hegel is discussed in *Being and Time* only briefly, but largely in the context of Aristotle and time (GA2, 428–36). If Aristotle and Descartes will receive most treatment here, it is worth first briefly noting the issues raised in Heidegger's reading of Kant.

In the *Critique of Pure Reason*, Kant attempts to separate out world and nature, despite the fact that they are often conflated. The world is the 'mathematical sum-total of all appearances', a totality, that is in its large form as an aggregate or composition [*zusammensetzung*], as well as in the small form through division. Nature is 'this same world . . . when it is viewed as a dynamical whole and one does not look at the aggregation in space or time so as to bring about a quantity, but looks instead at the unity in the existence of appearances'.[9] The world, therefore, is the *totum* of beings, a mathematical totality, and nature the dynamic totality (GA26, 226).[10] What we find in Heidegger's pursuit of this issue is crucial, since he separates out 'the mathematical categories of quantity and quality, and the dynamic categories of relation and modality' (GA26, 226). Although Heidegger is at pains to point out that neither mathematical or dynamic here means anything too close to the use of those terms in physics, there is something very revealing here. 'For Kant's general ontology, the exemplary being is, of course, nature, i.e., beings-in-themselves as discovered by the mathematical science of nature' (GA26, 227; see GA25, 43–5).[11]

Dynamic categories deal with the that-being, the existential attributes of the nature of beings; mathematical categories deal with the what-being, the essential characteristics (GA26, 228). While the way Heidegger discusses this notion here, and the following course which provides a more thorough historical overview and discussion of Kant in the second division on 'Philosophy and Worldview' (GA27, see especially 239–58),[12] is rather underdeveloped, he is opening up in a productive way an issue that would dominate his thinking from the mid-1930s on. This is the question of calculation, and how mathematical models of seeing the material world are reductive and ultimately dangerous. In the course devoted to Kant from 1927–28, designed to work through the first *Critique* in detail, Heidegger's question is 'how must nature be determined and thought in advance, so that the entirety of this being as such can be accessible to calculative knowledge in a fundamental way?'. His answer, drawing upon the changes initiated by Galileo and Kepler, but most fundamentally, as we shall see, in Descartes, is this:

> Nature must be circumscribed as what it is in advance, in such a way as to be determinable and accessible to inquiry as a closed system [*Zusammenhang*] of the locomotion [*Ortsveränderunen*] of material bodies in time. What limits nature as such – movement, body, place, time – must be thought in such a way as to make a mathematical determination possible. Nature must be *projected* [entworfen] in advance unto its mathematical constitution. (GA25, 30–1; see GA2, 362; GA41, 103/102–3; GA15, 313–14)

There are several crucial issues here, notably the way in which what nature is is determined *in advance*, in other words that it being as such is determined in order to make observations about its particularities. Nature is understood as the movement of bodies through place, *Ort*, in time – the determinate characteristics of modern physics – but determined in a thoroughly mathematical way. Mathematics here is a particular sense, a modern sense, of composition and division. The limits of the system, the composition of the thought of nature, become the limits of nature itself. Nature ceases to be what it might be except in terms of the system through which it is understood. 'It is only on the basis of disclosing the mathematical constitution of nature that the knowing determination of nature obtains meaning and justification according to measure, number and weight [*Maß, Zahl und Gewicht*]' (GA25, 31–2; see GA21, 204). In Kant's thought this gets played out in the conception that, instead of our cognition conforming to objects, objects actually must conform to our cognition;[13] and that the 'conditions of possibility of experience in general are simultaneously the conditions of possibility for the objects of experience'.[14] As Heidegger phrases it, 'there is already an *a priori* knowledge upon which each empirical measurement depends, i.e. to which this measurement must correspond and conform' (GA25, 56; see GA2, 362).

Heidegger returns to this theme again and again, adding nuance to his argument. His key point is that the break with previous understandings of nature is not that experiment is key, as the Greeks also experimented, nor that quantitative measure is used, because measuring and counting had been used in the Greeks and the middle ages (GA34, 61; GA41, 68–9/68). Nor is it that modern science works with facts and medieval science with concepts, because both work with both (GA41, 66/66). Rather, it is the way that they are conceived, in that in modern science 'a projection was made which *delineated* [umgrenzt] in advance what was henceforth to be *understood* as nature and natural process: a spatio-temporally determined totality of movement of masspoints [*Massenpunkten*]. In principle, despite all process and transformation, this projection of nature has not changed to the present day' (GA34, 61).[15] Indeed, following these changes, Heidegger suggests that philosophy itself demonstrates its propositions by geometrical means; *more geometrico*' (GA56/57, 18–19).

One of the telling instances is that Kant conceives of the proposition 'all bodies are extended' as an analytic judgment – that is, that the predicate is contained in the very idea of the subject – while 'some bodies are heavy' is a synthetic judgement, that is, it tells us something more, with an implicit stress on the 'some'.[16] Heidegger pursues this in a discussion of Kant's suggestion in the *Critique* that 'space is represented as an infinite magnitude [*Größe*] that is given'.[17] By magnitude, Kant does not mean a simple amount [*Großes*], that could be summed to another, but, Heidegger suggests, something like greatness [*Großheit*]. Kant uses the Latin *Quantum* rather than quantity [*Quantität*] to describe this. Where quantity is confined to the categories of unity, plurality and totality – modes of comparison – comparison is not the issue with *quantum*, magnitude. Heidegger cites Kant's *Reflexionen*, which suggests that 'the *quantum* wherein all quantities can exclusively be determined is . . . space and time'.[18] In other words, the quantum is the determination, the condition of possibility, for particular quantities: 'magnitude is that which makes possible anything that is determined as having a magnitude . . .

magnitude as greatness is itself neither big nor small [*Die Größe ist als Großheit nicht selbst groß oder klein*] (GA25, 118–20).[19]

It is worth remembering that, for the early Heidegger, as with so many other issues, his concern with measure and calculation is largely orientated around the reductive understanding of time. In the lecture on 'The Concept of Time', there is a brief discussion of measure in relation to Augustine's reflection of time in his *Confessions* (GA64, 111; see GA64, 18; GA60, 284–6; GA31, 120–1), and Heidegger bemoans the mathematicisation of time as a variable t to add to the mathematical coordinates of x, y and z later in the same lecture. 'Once time has been defined as clock time [*Uhrzeit*]', Heidegger declares, 'there is no hope of ever arriving at its original sense again' (GA64, 122).[20] It is in relation to this concern that we find most of the remarks in this topic in *Being and Time*, including brief discussions of Aristotle and Hegel on calculative time (GA2, 413–36; see also GA21, 251–62; GA24, 352ff; GA26, 256–9; GA64, 91–2),[21] although there are some additional comments in the discussion of the spatiality of worldhood (for example, GA2, 111–13).[22] Heidegger suggests that 'the connections between historical numeration, astronomically calculated world-time and the temporality and historicity of Dasein need further investigation' (GA2, 419 n. 4),[23] although Heidegger also references back to a lecture he gave in 1916 (GA1, 415–33).[24] These questions will be returned to in the discussion of Descartes below, for Descartes takes on a privileged position in Heidegger's reading of how the tradition has moved to this mathematical projection of nature. But before we move to this, we need to analyse how Heidegger thinks the question of number is determined in the Greeks.

Arithmetic and Geometry

Heidegger provides two detailed discussions of the question of number in his early work,[25] which are important both because they contain his most thorough discussion of ancient mathematics and because they are the foundation of his later work on issues of calculation more generally. The second is found in the Summer 1926 course on the *Basic Concepts of Ancient Philosophy*. Delivered at the very moment Heidegger was finalising the parts of *Being and Time* that were published – May to July 1926 – this course and the as yet unpublished one from the following semester on *History of Philosophy from Thomas Aquinas to Kant* (GA23) provide a broader but summary reading of almost the entire tradition. *Basic Concepts of*

Ancient Philosophy is interesting in general terms because it contains some of the most detailed discussions of the pre-Socratics to be found in the Heidegger of the 1920s.

Heidegger discusses how Thales, the first scientific philosopher, is also the first Greek mathematician, and this, he suggests, is not by chance. *Mathema*, that which can be taught, stands in place of science in general, and is useful both as a theory and as a practical tool, being related to maritime geography and the calculation of distances between coasts (GA22, 40, 51–2). Thales took the Egyptian geometry of empirical measurement, and turned it into an abstract and deductive process.[26] In relation to the Pythagorians and the representation of numbers in the geometric figure of the triangle, Heidegger contends that 'the Greeks did not think in a purely arithmetic manner, but more in the mode of spatial figuration and representation' (GA22, 221). He continues to suggest something whose implications, here, at least, are not worked through: 'Concerning this spatial figure, we apprehend the spatial as much as number. Number becomes *logos*, "concept", number makes possible the conceivable and definable nature of being' (GA22, 221). Elsewhere there is a brief discussion of Zeno of Elea, the thinker Aristotle would dispute in his analysis of movement in *Physics* Book IV (see GA22, 71–6, 237–40), and the notion of the *kenon*, the void, in relation to that of *topos* (GA22, 244–5, 319; see GA32, 176–7). This discussion culminates in the crucial assertion that the merit of Zeno's work is that it is neither time nor space which is the problem, but the continuum. The continuum – the mode of connection of being – is the phenomenon 'equally at the base of magnitude [*Größe*], space and time' (GA22, 76, see 239–40).[27]

The more important of the two discussions is found, yet again, in the crucial *Plato's* Sophist course. A few weeks into the course, Heidegger turns aside from his main aim at that point, which is the meaning of *sophia*, and discusses mathematics in some detail. It is this seemingly tangential discussion or excursus [*Exkurs*] that seems to me to contain the single most important *philosophical* discussion of number in his work. Indeed, as he declares immediately after this discussion, this is by no means unrelated to the wider concerns of this discussion: '*Metrein*, to take measure [*messen*], to determine, is the mode in which Dasein makes something intelligible. *Metron* and *arithmos* belong in the same realm as *logos*, namely the realm of *aletheuein*' (GA19, 126).[28]

The purpose of this excursus is first to examine *mathematike* in general, and second *arithmetike* and *geometria*. The mathematical sciences have as their theme *ta eks aphaireseos*, that which shows itself as withdrawn from something, specifically from what is immediately given – *phusika onta*. In other words, mathematics is an abstraction from being. This is generally accredited to Thales. This abstraction is recognised by Aristotle when he speaks of *khorizein*, a separating, which links to the important word *khora*, which Heidegger here translates as 'place' [*Platz*]. For Heidegger, therefore, mathematics takes something away from its own place. But mathematics itself does not have a *topos*. This might have the ring of a paradox, as *topos* is often translated as 'space' [*Raum*]: Heidegger prefers 'place' [*Platz*]. (We should note here that Heidegger therefore sees both *khora* and *topos* as *Platz*, though he clarifies the latter with the additional word *Ort*, which is usually translated as 'locale' or 'place'.) Heidegger suggests that the *khorizein*, the separating, is for Aristotle the way in which the mathematical becomes objective. This is clearly linked to the *khorismos* of Plato's ideas, where the ideas have their *topos* in the *ouranos*, the heavens (GA19, 100–1).

In the *Physics* Book II, discussing the scope of natural science, Aristotle examines the mathematical objects of *stereon* and *gramme* – solids and lines. Whilst these can be considered as *phusika*, with a surface as *peras*, the limit of a body [*als Grenze eines Körpers*], the mathematician considers them purely in themselves (193b32).[29] Heidegger suggests that this negative description of the mathematical in Aristotle – 'that it is *not* the *peras* of a *phusikon soma*' – means that 'the mathematical is not being considered as a "place" [*Ort*]. Therefore, this abstracting, this extraction [*Heraussehen*] of the essence of the mathematical from the realm of *phusikon soma*, is essential, but *oyden diaphora*, it makes no difference [*macht das keinen Unterschied*].' By this, Aristotle means that the abstracting does not turn them into something else, but the 'what' of the *peras* is simply taken for itself. The *khorizein* therefore, this extracting, does not distort. Such an extracting is at play in the ideas generally. Now *khorismos* has a justifiable sense in mathematics, but not where *beings* are concerned. For the *phusika onta* are *kinoumena*, related to motion, and hence cannot be removed from their *khora*, their place [*Platz*]. Being and presence are determined in relation to a place, a *topos* (GA19, 101–2).

In Aristotle, Heidegger contends, there is therefore a clear differentiation between arithmetic and geometry – the former is concerned with *monas*, the unit; the latter with *stigme*, the point. *Monas* is related to *monon*, the unique or the sole, and is indivisible according to quantity. *Stigme* is, like *monas*, indivisible, but unlike *monas* it has the addition of a *thesis* – a position, an orientation, an order or arrangement. *Monas* is *athetos*, unpositioned; *stigme* is *thetos*, positioned (*Metaphysics*, 1016b29–31). This addition – this *prosthesis* – is crucial in understanding the distinction between arithmetic and geometry. For those of us interested in the questions of space and place, it is frustrating that Heidegger does not provide an answer to the question of 'the meaning of this *thesis* which characterises the point in opposition to the *monas*?'. He recognises that a 'thorough elucidation of this nexus would have to take up the question of place and space', but at this point can only look at what is necessary to describe mathematics (GA19, 102–4).

In doing so, Heidegger clarifies the distinction [*Unterschied*] between *thesis* and *topos*; position [*Lage*] and place. Mathematical objects are for Aristotle, Heidegger says, '*ouk en topo*' (*Metaphysics*, 1092a18–20),[30] 'not any place [*nicht an einem Platz sind*]'. As I have discussed elsewhere, Heidegger is at pains to disregard any modern conception of space here, turning instead to *Physics* Book IV, which discusses the notion of *topos*.[31] The crucial issue is that *topos* has a *dunamis*, but this is not to be understood as force or power.

> *Dunamis* is here understood in a quite strictly ontological sense; it implies that the place [*Platz*] pertains to the being itself, the place constitutes precisely the *possibility of the proper presence* [Möglichkeit des eigentlichen Anwesendseins] of the being in question. This possibility, like every possibility, is prescribed in a determinate direction: every being has *its* place [*Jedes Seiende hat* seinen *Ort*]. The *dunamis* of the *topos* pertains to beings themselves as such . . . Each being possesses in its being a prescription toward a determinate location or place [*Platz, Ort*]. *The place is constitutive of the presence of the being.* [(GA19, 105–6)[32]

According to Aristotle, above/below, front/back and right/left are crucial to determining a place. But these determinations are not always the same, that is, though they are *absolute* within the world, they can also change in relation to people. This change is one of *thesis*, orientation, therefore *topos* is not the same as *thesis*. Geometrical figures have *thesis*, they can have a right or a left for us, but they do not occupy a place (208b22). Now if geometry does not have a place, what indeed is place? It is only because we perceive motion that we think of place, therefore only what is moveable [*kineton*] is in a place. Glossing two lines of the *Physics*, Heidegger contends that 'place is the *limit* [Grenze] *of the periekon*, that which delimits [*umgrenzt*] a body, not the limit of the body itself, but that which the limit of the body comes up against, in such a way, specifically, that there is between these two limits no interspace [*Zwischenraum*], no *diastema*' (GA19, 108).

While it is undoubtedly easier to take the extension of the material or the limit to the form as the place in itself, we should rather try to think place ontologically, remembering that place has a *dunamis*. Rather than an external determination of things in advance, place is rather an innate capacity of beings as such, their very constitute ability to be present: 'place is the ability a being has to be there [*Dortseinkönnen*], in such a way that, in being there, it is properly present [*dortseiend, eigentlich da ist*]' (GA19, 109).[33]

When geometry intervenes, what it extracts from the *aistheta* in order for it to become the *theton* is precisely the moment of place [*Ortsmomente*]. These moments of place are the *perata* of a physical body, and in their geometrical representation acquire an autonomy over and against the physical body. So geometrical objects are not in a place, but have directions – above/below, right/left, and so on. We can use this to give us insight into the positions as such, an *analysis situs*, even though geometry does not possess the same determinations. Every geometrical point, line, surface is fixed through a *thesis*, they are therefore *ousia thetos*. The *monas* does not bear an orientation, therefore they are *ousia athetos*.[34] Geometry therefore has a greater proximity to the *aistheta* than does arithmetic: arithmetic is more detached, more separate. The basic elements of geometry – point, line, surface – are the *perata* for the higher geometrical figures. But for Aristotle, in opposition to Plato, such higher geometrical figures are not *put together* out of such limits (231a24ff). A line will never arise out of points, nor a surface from a line, nor a body from a surface, for between any two points there is again and again a *gramme*. Heidegger takes this forward by discussing the unity that must arise in order for lines to be made of points, surfaces from lines, and so on. He relates these questions to arithmetic too, asking what is the mode of manifoldness of number? (GA19, 110–12).

In investigating this manifold [*Mannifgaltigen*], this mode of connection, Heidegger reminds us of the link between geometry and the *aistheta*. 'Everything in *aisthanesthai* possesses *megethos*; everything perceivable has stretch [*Erstreckung*]. Stretch, as understood here, will come to be known as continuity'. Aristotle derives this notion of continuity [*synekhes*] not from his work on geometry, but on physics.[35] This occurs in *Physics*, Book V, in the discussion of co-being, being-together [*Miteinanderseins*], the *phusei onta*. This *Miteinandersein* is, of course, not the same as the being-with-another of human community, discussed in Chapter One, but, as we shall see, there are some important issues in their relation. There are seven forms of co-being.

1. the *hama*, the concurrent – understood as something concerning place, not temporality. The *hama* is that which is in one place.
2. *khoris*, the separate – that which is in another place.
3. *haptesthai*, the touching – that whose ends are in one place [*hama*].
4. *metaksu*, the intermediate – that which something, in changing, passes through. Such as a boat moving in a stream, the stream is the *metaksu*, the medium.
5. *ephekses*, the successive – where something is connected to something else, and between them there is nothing 'of the same lineage of being'. There might be something else, but not another of the same.
6. *ekhomenon*, the self-possessed – an *ephekses* determined by *haptesthai*. In other words, a succession where the ends meet in one place, the *hama*.
7. *synekhes*, *continuum* – a complicated form, since it presupposes the other determinations. It is an *ekhomenon*, but more, a *hoper ekhomenon* – more originary, not only do the ends of the elements of a succession meet in the same place, but the ends of one are identical with the other (GA19, 113–15; see GA22, 318–19).

'These are the determinations of being-with-another. The *synekhes* is the structure that makes up the principle of *megethos*, a structure which characterises every stretch' (GA19, 115). *Monas* and *stigme* cannot be the same, shows Aristotle, for the mode of their connection is different. For points are characterised by *haptesthai*, by touching, indeed they are *ekhomenon* – an *ephekses* determined by *haptesthai*. But the units (of arithmetic), the *arithmos*, have only the *ephekses*. The mode of connection of the geometrical, of points, is characterised by the *synekhes*; the series of numbers – where no touching is necessary – by the *ephekses*. To consider geometrical figures, therefore, we must add something over and above the *ephekses*. These additions – *megethos*, *pros ti*, *thesis*, *topos*, *hama*, *hupomenon* – ensure that the geometrical is not as original as the arithmetical (GA19, 115–16).

Heidegger is now steering his excursus back to the issue of *sophia* through reference to Chapter Six of Aristotle's *Categories*, where there is a discussion of *poson*, quantity. Heidegger claims that what is posited in the *thesis* is nothing else than the continuum itself. 'This basic phenomenon is the ontological condition for the possibility of something like stretch, *megethos*: position and orientation are such that from one point there can be a continuous progression to the others; only in this way is motion understandable' (GA19, 118–19). The line, which is continuous, can have points extracted from it, but these points do not together constitute the line. The line is more than a multiplicity of points, it has a *thesis* (5a15–37). But with numbers there is no *thesis*, so the series of numbers has a constitution only by way of the *ephekses* (4b22–30). Because a *thesis* is not required to understand arithmetic, number, *arithmos*, is ontologically prior: it seeks to explain being without reference to beings – which is why Plato begins with number in his 'radical ontological reflection'. But Aristotle does not claim this. Instead, he shows that the genuine *arkhe* of number, the unit, *monas*, is no longer a number, precisely because it is without the mode of connection. Instead, the *monas* is that which is, the one, 'every *on* is a *hen*', every being is a one (GA19, 117). What this means is that 'for Aristotle the *monas*, the unit, is itself not yet number; instead the first number is two' (GA19, 111),[36] and therefore a more fundamental discipline is discovered, that which studies the basic constitution of beings, namely *sophia* (GA19, 120–1; see *Metaphysics*, 982a28).

We can see in this incredibly rich exegesis of Aristotle why Heidegger later suggests that '*Aristotle's* Physics *is the hidden, and therefore never adequately studied, foundational book of Western Philosophy*' (GA9, 242/185; see GA10, 92/63; GA69, 6).[37] It raises a large number of interesting and challenging points, of which this summary shows some of the ones I find most important or intriguing.

1. Mathematics is an abstraction, an extraction from, an extractive looking at [*Heraussehen*] being. There is therefore a *khorizein*, a separating, between mathematics and being.
2. Arithmetic's *monas*, the unit, is *athetos*, unpositioned; geometry's *stigme*, the point, is *thetos*, positioned.
3. Mathematical objects are positioned but do not have a place. For the Greeks, the objects they are abstractions from have a place. The modern concept of space is not present in either.
4. Place has a *dunamis*. This should be understood ontologically: every being has *its* place. Place is something belonging to beings as such: it is their capacity to be present.

5. The extension of material is not sufficient to understand place.
6. Motion is tied up with place. Only what is movable is in a place, but place itself does not move.
7. Everything perceivable has stretch, size, *megethos*. This is understood as *synekhes*, the *continuum*. This is a succession, not only where the ends meet in one place, but where the ends of one are identical with the next.
8. This is the crux of the difference between arithmetic and geometry: the mode of their connection is different.
   Arithmetic – succession where between the units there is nothing of the same lineage of being; and it is only with the second that there is truly number.
   Geometry – succession where the ends of one point are the ends of the next.
9. Therefore, though points can be extracted from a line, these points do not constitute the line. The line is more than a multiplicity of points, the surface more than a multiplicity of lines, the solid more than a multiplicity of surfaces.[38]

What Heidegger provides in this excursus is both illuminating as a gloss on Aristotle and crucial in opening up some issues in the history of the tradition. Is this distinction maintained, or does later thought challenge or ignore it? How does this happen and why is this important? It seems to me that the full implications of this excursus are not really returned to for many years. While Heidegger is interested in mathematical issues throughout his career, it is difficult to think of another passage where he discusses these issues *philosophically* in as much depth.

Descartes and Extension

Although geometry itself is mentioned only twice in *Being and Time* (GA2, 68, 112), it is behind the extensive critique of Descartes in that work, and was likely to have been explored in more detail in the promised but never published division (the second of Part Two) that was to treat Descartes explicitly (see GA2, 40).[39] As Heidegger notes, his preliminary remarks in the first division 'will not have been grounded in full detail until the phenomenological de-struction of the "*cogito sum*"' (GA2, 89). As I have tried to show in *Mapping the Present*, Heidegger's critique is both of Descartes' particular way of conceiving the subject, and also of the way in which he conceives of space. The more detailed discussion of this can be found in that earlier work.[40] Heidegger's point is that rather than encountering a room in a geometrical spatial sense, we react to it as *Wohnzeug*, equipment for dwelling (GA2, 68; see GA24, 414). The way we react to space is much closer to notions of near/far or close/distant, not *primarily* determined by geometry and measurable distance, but by the more prosaic notions of closeness or nearness [*Nähe*], de-distancing [*Ent-fernung*] and directionality [*Ausrichtung*]. Space is encountered in everyday life, and lived in, not encountered in geometrically measurable forms and shapes. It is part of the structure of our being-in-the-world. Geometry is an abstraction from the world, but the results of this abstraction are taken by Descartes and Kant as fundamentals of our way of being.

Indeed, we can see how Heidegger's critique of Kant is, in certain key respects, a continuation of the critique of Descartes. Kant's metaphysics of nature is an ontology of *res extensa*, while the metaphysics of morals – which does not explicitly concern us here – is an ontology of the other side of the Cartesian division, the *res cogitans* (GA24, 197–8; GA20, 237, 322).[41] Instead of actually interrogating the being of the *sum* of the *cogito ergo sum*, or, in Kantian terms, 'the subjectivity of the subject', Kant is prepared to take Descartes' position forward 'quite dogmatically'. In other words, like Descartes, Kant failed to address the problem of both being and Dasein (GA2, 24; see 318–21). If this will have to suffice for one side, it is worth working through in detail how Descartes actually conceives of *res extensa*, and how this is developed in the thought of Leibniz. Indeed, Heidegger suggests that the way Descartes is understood in the tradition is 'at best only a bad novel' (GA41, 100/99).[42]

In Descartes' *Meditations on First Philosophy*, there is a clear distinction proposed between mind and body, with mind as *res cogitans*, and matter as *res extensa* – thinking thing and extended thing.[43] Extension is therefore at the heart of his project, as the central characteristic of nature. Initially, in the *Meditations*, properties of materials are put, like other things, into doubt. Descartes suggests that senses may be misleading, and therefore he will treat 'body, shape, extension, movement, and place' as figments of his imagination.[44] But, of course, all of these things put into doubt are retrieved in the movement of his thought.

> By 'body' I understand all that is suitable for being bounded by some shape, for being enclosed in some place, and thus for filling up space, so that it excludes every other body from that space.[45]

Descartes then discusses a thought experiment with a piece of wax. 'Let us direct our attention to this and see what remains after we have removed everything which does not belong to the wax: only that it is something extended, flexible, and subject to change'.[46] It seems clear that motion and change of shape have to be thought in relation to the substance to which they are attached, that is, an *extended* substance. Extension, Descartes contends, is contained within these concepts.[47]

> The unavoidable conclusion, then, is that there exists something extended in length, breadth and depth and possessing all the properties which we clearly perceive to belong to an extended thing. And it is this extended thing we call 'body' or 'matter'.[48]

The central properties of corporal things are 'namely, magnitude, or extension in length, breadth, and depth; shape, which arises from the limit of the extension; position, which the various shaped things possess in relation to one another; and motion, or the alteration of this position; to these can be added substance, duration and number'.[49] Where extension in length, breadth and depth constitute the being of the substance of nature,[50] the last three are derived from the analysis of the self, which Descartes distinguishes from a body in the following way: 'I am a thing that thinks and not an extended thing, whereas a stone is an extended thing and not a thing that thinks'.[51]

> I distinctly imagine that quantity, which philosophers commonly call 'continuous': namely, the extension of its quality, or rather the extension of the thing having quantitative dimensions of length, breadth, and depth. I enumerate the thing's various parts. I ascribe to these parts certain sizes, shapes, positions and movements from place to place; to these movements I ascribe various durations.[52]

This is the determination of the world, for Descartes, being is substance, extensible.[53] Geometry is the science that allows us best access to it. Descartes' *Discourse on the Method* is a theoretical prelude, to be followed by three examples – the *Dioptrics*, *Meteorology* and *Geometry*. With the first two, Descartes is merely trying to persuade us that his method is better than the ordinary one. But with the *Geometry*, he claims to have 'demonstrated it'.[54] There are two key points that I want to address: first, the distinction between Descartes' understandings of space and those of the scholastics; second, the revolution in geometry he undertakes. In the first the issue is the object of study; in the second it is the method.

There is a fundamental differentiation in scholasticism between *locus internus*, the space occupied by a body; and *locus externus*, the space or the external surface containing a body.[55] In the *Principles of Philosophy*, Descartes confronts this head-on.

> There is no real distinction between space [*spatium*], or internal place [*locus internus*], and the corporeal substance contained in it; the only difference lies in the way in which we are accustomed to conceive of them. For in reality the extension in length, breadth and depth which constitutes a space is exactly the same as that which constitutes a body. The difference arises as follows: in the case of a body, we regard the extension as something particular, and thus think of it as changing whenever there is a new body; but in the case of a space, we attribute to the extension only a generic unity, so that when a new body comes to occupy the space, the extension of the space is reckoned not to change but to remain one and the same, so long as it retains the same size and shape and keeps the same position relative to certain external bodies which we use to determine the space in question.[56]

The following article of the *Principles* pursues this point, and relates back to the experiment with the wax. Any attributes of a body can be removed – weight, colour, hardness, and so on – without it ceasing to be a body, save for the notion of extension. And extension, for Descartes, is exactly that 'comprised in the idea of a space', even an 'empty' [*vacuum*] space.[57]

> Thus we always take a space to be an extension in length, breadth and depth. But with regard to place, we sometimes consider it as internal to the thing which is in the place in question, and sometimes as external to it. Now internal place is exactly the same thing as space; but external place may be taken as being the surface [*superficiem*] immediately surrounding what is in the place.[58]

This is then very important, because Descartes is both introducing a notion of space, *spatium*, but erasing some of the distinctions hitherto felt essential. 'The terms "place" and "space", then, do not signify anything different from the body which is said to be in a place; they merely refer to its size, shape and position relative to other bodies.'[59] Place, for Descartes is more akin to position; and space to size or shape. Two different things in size and shape can occupy the same *place*, but clearly not the same *space*. And when something moves, it is its place that has changed, not its size or shape.[60] This is crucially important, because it is space not place which lays claims for exclusivity. For Descartes, all corporeal nature 'is the object of pure mathematics'.[61]

Heidegger comments on this:

> Descartes asserts that what is distinctive in the *res naturae* is extensio, extension [*Ausdehnung*]; the natural thing is *res extensa*. Spatial spread [*Ausbreitung*] is indisputably one characteristic belonging to the things of nature experienced by us, but why did Descartes make this so distinctive, putting it forth as the fundamental determination? His intention is decisively a critical one, simultaneously negative and positive; negative: against the explanation of nature in medieval scholasticism, against the assumption of concealed forces; positive: with the intent of thus achieving a determination of the things and processes of nature, their movement, that makes scientific knowledge possible, with its corresponding provability and determinacy. Scientific knowledge is, however, mathematical . . . This is the construction of an idea of knowledge which presents itself first of all in the mathematical. But because mathematical knowledge is primarily related to what is spatial, extension is put forth as the primordial characteristic of substance . . . (GA33, 95/80)[62]

The second issue, that of the mathematical knowledge which is brought to bear on this issue is well illustrated in a letter to Mersenne. Mersenne had written mentioning that the mathematician Desargues has heard Descartes is giving up geometry. Descartes replied:

> I have only resolved to give up abstract geometry, that is to say, research into questions which serve only to exercise the mind; and I am doing this in order to have more time to cultivate another sort of geometry, which takes as its questions the explanation of the phenomena of nature.[63]

What we find here is in some ways a reversal of the move made by Thales. Geometry is no longer the Platonic ideal of mental exercise, but a science of the real world. Geometry and physics have the same *objectum*, 'the difference consists just in this, that physics considers its object not only as a true and real being, but as actually existing as such, while mathematics considers it merely as possible, and as something which does not actually exist in space, but could do so'.[64] For example, in the *Discourse on the Method*, Descartes says that the 'object dealt with by geometricians' is '*like* [emphasis added] a continuous body or a space indefinitely extended in length, breadth, and height or depth, divisible into various parts which could have various shapes and sizes and be moved or transposed in all sorts of ways'.[65] Geometry is no longer simply an *abstraction* from being, but is seen as a generalisation of being. What Descartes does is to see geometry as equivalent to algebra. Just as algebra is symbolic logistic, geometry is a symbolic science. It is this, rather than the simple equation of arithmetic and geometry, that is his most radical break with the past.[66]

As Heidegger's ex-student Jacob Klein has shown, 'extension has, accordingly, a *twofold* character for Descartes: It is "symbolic" – as the object of a "general algebra", and it is "real" – as the "substance" of the corporal world'.[67] So, not only is Descartes moving geometry from abstract mental exercise to practical science – the foundation of physics, a study of the world – he assumes that the insights of geometry can tell us about the world. The concept of extension is not simply a geometrical property, *but a physical property*. Indeed, as Heidegger recognises, it is for Descartes 'the fundamental ontological determination of the world' (GA2, 89; GA22, 241, 244). As we noted above, it is a critique of scholasticism and provides the foundation for scientific knowledge (GA33, 94/80).

> The being of the world is nothing other than the *objectivity of the apprehension of nature through calculative measurement*. Contrary to all ancient and medieval knowledge of nature, physics is now *mathematical physics*. Only what is mathematically defined in the world can be properly known in it, and only what is thus mathematically known is *true* being . . . The proper being of the world is defined *a priori* by way of a particular and in fact possible kind of knowledge of the world as nature. (GA20, 245)

It is the *symbolic* objectivity of extension within the framework of the *mathesis universalis* that allows it to explain the being of the corporal world. 'Only at this point has the conceptual basis of "classical" physics, which has since been called "Euclidean space", been created'.[68] Newton is able to build on the developments through scholasticism and Descartes' work, and it reaches 'its first systematic and creative culmination' in his work (GA41, 77/76). For example, the first law of motion – that 'every body preserves in its state of being at rest, or of moving uniformly straight forward, except insofar as compelled to change that state by force impressed'[69] – is, according to Heidegger, discovered by Galileo, who only 'applied it in his last works and did not even express it as such', articulated by Baliani, attempted to be grounded metaphysically by Descartes, and then a metaphysical law in Leibniz (GA41, 78–9/78). What this heritage provides is 'the foundation on which Newton will raise the structure of his mathematical science of nature'.[70]

What this means, and this is the crucial point, is that not only is the understanding of space as 'non-Euclidean' possible, but there is no such thing as Euclidean space. What we call Euclidean space is actually a seventeenth-century invention, based no doubt on the postulates of Euclid's *Elements*, but crucially introducing the idea that this is constituent of reality. Euclid, like Plato, sees his geometry as a mathematical system. It is the generalisation of this to explain the world that is the crucial element introduced in the seventeenth-century.[71] As David Lachterman, a student of Klein, has noted, we should ask *where* the lines, planes and points of geometry are actually found or installed. The conventional answer – 'Euclidean space' – has, he suggests, become so installed, so unrevolutionary, that we find it self-evident that some conception of 'space' *must* lie in the background of Greek geometry. But such an answer is so close to the need for such a 'space' in a modern mathematical physics of extended corporal entities and their motions that we should guard against accepting it as ahistorical. 'The locale of Greek geometry may be foreign to the modern conceptions of extension and space'.[72] Indeed, this is precisely what Lachterman argues. There is, he suggests, no term corresponding to or translatable as 'space' in Euclid's *Elements*.[73] To *khorion* 'is the area within a perimeter of a specific figure, while *topos* and *thesis* in the *Data* have functions determined by the contextual aims of that work as a "dialectical" foil to the *Elements*, not by a physics of space hidden in the background'.[74]

Lachterman's work is most valuable in showing that Euclid, who wrote in the wake of Plato's thought (though he never references him[75]), did not rely on this understanding of space defined by extension: indeed, not on a view of 'space' at all. So, Descartes' revolution is that not only does he introduce this word 'space' but, by conceiving of geometrical lines and shapes in terms of numerical co-ordinates, which can be divided, it turns something that is *thetos* into *athetos*; positioned into unpositioned. Indeed, for Descartes, it is the very nature of a body, *res extensa*, that it is divisible.[76] Atoms are impossible for Descartes, because we can continue to divide indefi-nitely. 'For if there were any atoms, then no matter how small we imagined them to be, they would necessarily have to be extended and hence we could in our thought divide each of them into two or more extended parts, and hence recognise their divisibility'.[77]

In this discussion I have considered only curves that can be described upon a plane surface, but my remarks can easily be made to apply to all those curves which can be conceived of as generated by the regular movement of the points of a body in three-dimensional space [*par le mouuement regulier des poins de quelque cors, dans un espace qui a trois dimensions*].[78]

At the very beginning of the *Geometry,* Descartes boasts that 'all problems in geometry can be simply reduced to such terms that a knowledge of the lengths of certain straight lines is sufficient for their construction'.[79] Later he notes that 'in the method I use all problems which present themselves to geometers reduce to a single type, namely, to the question of finding the values of the roots of an equation'.[80] That is, geometric problems can be reduced to equations, the length (that is, quantity) of lines: a problem of number. The *continuum* of geometry is transformed into a form of arithmetic. The mode of connection of the geometrical for the Greeks is characterised by the *synekhes*; the series of numbers – where no touching is necessary – by the *ephekses*. Descartes' geometry, because of its divisibility, can only be *ephekses*. Descartes' understanding of space in terms of extension, in terms of mathematical co-ordinates, is a radical break with Greek thought. It is not a spatialising of calculation, but a calculation of space. The *continuum* is now a sequence of numbers, a multiplicity composed of units, *monas* as *hen*.[81] Geometry loses position just as place is transformed into space.

We will come on to some of the implications this has in a moment. While Heidegger certainly considers Descartes to be the essential and crucial break, it is important to note Leibniz here. Although Leibniz is not mentioned in *Being and Time*, Heidegger certainly recognises both the continuity and the distinction between his thought and that of Descartes in some of his early courses (see, for example, GA20, 241, 246, 322–5). In 1928, shortly after *Being and Time* was published, he devoted a lecture course to Leibniz in relation to logic (GA26) and the engagement continues into the following course (GA27). Heidegger also mentions that he discusses the *Monadology* in a 1929–30 seminar on 'truth and certainty in Descartes and Leibniz' (GA26, 87 n. 1); and in 1933–34 he gave a full seminar on this text. Related seminars – at least from their titles – were given in 1935–36, 1940–41 and 1944–45.[82]

In the 1928 course, Heidegger shows how the Cartesian move makes organic nature amenable to mathematical-geometrical theory. This was in particular a way of thinking about animals and plants, matter in motion, a mechanistic understanding. When Descartes attempted to think about locomotion – that is *motio localis*, change of place, of movement – he did so without recourse to an understanding of force, partly because of its association with scholastic philosophies of nature (GA26, 91).[83] Leibniz, on the contrary, is concerned with reintroducing precisely this notion, that is, *dunamis* in a transformed Aristotelian sense: 'what remains invariable and constant is not the quantity of motion but the magnitude of force [*nicht die Quantität de Bewegung, sondern die Größe der Kraft*]' (GA26, 93).[84] To equate the extended with extension is mistaken, because it turns the magnitude of space into a substance itself (GA20, 323).[85] This theme is extended in a minor digression in the course on Aristotle's *Metaphysics* Book Θ from 1931.

> Leibniz turns against this determination of the being of natural things and says: The being of these substances does not lie in extension (*extensio*) but in activity [*Wirken*] (*actio, agere*). Two things must be noted in this new articulation of the being of natural things: (1) With this Leibniz does not want to eliminate the determination of *extensio*. This remains intact, but in such a way that it is acknowledged as grounded upon a more original determination of being in the sense of acting. (2) This concept of acting is now grasped in the context of our present problem such that the beings which are determined in this way now more than ever admit a mathematical determinacy. In this way it comes about that, in comparison with Descartes, a much more intimate and essential connection becomes possible between the mathematical method of measuring movement (infinitesimal calculus [*Infinitesimalrechnung*]) and the kind of being which is knowable, something we shall not enter into here. (GA33, 95–6/80–1)

For Leibniz, extension is thus not the fundamental determination, but a second order issue. That said, it does not lose its importance as an issue in itself. Second, acting, as the ground of extension, is itself mathematical. As Heidegger elaborates, the 'basic implications of this new formulation of the being of substances' applies to 'all substances, that is, all beings, not just the material things of nature' (GA33, 97/82). In a reassertion of Aristotle, Leibniz maintains that force is equally essential to the constitution of things, and that matter is but one part of the question,[86] something he developed philosophically in his *Monadology* (GA33, 101/86). Mathematical physics, with its understanding of force and the essentially mathematical characterisation of the world, emerges here (see GA33, 94/79).

The Measure of All Things

It is therefore clear that Heidegger has thought through numerous issues around the questions of calculation by the early 1930s. There are three key sources in the mid-1930s, all post-dating the Rectorial period, in which Heidegger returns to these themes with renewed vigour. These are the *Nietzsche* lectures; a course on Kant (1935–36); and the *Beiträge zur Philosophie (Vom Ereignis)*.[87] The *Beiträge* is a collection of manuscripts written in the years 1936–38, and first published in 1989, the centenary of Heidegger's birth and some thirteen years after his death (GA65). It is a vast book, over 500 pages in the German original, and it has often been seen as Heidegger's second major work, ranking with *Being and Time* in its importance.[88] This is an over-estimation, as the book we have is rather something of a workshop, a working out in rough form of a number of ideas that – originally intended for Heidegger's eyes only – are slowly brought to public attention in his lectures and publications. Nonetheless, it contains some remarkable possibilities.

While the detailed critique of Descartes in Heidegger's work in the *Nietzsche* lectures is in many respects close to what Heidegger said before, and is almost certainly a glimpse of what would have gone on in the unwritten Part Two of *Being and Time*, it is now developed in some important ways. Similarly, the lecture course on Kant is also close to previous material, but contains some important analyses. This particular course demonstrates in particular Heidegger's breadth of knowledge of classical and modern physics. However, it is in the *Beiträge* that the importance of these issues really becomes evident, because here we find the *political* issues explored in most depth.

One of Heidegger's central claims in *Being and Time* is that we have forgotten the question of being. Traditional philosophy, for Heidegger, has neglected the question of being in favour of studying beings. It is for this reason that at the very beginning of that book he quotes the passage from Plato's *Sophist* where the Eleatic stranger wonders what is meant by the expression 'being' (244a; GA2, 1). In the *Beiträge*, Heidegger suggests that there are three things that cause us to forget being: three concealments [*Verhüllungen*]. These are calculation [*die Berechnung*], acceleration [*die Schnelligkeit*] and massiveness [*Massenhaften*]. As we might expect from the three terms, the second two are dependent on the first. Calculation is grounded by the science or knowledge of the mathematical, and is set into power by the machination of technology. This is somewhat ambiguous, and could seem to suggest that calculation is dependent on technology, but the suggestion is the reverse: technology is dependent on calculation, which is grounded in a particular way of thinking the mathematical. Technology merely makes this more apparent. This sense of calculation requires all things to be adjusted in this light; the incalculable is only the not yet calculable, and *organisation* is given priority. Acceleration, or the celebration of quantitative enhancement, particularly celebrated by the Futurists, is likewise so grounded, and massiveness is a particular way of reckoning, based on number and calculation (GA65, 120–1; see GA66, 217–20).

Heidegger suggests that it is with Descartes that this shift in understanding the mathematical occurs. The notion of *logos* had long since become distanced from the idea of speech, and had become the Latin *ratio*. But this becomes mathematical only in Descartes.

> By a certain interpretation of being (as *idea*) the *noein* of Parmenides becomes the *noein* of *dialegesthai* in Plato. The *logos* of Heraclitus becomes the *logos* as statement [*Aussage*] and becomes the leading theme [*Leitfaden*, textbook] of the 'categories' (Plato's *Sophist*). The combining of both into *ratio*, that is the related comprehension of *nous* and *logos*, is prepared in Aristotle. With Descartes *ratio* becomes 'mathematical'; only possible because since Plato this mathematical essence has been the focus, and is *one* possibility grounded in the *aletheia* of *phusis*. (GA65, 457)[89]

In Descartes, as we have seen, the *continuum* of geometry is transformed into a form of arithmetic. Geometrical lines and shapes are conceived in terms of numerical co-ordinates, which can be divided; and this is a mode of access to the material bodies of nature.

To illuminate the importance of this shift in terms of a human understanding of measure, it is worth considering Heidegger's comparison of Descartes to Protagoras. He does this by analysing Protagoras' saying '*panton khrematon metron estin anthropos*'.[90] Although Heidegger regularly returned to this topic, the most important discussion is from 1940, in a lecture course on Nietzsche entitled *European Nihilism*.[91] As Heidegger notes, this is usually translated as 'man is the measure of all things'. At first he suggests 'one might suppose that it is Descartes who is speaking here' – before clearly distancing himself from that way of reading it: 'we would be falling prey to a fatal illusion if we wished to presume a sameness [*Gleichartigkeit*] of basic metaphysical positions here on the basis of a particular sameness [*Gleichheit*] in the words and concepts used' (GA48, 175–6; N, IV, 91–2). While it might appear that 'all metaphysics – not just the modern version – is in fact built on the standard-giving role of man within beings as a whole' (GA48, 161; N, IV, 86), this is a dangerous point to assume.

However, in the context of these lectures it appears evident that Nietzsche's role as the evaluator, and the revaluation of all values, equally falls into this model (GA48, 161–2; N, IV, 86–7). As Heidegger suggests, 'value translates the essentiality of essence (that is, of beingness) into the calculable, something that can even be estimated in terms of quantity and spatial extension [*Zahl und Raummaß*]' (GA47, 288; N, III, 176). This critique of values as calculative, of the relation between evaluation and accounting, is a key theme in the *Nietzsche* lectures, and indeed had been an early concern, dating from at least as early as the 1919 course *Phenomenology and the Transcendental Philosophy of Value* (GA56/57).[92]

But while Cartesian thought can even be found in the avowedly anti-Cartesian Nietzsche, Protagoras' phrase needs to be understood in a rather different manner. Heidegger suggests that 'experienced in a Greek way, the human of the basic relationship with beings is *metron*, measure [*Maß*]'. What he means is that they let 'their confinement [*Mäßigung*, moderation] to the . . . restricted radius [*Umkreis*] of the unconcealed become the basic trait of their essence' (GA48, 178; N, IV, 94). Indeed, the continuation of Protagoras' phrase is that 'man is the measure of all things, of beings that they are, of non-beings, that they are not' (see GA33, 197–203/169–74). The ellipsis above masks Heidegger's qualification that the restriction is particular [*jeweilige*] to the individual; his use of the word 'unconcealed' [*Unverborgenen*] is intended to make us think of the notion of *aletheia*. In this example of Greek thought, Heidegger suggests, being is presence, truth is unconcealment, and measure is of the unconcealed. Equally, we should remember that *khremata* is not just any old things, but specifically those things as they are used, things with value (see GA5, 103/78; GA41, 70/70; GA8, 190–1/186–8). The human 'I', rather than being the subject of a later period, is seen in relation to the beings it belongs to. In other words, to be the measure of all things – for the Greeks – is that the human lets themselves be revealed through the disclosing of *aletheia*. The measure of all things is the human.

In Descartes, the position is somewhat different. Heidegger suggests that

The 'mathematical' is a standard of measure [*maßgebend*] for Descartes' conception of knowledge and knowing. But it remains for us to ask here, does Descartes simply take the already present and practised form of 'mathematical' knowledge as the model for all knowledge, or does he on the contrary newly define – in fact, metaphysically define – the essence of mathematics? The second is the case. (GA48, 201; N, IV, 113–14)

The mathematical – conceived in a new way – is the measure. Heidegger makes this point in a number of ways – essentially, the mathematical is not grounded in number, but number is grounded in the mathematical. Because mathematics is something grounded in *ta mathematica*, that is, the observation of what is, *mathesis* is learning, *ta mathematica* what is learnable. In these terms, 'modern science, modern mathematics and modern metaphysics sprung from the same root of the mathematical in the wider sense' (GA41, 98/97, see 69–71/ 69–71, 74–5/74; GA5, 78/59). Particular versions of mathematics – analytic geometry in Descartes, infinitesimal calculus in Newton and differential calculus in Leibniz – are all grounded on the 'basically mathematical character of the thinking' (GA41, 94/94). See, for example, the way in which, in *Rules for the Direction of the Mind*, Descartes inquires into *mathesis* as the basis for later inquiries into arithmetic, geometry and other sciences, and declares that 'the exclusive concern of *mathesis* is with questions of order or measure [*ordo vel mensura*]'.[93] In other words, the developments in new forms of mathematical thinking are not the reason for the predominance of mathematics, but the consequence of it (GA42, 52/30). Now, of course, Descartes' understanding of *res extensa* is dependent on his understanding of *res cogitans*, the human subject, the initial 'I am'. The *cogito* forms the basis for all that is knowable, *mathesis* in its broad sense. Such a shift also forces us to rethink the nature of truth, which is no longer understood as the unconcealment Heidegger finds in the Greeks, but as veracity, certitude, accord. The human subject takes the place of the integrated human (see GA48, 187; N, IV, 102). As Heidegger suggests:

> Descartes, with his principle of the *cogito sum*, forced open the gates of the domain of such a metaphysically comprehended domination. The principle that lifeless nature is *res extensa* is simply the essential consequence of the first principle. *Sum res cogitans* is the ground, the underlying [*der Grund, das zum Grunde Liegende*], the *subiectum* for the determination of the material world as *res extensa*. (GA48, 205; N, IV, 117)

As Heidegger notes in the *Beiträge*, the establishment of individual identity grounds the identity of other things. The principle of identity

'A = A' is *'grounded* [gegründet] in I = I [*Ich = Ich*]', rather than 'I = I as an exceptional instance of A = A' (GA65, 201). The fundamental determination of the world is extension, *res extensa*, but this is grounded on thinking, *res cogitans*. 'Man establishes himself as the measure of all measures [*Maßgabe für all Maßstäbe*] with which whatever can count as certain – i.e. as true, i.e. as in being – is measured off and measured out (reckoned up) [*ab- und ausgemessen (verrechnet)*]' (GA5, 110/83). A human notion becomes the measure of all things.[94]

Our view of the world is therefore not only shaped by our perception, it is also limited by it. The ontological foundation of modern science – this notion of calculation – acts to limit the ontic phenomena it, and we, are able to experience and to encompass. 'The step taken by Descartes is already a first and decisive consequence [*Folge*], a 'compliance' [*Folgeleistung*] by which machination assumes power as transformed truth (correctness), namely as certainty' (GA65, 132). It is worth noting here an important discussion of the notion of exactness in science. For Heidegger, the concept of 'exact' is ambiguous. We usually understand it to mean precise or accurate [*genau*], measured from [*abgemessen*], careful [*sorgfältig*], but if that is so then all sciences are exact in that they are careful to use the method appropriately. But 'exact' can also be seen to mean 'determined, measured and calculated according to the measure of numbers [*zahlenmäßig bestimmt, gemessen und errechnet*]', and then 'exactness is the character of the *method itself*, not merely how it is used' (GA65, 149–50).[95] In order for science to have some purchase on its subject matter, it must work with the way that subject matter is determined. When the modern concept of nature is conceived – as it is by Descartes – as 'accessible only to quantitative measuring and calculation', science must be exact (GA65, 150; see also GA5, 76–7/58, 79/60). We saw this in the discussion of world in relation to Kant above. Elsewhere, Heidegger cites Max Planck's statement that 'that is real which can be measured' (GA7, 52). In the Modern period, 'beings became transparent objects capable of being mastered [*beherrschbaren*] by calculation' (GA5, 65/48). But in so doing, making measure the determination, science allows what is essential to slip through our fingers. Though putting a stone on a scale will measure its heaviness as a calculated weight, a number, the burden has escaped us (GA5, 33/25; see GA65, 275–6; GA7, 171–2).

But though, like Heidegger, we might want to criticise this conception of the material world, of nature, as *res extensa*, it has enormous consequences. The modern notion of measure, which derives from Descartes, sees beings as calculable, as quantitatively measurable, but as a determination of the world, 'it is the first resolute step through which modern machine technology, and along with it the modern world and modern mankind, become metaphysically possible for the first time' (GA48, 204–5; N, IV, 116–17). The modern physical theory of nature prepares the way not simply for technology but for the *essence* of modern technology, which is not in itself technological, but is a way of seeing things as calculable, mathematical, extended and therefore controllable. Technological domination means the destruction [*Zerstörung*] of nature (GA45, 53). This is the modern worldview, worldpicture [*Weltbild*], the world as picture – not a picture of the world, but 'the world grasped as picture' (GA5, 89/67).

The discussion is developed and continued in Heidegger's consideration of the issue of worldview [*Weltanschauung*]. In a very early course he had suggested that this is '*the task of philosophy*' and that '*therefore* a philosophical-historical consideration of the manner in which philosophy performs this task' is an essential inquiry (GA56/57, 8). In the *Beiträge*, though, Heidegger suggests that ' "Worldview", like the domination of "worldpictures" is an outgrowth [*Gewächs*] of modernity, a consequence [*Folge*] of modern metaphysics' (GA65, 38). In a contemporaneous lecture course on Schelling, he notes that Kant coins the term, and that it develops from insights in Leibniz's work (GA42, 29/17). It is interesting to note here that a word given important currency by the National Socialist movement – who saw their 'system' of beliefs to be a *Weltanschauung* rather than an ideology[96] – is now criticised in a way which is akin to Nazi medical discourse: worldview is a tumour, an ulcer, a festering sore on the problem of modernity.[97]

The Politics of Calculation

What has been shown by the examination of Protagoras and Descartes is that in the first case measure is taken from the world to understand the human; in the second a human notion of measure is used to understand the world. Increasingly, Heidegger realises this is a political issue: indeed, it can be generally said that when Heidegger develops his earlier ideas on calculation after the Rectorial period there is a new political urgency. The *Beiträge*, for example, is an explicitly political text, written in secret, and both a product of Heidegger's political career and a response to it.[98] It needs to be seen within the context of the time much more than is usually acknowledged. In particular, a running theme of the *Beiträge* concerns the problems of mechanistic, calculative ways of looking at the world. To take a few examples, the Nuremburg laws had been promulgated in 1935; September 1936 saw the Four Year Plan announced; the *Anschluß* with Austria, the Munich Agreement and *Kristallnacht* all happened in 1938.[99] The political themes of the *Beiträge* are not disconnected comments about world events at the time of writing but a very real response to them.

The word measure is *Maß*, which derives from *messen*, to measure or gauge. It is also related to the term *Masse* – the mass or the group.[100] Heidegger continually works with words that share this stem. We have already seen in the discussion of *Introduction to Metaphysics* in Chapter Two *Massenversammlungen*, the mass meetings; *Vermassung*, the reduction to a mass or measure, levelling down; and *Lebensmasse*, vital resources. In that period, Heidegger suggested that all had been condensed to extension and number. We have seen here how that measuring is indebted to Descartes. One of the most important related words in a political context is *Gemäßheit*, a word vital to National Socialism, which means conformity or accord, the removal of dangerous elements as things are brought together around a fixed measure or norm. *Ge-* denotes a bringing together, therefore *Gemäße* is a bringing together of measure, or a bringing things to the same measure. In this, it is directly related to the better known concept of *Gleichschaltung*, which implies political co-ordination, literally 'same wiring' or 'connection', the bringing into line and elimination of opposition, subordinating things to a common measure.[101] *Schalten* is to direct, govern or rule; *Schaltung* is connection or wiring. Because *Gleich* means same or identical, this implies a making similar, a forced conformity, an ordering around a prescribed norm.[102] Aside from the sarcastic reference noted in Chapter Two (GA38, 11), Heidegger does not explicitly analyse this notion but he does make some ambiguous comments about the related terms *eingeschalten* and *einschalten* – to switch on or connect up – in terms of the transformation of society, of peasants into workers in the 'provisions industry', 'of leading scholars into the managing director of a research institute' (GA51, 38). Rather, in the notion of measure, the issues are there in muted form.

The other key background theme is the gearing up of the economy, particularly in the Four Year Plan.[103] Section 74 of the *Beiträge*, for example, which is entitled ' "Total Mobilisation" as Consequence of Originary Forsaking of Being', takes issue with the putting to use of the resources of the country and the people within it. Heidegger characterises 'total mobilisation' [*totale Mobilmachung*], a notion developed in Ernst Jünger's work, as 'purely setting-into-motion'.[104] While the masses [*der Massen*] are put to service, the purpose is unclear (GA65, 143; see GA7, 70).[105] Equally, the calculative understanding of time found in Aristotle, Heidegger notes, does not simply begin the path toward mathematical basis of physics, but also for the ordering of all human comportment, including the time of the worker, *der Arbeiter* (GA54, 210; see GA52, 104).

It becomes increasingly clear to Heidegger, both in the *Beiträge* and perhaps more obviously in the *Nietzsche* lectures given in the period 1936–40, that neither Nietzsche nor Nazism is a solution to the problem of technology and the spectre of nihilism. As he suggests in 1940, following France's defeat, the modern 'machine economy', that is, 'the machine-based calculation of all activity and planning', requires new kinds of humans: 'it is not sufficient that one possesses tanks, airplanes and communication equipments; nor is it sufficient that one has humans, who can service them . . . only the Over-man [*Übermensch*] is appropriate to an absolute "machine economy"'. While it was Descartes who 'forced open the gates of this domain' (GA48, 204–5; N, IV, 116–17), Germany has beaten them at their own game.[106]

> The prepotence of Being in this essential configuration is called *machination*. It prevents any kind of grounding of the 'projections' that are under its power and yet are themselves none the less powerful. (GA47, 287; N, III, 175)

While, as before, time and space are discussed in terms of their calculative aspects,[107] there is the introduction of a new notion, that of 'the gigantic' [*Das Riesenhafte*] (GA65, 441–3). There are three obvious candidates for giganticism in 1930s Germany: the Leviathan, a state of unlimited and undivided sovereignty on the Hobbesian model; the Behemoth that became the symbol of the Nazi war machine; and the Hindenberg airship which had burst into flames in 1937.[108] But Heidegger means something more than this:

> The gigantic was determined as that through which the 'quantitative' is transformed into its own 'quality', a kind of magnitude [*Größe*]. The gigantic is thus not something quantitative that begins with a relatively high number (with number and measurement) – even though it can appear

superficially as 'quantitative'. The gigantic is grounded upon the decided-
ness and invariability of 'calculation' and is rooted in a prolongation
of subjective re-presentation unto the whole of beings (GA65, 441; see
GA5, 95/72).

This theme of the quantitative as a quality in itself is important. The
quale of something is its whatness, effectively its way of being, or, in
the traditional sense, its essence. That the quantitative has become a
quality is an important shift. The gigantic, for Heidegger, is not merely
a quantity of dramatic proportions, but his name for this shift.
Descartes sees the world as 'mechanical nature, that is, extension'
(GA42, 103/59). What is important here is how the shift to seeing
what is as what can be calculated plays out politically. As Heidegger
notes in his 1937–38 course, the crisis of science is not to be understood in terms of minor problems that can be resolved within the
existing order, but from something much deeper. It stems 'not from
1933, and not from 1918, and not even from the much-criticised
nineteenth century, but from the beginning of the modern age'. The
two dates Heidegger picks are significant – Hitler taking power and
the end of the First World War. As Heidegger continues, though, this
'was not a mistake but a fate [*Schicksal*], and only a fate will overcome
it' (GA45, 53–4). Essentially, the current malaise is seen in terms of the
twin themes of order [*Ordnung*] and calculation. These two are
related to each other in that dividing something into elements helps
to establish control over it, as these can be organised, rendered and
further divided, or grouped and forced into similarity.[109]

All calculation lets what is countable [*Zählbare*] be resolved into something counted [*Gezählten*] that can then be used for subsequent counting
[*Zählung*]. Calculation refuses to let anything appear except what is
countable. Everything is only whatever it counts. What has been counted
in each instance secures the continuation of counting. Such counting
progressively consumes numbers [*Zahlen*], and is itself a continual self-
consumption. The calculative process of resolving beings into what has
been counted counts as the explanation of their being. Calculation uses all
beings in advance as that which is countable, and uses up what is counted
for the purpose of counting. This use of beings that consumes them betrays
the consuming character of calculation. Only because number can be
infinitely multiplied, irrespective of whether this occurs in the direction of
the large or small, can the consuming essence of calculation hide behind its
products and lend to calculative thinking the semblance of productivity –
whereas already in its anticipatory grasping, and not primarily in its

subsequent results, such thinking lets all beings count only in the form of what can be set at our disposal and consumed. Calculative thinking compels itself into a compulsion to master everything on the basis of the consequential correctness of its procedure. (GA9, 308–9/235)

Indeed, in Heidegger's discussion of the Nazi concept of 'new order' [*Neue Ordnung*] and the notion of *Lebensraum* the implied critique is notably not moralising, nor even explicitly political, but from the perspective of the greater problem of nihilism and the culmination of metaphysics in technology (GA48, 139–41).[110]

> Space and time comprise the framework for our calculative dominating ordering of the 'world' as nature and history. This calculating, discovering and conquering by measurement of the world [*Diese rechnende, entdeck-ende, erobernde Durchmessung der Welt*] is undertaken by modern human beings in a way whose distinctive metaphysical feature is modern machine technology. Metaphysically, it remains undecided in this process whether this procedure on the part of modern human beings – a procedure of conquering space and of time-lapse – serves merely to bring about a position within the planet as a whole that secures this humanity a suitable 'living space' [*gemäßen »Lebensraum«*] for its lifetime [*Lebenszeit*], or whether such securing of space and time is intrinsically determined in such a far-reaching manner as to attain new possibilities of this procedure of conquering space and of time-lapse and to intensify this procedure. Metaphysically, it remains undecided whether, and in what way, this will to planetary ordering will set itself its own limit. (GA53, 59)

Calculability is therefore the essential prerequisite for mechanism (GA65, 376), and more generally the notion of machination is dependent on this particular way of grasping the world. This is not merely to discuss the problems of Germany, but also – as was seen in *Introduction to Metaphysics* – Soviet Russia. Interpreting Lenin's famous suggestion that 'Bolshevism is Soviet power + electrification', Heidegger suggests that this means that 'Bolshevism is the "*orga-nische*", that is the organised, calculating (and as +) conclusion of the unconditional power of the party along with complete technicisation'. What is decisive is not that, for example, they are 'always building more tractor factories', but rather 'the complete technical organisation of the world is already the metaphysical foundation for all plans and operations' (GA54, 127; see GA67, 150).

The notion of the gigantic would bear fruitful comparison with contemporary discussion of 'globalisation'.[111] Rather than conceive of globalisation as a radical break with modern, state-based, territorial politics, we can recognise that it is, ontologically at least, the same, merely extending the calculative understanding of space to the globe instead of a single nation.[112] Similarly, the remarks on the link between 'the machine and machination (technology)' may illuminate this and related contemporary issues:

> The machine, its essence. The service that it demands, the uprooting that it brings. 'Industry' (operations [Betriebe]); industrial workers, torn from homeland and history [Heimat und Geschichte], exploited for profit. Machine-training, machination and business. What recasting of man gets started here? (World-earth?) Machination and business [Machenschaft und das Geschäft]. The large number [die große Zahl], the gigantic, pure extension [Ausdehnung] and growing levelling off and emptying. Falling necessarily victim to kitsch and imitation [Unechten]. (GA65, 392)[113]

Machination, in this sense, is closely related to the notion of technology, a recurrent theme of work in the late 1940s, which Heidegger also talks about in the later essays of the Nietzsche volumes.[114] It is the idea of 'completed [vollendete] metaphysics' (GA7, 79), dependent on a process initiated by Descartes, which has its 'own greatness [eigene Größe]' (GA5, 99/75). Technology, as will later be elaborated, 'contains the recollection of tekhne', a fundamental term in the development of Western thought, but also 'makes it possible for the planetary factor of the completion of metaphysics and its rule to be thought without reference to historiographically demonstrable changes in nations [Völkern] and continents' (GA7, 79; see 97). World-wars and their 'totality' are consequences of the forgetting of being; humans become raw material; leadership becomes the 'planning calculation of the guarantee of the whole of beings' (GA7, 91–2). Heidegger goes on to draw total mobilisation and worldviews into this orbit, along with organisation, and service. 'Such worldviews drive all calculability of representation and production to the extreme, originating as they do essentially in mankind's self-imposed instauration of self in the midst of beings – in the midst of mankind's unconditioned hegemony over all sources of power on the face of the earth, and indeed its domination over the globe as such' (GA6.2, 14–15; N, III, 175; GA67, 113–22).

One of the problems of worldviews is precisely this totalising aspect. If they claim to regulate all kinds of action and thinking, then necessity (something which would be outside their control) is necessarily a problem. The idea of creativity, questioning the ground on which they stand, is impossible. Creativity becomes replaced by operations or management [*Betrieb*] (see GA5, 83–4/63–4; 97–8/73–4). We can note here the clear relation this has to the notions of *Gemäßheit* and *Gleichschaltung* – the removal of dangerous elements, the elimination of opposition, the bringing under a common measure. As Heidegger notes, the precedence of beings over being means that being is seen as '*koinon* in terms of the *hen*', the common is reduced to the one (GA6.2, 417). Heidegger suggests that, though they are incompatible, total political faith [*totale politische Glaube*] and total Christian faith are nevertheless both engaged in adjustment [*Ausgleich*] and tactics. This is because they share the same essence [*Wesens*]. Their total posture [*totalen Haltunzugrunde*] makes their struggle [*Kampf*] 'not a creative one, but rather "propaganda" and "apologetics"' (GA65, 41; see GA7, 92). Totalitarianism is dependent on this totalising understanding of the world, this conception of worldpicture.[115]

Somewhat cryptically, Heidegger suggests that

> Worldview is always 'machination' over and above what is passed to us, with the aim of overcoming and subduing it, with the means which are proper to, prepared by, though not brought to fruition – all of this slid over into 'lived-experience'. (GA65, 38)

The first part of this follows from what has been thus far discussed. The second, however, the link to the notion of 'lived-experience', is worth a little explanation. Elsewhere Heidegger asks 'What does machination mean?', and answers 'machination and constant presence: *poiesis – tekhne*. Where does machination lead? To *lived-experience*' (GA65, 107).[116] In a lecture course delivered at the time the *Beiträge* was being written, *Basic Questions of Philosophy*, Heidegger explains:

> At the beginning of modern thought, Descartes for the first time posited the certainty of the ego [*Ichgewißheit*], in which the human is made secure of beings as the object of their representations, and is the germ of what today, as 'lived experience' and 'experience' [»*Erlebnis*« *und* »*Erleben*«], constitutes the basic form of being human. It is one of the ironies of history that our age has discovered – admittedly very late – the need to refute Descartes, and takes issue with him and his 'intellectualism' by appealing to 'lived experience', whereas 'lived experience' is only a base descendent of the Cartesian *cogito ergo sum*. (GA45, 149)

A concept appealed to – particularly by the Nazi regime[117] – as a more authentic, more rooted way of dealing with the world than the cold calculation of technology is grounded in the same way of thinking which takes a human notion as the measure of all things. In the *Beiträge*, Heidegger is even more explicit:

> Now, however, since beings are abandoned by being [*Seyn*], the opportunity arises for the most insipid 'sentimentality'. Now for the first time everything is 'experienced' [*erlebt*] and every undertaking and performance drips with 'lived-experience' [*Erlebnisse*]. And this lived-experience proves that now even the *human* as a *being* has incurred the loss of being [*Seyn*] and has fallen prey to their hunt for lived-experiences. (GA65, 123–4)[118]

Although Heidegger had used the term in a number of places, notably a 1919 course, even there he recognised that 'the term "lived experience" [*Erlebnis*] is today so faded and worn thin that, if it were not so fitting, it would be best to leave it aside. Since it cannot be avoided, it is all the more necessary to understand its essence' (GA56/57, 66). For Heidegger, this is tied into the notion of *Ereignis*, which will assume centre stage in his late thought, and which is first worked through in detail in the *Beiträge*. An *Erlebnis*, in this sense, is an event, or a propriation [*Er-eignis*] (GA56/57, 69).

The key example of an *Erlebnis* in this course is our way of encountering a lectern. Heidegger suggests that when his students come into the lecture room they go to *their* usual place. He suggests they put themselves in his place – when he comes into the room he sees a lectern. Does he see it as brown surfaces, at right angles? Does he see it as a largish box with a smaller one on top of it? No. Rather he sees a lectern, which he has spoken at before. He does not first see the surfaces, then the surfaces as a box, then the purpose of it; rather a lectern, within an environment. The lectern only becomes an issue if it is too high, or there is something – a book, for example – obstructing its use. This way of taking an everyday object and discussing how we experience it is reminiscent of the kitchen table in the later lecture course *Ontology: The Hermeneutic of Facticity* or the hammer in *Being and Time*. Heidegger goes on to argue that a Black Forest farmer or a native from Senegal would experience the lectern in a different way. The farmer would equally not see the lectern as a box, but as the 'place for the teacher'; the native as something 'which he does not know what to make of'. Heidegger calls the latter 'instrumental strangeness' (GA56/57, 70–3). But in all cases essentially the same thing is happening:

> In seeing the lectern I am fully present in my 'I'; it resonates with the experience, as we said. It is an experience proper to me and so do I see it. However it is not a process [*Vorgang*], but rather a *propriation* [*Ereignis*] (non-process, in the experience of the question a residue of this propriation). Lived experience [*Das Er-leben*] does not pass in front of me like a thing, but I appropriate [*er-eigne*] it to myself, and it appropriates itself according to its essence. If I understand it in this way, then I understand it not as process, as thing, as object, but in quite a new way, as propriation. (GA56/57, 75)

Rather than the Cartesian division of subject and object, the division of human from the world, grounded on the *cogito* and the split between *res cogitans* and *res extensa*, we have a way of understanding that looks at the way we comport ourselves always already within a world [*Welt*]. Heidegger's hyphenated term being-in-the-world, used in *Being and Time*, shows that what we call 'being' is indivisible from the world or environment [*Umwelt*]. 'The world that is closest to us is one of practical concern. The environing world [*Umwelt*], and its objects are in space, but the space of this world is not the space of geometry'.[119] As he puts it in the *Kriegsnotsemester*, 'es weltet', 'it worlds'. This use of the impersonal 'it' is related to Heidegger's interest in the term *es gibt*, which literally means 'it gives', and has the sense of 'there is', in the impersonal sense of the French *il y a*.[120] For Heidegger, both in this early lecture course and the *Beiträge*, it is *Ereignis* that *gives* being, time, space. In opposition to the worldview, to the view the human has of the world, the grid they use to comprehend, order and exploit the world, the world rather gives to us the view, the comportment (GA2, 211). It is this sense of experience, as a propriation, an *Ereignis*, that can be used to refute Descartes, rather than the 'lived-experience' that too stems from Descartes. In a sense, this is a reversal of the reversal of Protagoras: rather than the human being the measure of all things, the measure of all things is the human.

Just as he wants to try to rethink *Erlebnis* in a more originary way, so too with the notion of machination [*Machenschaft*], which Heidegger says is a mode of making [*machen*], and, although etymologically distinct, is related to the notion of *Macht*, power. The notion of *Machenschaft* is usually associated with 'a "bad" type of human activity and plotting for such an activity', but Heidegger is interested in retrieving a sense of how it impacts on the question of being (see also GA69, 26–7, 46–7, 62–71, 228). The notion of *machen* is, however, unquestionably a human comportment: Heidegger adds '*poiesis, tekhne*' in parentheses here to underline the point. That said, he wants to stress that this comportment is only possible on the basis of a particular interpretation of beings, that is of *phusis*, the Greek term that encompasses nature and the physical more generally. *Phusis* is thought in relation to *tekhne*, 'so that what counts now is the preponderance of the makeable and the self-making [*Machbare und Sich-machende*] . . . in a word: machination' (GA65, 126). *Phusis* is not *tekhne*, but a reduction of the former into the latter is pronounced.[121]

> What does *machination* mean? That which is let loose into its own shackles? Which shackles? The pattern of generally calculable explainability [*berechnenbaren Erklärbarkeit*], by which everything draws nearer to everything else in the same measure [*gleichmäßig*] and becomes completely alien to itself – yes, totally other than just alien [*ja ganz anders als noch fremd wird*]. The relation of non-relationality [*Der Bezug der Unbezüglichkeit*]. (GA65, 132)

Heidegger provides a few examples of how he thinks calculative thinking holds sway in the contemporary age. For example, he shows how *Geisteswissenschaft* will increasingly 'be transmogrified into a pedagogical tool for inculcating a "political worldview"'. Heidegger has already noted how the major branches of industry and military Chiefs of Staff [*der Generalstab*] are more attuned to the uses of the mathematical, technical sciences (GA44, 15; N, II, 16). Science cannot be preserved in its old ways and means, but crucially, 'nor will the technical style of modern science, prefigured in its very beginnings, be altered if we choose new goals for such technology. That style will only be firmly embedded and absolutely validated by such new choices' (GA44, 16; N, II, 17). Philosophy is something entirely different, which seems to be the point of this discussion, but the issue is important. Here, in 1937, Heidegger is outlining the point of his technology essay.

In the second *Nietzsche* lecture course there is a discussion of the difference between Nietzsche's thought of force [*Kraft*] and that of physics. 'Physics, whether mechanistic or dynamic in style, thinks the concept of force always and everywhere as a quantitative specification

within an equation [*Maßbezeichnung innerhalb der Rechnung*]; physics as such, in the way it takes up nature into its representational
framework, can never think force as force' (GA44, 90; N, II, 86; see
GA7, 59).[122] Before he goes on to show that Nietzsche thinks force in
a very different way, he notes that to call Nietzsche's thought dynamic
would require us to think the Greek *dunamis*, and to realise that the
opposition of the dynamic and the static is misleading.

> Given its frame of reference, physics always deals with sheer relations of
> force with a view to the magnitude of their spatio-temporal appearance.
> The moment physics conducts nature into the domain of the 'experiment',
> it co-posits in advance the calculative, technical relation [*die rechnerische,
> technische Beziehung*] (in the broader sense) between sheer magnitudes of
> force and effects of force, and with calculation it co-posits rationality [*mit
> der Rechnung aber die Rationalität*]. (GA44, 90; N, II, 86)

The last point is crucial, in that Heidegger is showing the integral
relation between modern understandings of rationality and calculation. Rationality, *ratio*, has become mathematical, rather than concerned with relation and balance, or to the Greek term *logos*, much
more associated with language than number.

One of the most extensive discussions of related themes comes in a
course delivered shortly after the conclusion of those on Nietzsche,
Basic Concepts.

> The modern habit of thinking time together with 'space' (already pre-
> figured in the beginning of metaphysics with Aristotle) leads us astray
> [*führt irre*]. For according to this way of thinking time is considered
> solely in terms of its extension [*Erstrekung*], and this as a counting up
> [*Rechnung*] of fleeting now-points. Thought in modern terms, time like
> space is a parameter [*Parameter*], a standard scale [*Maßstab*] according to
> which something is measured and estimated [*gemessen und gerechnet*].
> Space and time are essentially related to 'calculation' [*»Rechnung«*].
> (GA51, 120; see GA53, 47–50, 53)

Heidegger highlights what he calls 'a metaphysical subjugation to
technology', and notes that 'accompanying this subjugation within us
is an attitude that grasps everything according to plan and calculation,
and does so with a view to vast time-spans in order wilfully and
knowingly to secure what can last for the longest possible duration'
(GA51, 17). Here we find a reduction of the world to calculation and
planning. Such comments clearly follow from those outlined since at
least 1935.

> It is one thing when empires [*Reiche*] endure for millennia because of their continuing stability. It is something else when world dominions [*Weltherrschaften*] are knowingly planned to last millennia and the assurance of their existence is undertaken by *that* will whose essential goal is the greatest possible duration of the greatest possible order of the largest possible masses [*Massen ein wesenhaftes Ziel*]. (GA51, 17)

The obvious reference to the thousand-year Reich is put in language of range and scope – temporal extent, duration, order, mass – terms that a moment before were used to illustrate the problem of technology and its metaphysical subjugation. For Heidegger, 'this will has been the concealed metaphysical essence of modernity for the last three centuries', which means that Hitler here is a symptom of a much wider malaise. Indeed, the essence of modern technology is the same as the essence of modern metaphysics (GA5, 75/57).

> It appears in various predecessors and guises that are not sure of themselves and their essence. That in the twentieth century this will would attain the shape of the unconditional, Nietzsche had clearly thought in advance. (GA51, 17–18)

So while it existed in previous forms, it is in Nietzsche's thought that the unconditional form of the modern period (1941) first appears with clarity. Nietzsche here is seen both as the diagnostic, and potentially the problem.

> Participation in this will to man's unconditional mastery over the earth, and the execution of this will, harbour within themselves that subjugation to technology that does not appear as resistance and resentment [*Widerwille und Unwille*]. That subjugation appears as will, and that means it is also effective here . . . However, where one interprets the execution of this metaphysical will as a 'product' of the self-obsession and arbitrariness [*Eigensucht und Willkür*] of 'dictators' and 'authoritarian states', there speak only political calculation and propaganda, or the metaphysical naïveté of a thinking that ran aground centuries ago, or both. (GA51, 18)

In other words, those that think that this is *caused* by the actions of single individuals or states are mistaken. This is a wider problem. This is not based on the 'chance arbitrariness [*Zufälligen Willkür*] of dictators but in the metaphysical essence of modern actuality in general' (GA53, 118). Whether this attribution be through critique or celebration, it is flawed thinking.

> Political circumstances, economic situations, population growth, and the like, can be the proximate causes and horizons for carrying out this metaphysical will of modern world-history. But they are never the ground of this history and therefore never its 'end'. The will to preservation, and that always means the will to enhance life and its lastingness, works essentially against decline and sees deficiency and powerlessness in what lasts only a short while. (GA51, 18)[123]

Again, the very real crises of the modern ages are symptoms of a wider malaise. The will to power, to domination, to preservation and all the metaphysical baggage it carries is another stage in the long-running problem. The concluding lines of the published *European Nihilism* course provide Heidegger's summary assessment of the importance of this topic:

> The age of the fulfilment of metaphysics – which we descry when we think through the basic features of Nietzsche's metaphysics – prompts us to consider to what extent we find ourselves in the history of being. It also prompts us to consider – prior to our finding ourselves – the extent to which we must experience history as the release of being into machination, a release that being itself sends, so as to allow its truth to become essential for man out of man's belonging to it. (GA6.2, 229; N, IV, 196)

It is in the *Beiträge* that Heidegger makes many of these points for the first time, a working through of issues surrounding him. Mournfully, he remarks that the human 'might for centuries yet pillage and lay waste to the planet with their machinations, the gigantic character of this driving might "develop" into something unimaginable and take on the form of a seeming rigour as the massive regulating of the desolate as such – yet the greatness of being [*Seyn*] continues to be closed off' (GA65, 408). Heidegger argues that the originary, more rooted sense of *phusis* is lost as nature is seen as a being itself, 'and, after this demoting [*Absetzung*], ultimately reduced to the full force of calculating machination and economy' (GA65, 277). Nature becomes *res extensa*, an extended material resource. The natural no longer has any 'immediate relation to *phusis*, but rather is fully set-up [*gestellt*] according to the machinational' (GA65, 133). Heidegger talks of the human reduction and '*transition to a technicised animal*, which begins to replace the instincts, which have already grown weaker and less refined by the giganticism of technology [*der Technik*]' (GA65, 98). In this reduction, nature becomes merely scenery and a place for recreation, and even in this arranged for the masses as a form of the gigantic (GA65, 277).

Very similar language would be used for the Rhine river in the later 'Question Concerning Technology' essay (GA7, 16–17). Here, Heidegger suggests that 'modern science's way of representing pursues and entraps nature as a calculable coherence of forces', it 'sets nature up to exhibit itself as a coherence of forces calculable in advance' (GA7, 22; see ID, 98–9/34–5). This way of thinking, as we have seen, prepares the way for technology, but more, for the *essence* of technology. Heidegger uses the crucial term *Ge-Stell*, framework or the set-up, to name this essence. Exact physical science is dependent on the particular casting of beings, essentially their calculability, in order to exist in itself, and for it to be the foundation of technology. The essence of technology is therefore prior to both. In the earliest form of this lecture, from 1949, the title itself was 'Das Ge-Stell' (GA79, 24–45).[124] In this piece, revised for delivery in 1953, Heidegger reaches a level of concision and clarity that the early sketches rarely achieve. But, in its published form, this essay appears peculiarly apolitical. What is striking is that the *Beiträge* dates from more than a decade before, in a very different situation, and that it and lectures from this time anticipate so many of the later essays' concerns. Indeed, realising the explicitly political context of the development of these ideas is extremely useful in both recognising their political import and understanding some of their more problematic claims.[125]

What we find in the writings and lectures of Heidegger in the 1940s is a curious balance of political remarks and a seeming depoliticising of his thought. In 1942, he comments on the entry of the USA into the war (GA53, 68); and later in the same course talks of the 'historical uniqueness' or singularity of National Socialism (GA53, 98, 106). After Stalingrad, with German defeat looking more and more likely, he notes that the 'planet is in flames' and calls for Germans to be 'strong enough in their preparedness for death' (GA55, 123, 181). And yet, when he returns to the notion of the *polis* and the determination of the human as the *zoon politikon*, although he again ties this to the *zoon ekhon logon*, no contemporary resonances are heard, and indeed Heidegger goes out of his way to deny them. In particular, he insistently argues that the *polis* simply cannot be understood as a 'state' (GA53, 100–7; see GA54, 100–1); and that we think the political in a Roman, rather than Greek way, that is imperially (GA54, 63), in relation to command and arrangement (GA54, 65). While there is undoubtedly here an implicit criticism of modern ways of thinking the political, there is also a muted reinterpretation of some of Heidegger's own claims about the political going on. We find this, for instance, in the reading of the myth of the cave in the 1942–43 course, which, like the essays published around the same time on this subject, are seemingly almost entirely apolitical. What, then, is the political legacy of Heidegger's thought?

Notes

1. For a reading of this in terms of space, see Stuart Elden, *Mapping the Present: Heidegger, Foucault and the Project of a Spatial History*, London: Continuum, 2001, especially Chapter One.
2. There is a discussion of the world as *kosmos* in GA26, 218–23. For important developments, see Eugen Fink, *Spiel als Weltsymbol*, Stuttgart: Kohlhammer, 1960; and Kostas Axelos, *Le jeu du monde*, Paris: Éditions de Minuit, 1969.
3. See Thomas Sheehan, 'Heidegger's *Lehrjahre*', in John Sallis (ed.), *The Collegium Phaenomenologicum*, Dordrecht: Kluwer, 1988, pp. 77–137 for details; and John van Buren, *The Young Heidegger: Rumor of the Hidden King*, Bloomington: Indiana University Press, 1994, pp. 58–9.
4. Martin Heidegger, 'Wilhelm Dilthey's Research and the Struggle for a Historical Worldview (1925)', in *Supplements: From the Earliest Essays to Being and Time and Beyond*, edited by John van Buren, Albany: State University of New York Press, 2002, p. 171.
5. Letter of Heidegger, 2 July 1915, cited in Sheehan, 'Heidegger's *Lehrjahre*', p. 78.
6. Sheehan, 'Heidegger's *Lehrjahre*', p. 107; see Sheehan, 'Reading a Life: Heidegger and Hard Times', in Charles Guignon (ed.), *The Cambridge Companion to Heidegger*, Cambridge: Cambridge University Press, 1993, pp. 70–96.
7. See Edmund Husserl, *Philosophy of Arithmetic: Psychological and Logical Investigations*, translated by Dallas Willard, Dordrecht: Kluwer, 2003; and *Early Writings in the Philosophy of Mathematics*, translated by Dallas Willard, Dordrecht: Kluwer, 1994. For discussions, see J. Philip Miller (ed.), *Numbers in Presence and Absence: Study of Husserl's Philosophy of Mathematics*, Dordrecht: Kluwer, 1982; Robert S. Tragesser, *Husserl and Realism in Logic and Mathematics*, Cambridge: Cambridge University Press, 1984; Françoise Dastur, *Husserl:*

Des mathématiques à l'histoire, Paris: PUF, 1995; and the introduction to Edmund Husserl, *L'origine de la geometrie*, translated and introduced by Jacques Derrida, Paris: Presses Universitaires de France, 1962. Heidegger discusses Husserl's idea of formal analysis and ontology as *mathesis universalis* in GA56/57, 108.

8. See Elden, *Mapping the Present*, Chapter One.

9. Immanuel Kant, *Kritik der reinen Vernunft*, Hamburg: Felix Meiner, 1956; translated by Paul Guyer and Allen W. Wood as *Critique of Pure Reason*, Cambridge: Cambridge University Press, 1988; A418–9/B446–7.

10. Compare GA21, 245. In *Being and Time* (GA2, 244 n. 1), Heidegger suggests that the distinction between the whole and a sum – *holon* and *pan* in Greek, *totum* and *compositum* in Latin – has been familiar since the time of Plato and Aristotle (see also GA19, 81–2).

11. See also GA27, 43, 186–8; and on the distinction between mathematical and dynamical in Kant, see also GA31, 160–1; GA41, 193–5/190–1.

12. See also 'Vom Wesen des Grundes' in GA9, 123–75/97–135; and GA24, 5–14.

13. Kant, *Kritik der reinen Vernunft*, Bxvi.

14. Kant, *Kritik der reinen Vernunft*, A158/B197.

15. For a discussion, see Miguel de Beistegui, *Thinking with Heidegger: Displacements*, Bloomington: Indiana University Press, 2003, Chapter Four, especially pp. 90–1.

16. The examples come from Immanuel Kant, 'Prolegomena zu einer jeden künftigen Metaphysik die als Wissenschaft wird auftreten können', §2a, in *Kant's Gesammelte Schriften, Akademieausgabe*, Berlin: Georg Reimer and Walter de Gruyter & Co, 1900ff, Vol. 4, p. 266; translated by Gary Hatfield as 'Prolegomena to any Future Metaphysics That Will be Able to Come Forward as Science', in *Theoretical Writings After 1781*, edited by Henry Allison and Peter Heath, Cambridge: Cambridge University Press, 2002, p. 62. See GA41, 164/161.

17. Kant, *Kritik der reinen Vernunft*, A25, see B39.

18. Heidegger's reference is to 'II, 1038', though it is not clear to what edition this refers.

19. For a much longer discussion a decade later, see GA41, 198–204/195–201; 251–2.

20. See also Heidegger, 'Wilhelm Dilthey's Research and the Struggle

for a Historical Worldview (1925)', p. 172; and GA53, 47–50.

21. This is briefly discussed in Elden, *Mapping the Present*, pp. 13–14. Of Heidegger's later work, see GA54, 210–11; ZSD, 11/11, 14–15/14.

22. See also the discussion in relation to Hegel, especially the *Philosophy of Nature*, in GA2, 428–32. Hegel's Jena lecture course on this is described as 'very obviously nothing but a speculative paraphrase of Aristotelian physics' (GA32, 176).

23. See also the notes on calculated time in GA42, 188; and GA49, 112.

24. See also GA67, 126.

25. See also the discussion in relation to Kant, GA21, 380–7.

26. See Edward A. Maziarz and Thomas Greenwood, *Greek Mathematical Philosophy*, New York: Frederick Ungar, 1968, p. 7. The notion of geometry as a land-measuring device of the Egyptians is described in Herodotus, *The Histories*, translated by Robin Waterfield, Oxford: Oxford University Press, 1998, 109.

27. See GA56/57, 171–2, on the continuum in Rickert's work.

28. Jacob Klein, *Lectures and Essays*, edited by Robert B. Williamson and Elliott Zuckermann, Annapolis: St John's College Press, 1985, p. 23, notes that *arithmos* is *Anzahl*, a definite number, rather than *Zahl*, number in general. See also the essay 'The Concept of Number in Greek Mathematics and Philosophy' in this collection, and his *Greek Mathematical Thought and the Origin of Algebra*, New York: Dover, 1992 [1934].

29. See Plato, *Meno*, 76a: 'shape is that in which a solid terminates [*perainei*, that is, comes to a limit] . . . shape is the limit of a solid [*stereon peras skhema einai*]'. Compare Euclid, *The Thirteen Books of Euclid's Elements*, with introduction and commentary by Thomas L. Heath, New York: Dover, three volumes, Second Edition, 1956, Vol. I, p. 153: 'a limit [*oros*] is that which is an extremity [*peras*] of anything . . . a shape [*skhema*] is that which is contained by any boundary or boundaries [*periekhomenon*]'. Heath provides the Greek in his commentary on pp. 182–3. I have altered the translation.

30. The full sentence reads 'for place is peculiar to the individual things, and hence they are separate in place [*khorista topo*]; but mathematical objects are not anywhere [*pou*]'. Heidegger is therefore not quite justified in his interpolation of '*ouk en topo*' to Aristotle: such a formulation is not found in the text.

31. See Elden, *Mapping the Present*, pp. 19–20; GA9, 248–9/190; and GA53, 65–6. In GA54, 174, Heidegger describes *topos* as 'not mere position in a manifold of points, everywhere homogeneous'.

32. For a discussion of *dunamis* in relation to geometry, see GA33, 58–61/48–52. This course as a whole provides Heidegger's most sustained treatment of *dunamis* in Aristotle. See also GA22, 307–8, 317; GA41, 85–6/85; and GA9, 280/214, 285/218.

33. 'Being there' [*dortsein*] in this phrase *can* be understood in the concrete sense of being in place, being somewhere. It is *not* the same as Dasein, which has been translated as 'being there'. Dasein more properly understood is existence, being-*the*-there, the open, the clearing.

34. See Maziarz and Greenwood, *Greek Mathematical Philosophy*, p. 23, where they suggest this was found in the Pythagoreans, who saw 'the unit as a "point without position", and the point as "a unit having position"'.

35. See also GA18, 174, 186–7.

36. Heidegger's references are the *Metaphysics*, 1016b18, 1016b15, 1021a13; *Physics*, 220a17ff. See also the discussion in the Plato part of this course, concerning the one, the both or some, and the more, dependent on language rather than 'a mathematical interpretation of the world' (GA19, 420–1; see also GA18, 31–3).

37. For valuable discussions, see Helen S. Lang, *Aristotle's* Physics *and its Medieval Varieties*, Albany: State University of New York Press, 1992; and her *The Order of Nature in Aristotle's* Physics: *Place and the Elements*, Cambridge: Cambridge University Press, 1999. For a useful situation of Descartes in relation to these debates, see Jorge Secada, *Cartesian Metaphysics: The Late Scholastic Origins of Modern Philosophy*, Cambridge: Cambridge University Press, 2000.

38. While this is the case for place, it is not the case for time. For a full discussion, see especially GA24, 352ff.

39. The most extensive discussion of Descartes from this period is found in GA17, but this is largely tied to the concerns of this course with phenomenology, truth and falsehood and the *cogito* rather than geometry.

40. See Elden, *Mapping the Present*, especially Chapter One. For a critique of Heidegger's reading of Descartes on the subject, see Étienne Balibar, 'Citizen Subject', in Eduardo Cadava, Peter

Connor and Jean-Luc Nancy (eds), *Who Comes After the Sub-ject?*, London: Routledge, 1991, pp. 33–57. For a discussion, see Simon Critchley and Peter Dews (eds), *Deconstructive Subjectiv-ities*, Albany: State University of New York Press, 1996.

41. See GA6.2, 232; N, IV, 175–6; see GA48, 308: 'Kant does not simply repeat what Descartes had already thought before him. Kant is the first to think transcendentally, and he explicitly and consciously conceptualises what Descartes posited as the begin-ning of inquiry against the horizon of the *ego cogito*. In Kant's interpretation of being, the beingness of beings is for the first time expressly thought as a "condition of possibility", thus clearing the way for the development of value thinking in Nietzsche's metaphysics. Nevertheless, Kant does not yet think being as value. But neither does he any longer think of being in Plato's sense, as *idea*'.

42. On Heidegger's reading of Descartes generally, picking up on this phrase, see Robert Bernasconi, 'Descartes in the History of Being: Another Bad Novel?', *Research in Phenomenology*, Vol. XVII, 1987, pp. 75–102.

43. René Descartes, *Meditationes de Prima Philosophia*, in *Oeuvres de Descartes*, publiées par Charles Adam et Paul Tannery, Paris: Vrin, 1964ff, thirteen volumes, Vol. VII, p. 44; translated by Donald A. Cress in *Discourse on the Method* and *Meditations on First Philosophy*, Indianapolis: Hackett, 1980, p. 73.

44. Descartes, *Meditationes*, Vol. VII, p. 24; *Meditations*, p. 61.

45. Descartes, *Meditationes*, Vol. VII, p. 25; *Meditations*, p. 62.

46. Descartes, *Meditationes*, Vol. VII, p. 31; *Meditations*, p. 65.

47. Descartes, *Meditationes*, Vol. VII, pp. 78–9; *Meditations*, p. 93.

48. Descartes, *Principia Philosophiae*, in *Oeuvres*, Vol. VIII–1, p. 41; *Principles of Philosophy*, in *The Philosophical Writings of Des-cartes*, Cambridge: Cambridge University Press, two volumes, 1985, Vol. I, p. 223.

49. Descartes, *Meditationes*, Vol. VII, p. 43; *Meditations*, pp. 72–3.

50. Descartes, *Principia Philosophiae*, Vol. VIII, pp. 52–3; *Principles of Philosophy*, pp. 232–3.

51. Descartes, *Meditationes*, Vol. VII, p. 44–5; *Meditations*, p. 73.

52. Descartes, *Meditationes*, Vol. VII, p. 63; *Meditations*, p. 85.

53. On this, see in particular GA20, 215–26.

54. Descartes, letter to Mersenne, December 1637, *Oeuvres de Descartes*, Vol. I, p. 478.

55. See the editors' note, *Principles of Philosophy*, p. 227.

56. Descartes, *Principia Philosophiae*, Vol. VIII-1, p. 45; *Principles of Philosophy*, p. 227. See also *Regulae ad Directionem Ingenii*, in *Oeuvres de Descartes*, Vol. X, p. 442.
57. Descartes, *Principia Philosophiae*, Vol. VIII-1, p. 46. *Principles of Philosophy*, pp. 227–8. On Descartes in this regard generally, see Alexandre Koyré, *From the Closed World to the Infinite Universe*, Baltimore: Johns Hopkins University Press, 1957, p. 88–109.
58. Descartes, *Principia Philosophiae*, Vol. VIII-1, p. 48. *Principles of Philosophy*, p. 229.
59. Descartes, *Principia Philosophiae*, Vol. VIII-1, p. 46. *Principles of Philosophy*, p. 228.
60. Descartes, *Principia Philosophiae*, Vol. VIII-1, pp. 47–8. *Principles of Philosophy*, p. 229.
61. Descartes, *Meditationes*, Vol. VII, p. 71; *Meditations*, p. 89.
62. The most sustained reading along these lines is found in GA2, 89–101. See, in particular, the questions to be answered in the unpublished division on Descartes at GA2, 101. On mathematical construction, see also GA6.2, 382.
63. Descartes, letter to Mersenne, 27 July 1638, *Oeuvres de Descartes*, Vol. II, p. 268.
64. Descartes, *Oeuvres de Descartes*, Vol. V, p. 160; *Conversation with Burman*, translated by John Cottingham, Oxford: Oxford University Press, 1976, p. 23.
65. Descartes, *Discours de la méthode*, in *Oeuvres de Descartes*, Vol. VI, p. 36; *Discourse on the Method*, p. 19.
66. Klein, *Greek Mathematical Thought and the Origin of Algebra*, p. 206.
67. Klein, *Greek Mathematical Thought*, pp. 210–11.
68. Klein, *Greek Mathematical Thought*, p. 211; see his *Lectures and Essays*, p. 21.
69. Isaac Newton, *The Principia: Mathematical Principles of Natural Philosophy*, Berkeley: University of California Press, 1999, p. 416, reading with the first edition.
70. Klein, *Greek Mathematical Thought*, p. 211. See GA68, 108.
71. See Maziarz and Greenwood, *Greek Mathematical Philosophy*, p. 256. Compare to the birth of the classical *episteme* as outlined in Michel Foucault, *Les mots et les choses*, Paris: Gallimard, 1966.
72. David Rapport Lachterman, *The Ethics of Geometry: A Genealogy of Modernity*, New York: Routledge, 1989, pp. 27–8. For

good examples of this assumption, see Jeremy Gray, *Ideas of Space: Euclidean, Non-Euclidean and Relativistic*, Oxford: Clarendon Press, Second Edition, 1989; and Hermann Weyl, *Space – Time – Matter*, Dover, 1950.

73. This is confirmed by the work of Thomas Heath, both in his translation of the *Elements*, and his *A History of Greek Mathematics*, New York: Dover, 1981, two volumes. Although Heath occasionally uses the word 'space' in his translations, his glossary to the latter work (Vol. II, pp. 563–69) includes no word that is the equivalent of 'space', however, the entry for '*khorion*' reads 'area . . . *khorein apotome, sectio spatii*'. This lends support to the suggestion that the shift is made in the transition from Greek to Latin thought.

74. Lachterman, *The Ethics of Geometry*, p. 80.

75. Maziarz and Greenwood, *Greek Mathematical Philosophy*, p. 242: '[Euclid's] works make no allusion to Plato or Aristotle, or even to their strictly methodological views'.

76. Descartes, *Meditationes*, in *Oeuvres de Descartes*, Vol. VII, pp. 85–6; *Meditations*, p. 97.

77. Descartes, *Principia Philosophiae*, Vol. VIII-1, p. 51; *Principles of Philosophy*, p. 231.

78. Descartes, *The Geometry of René Descartes*, French–Latin–English edition, translated by David Eugene Smith and Marcia L. Latham, New York: Dover, 1954, p. 146/147.

79. Descartes, *The Geometry*, p. 2/3.

80. Descartes, *The Geometry*, p. 216/217.

81. See Euclid, *The Thirteen Books of Euclid's Elements*, Book VII, Definition 2, in Vol. 2, p. 277. As Alain Badiou puts it, 'the being of number is the multiple reduced to the pure combinatorial legislation of the one' – *Court traité d'ontologie transitoire*, Paris: Seuil, 1998, p. 141; *Theoretical Writings*, edited and translated by Ray Brassier and Alberto Toscano, London: Continuum, 2004, p. 59. See his *Le nombre et les nombres*, Paris: Seuil, 1990.

82. William J. Richardson, *Heidegger: Through Phenomenology to Thought*, The Hague: Martinus Nijhoff, Third Edition, 1974, pp. 667–70. In his notes to Richardson, Heidegger adds that the last was broken off after an hour as he was co-opted into the *Volkssturm*. On Leibniz, see also the extensive discussion in GA6.2, 397–416; and GA10.

83. Descartes, *Principia Philosophiae*, Vol. VII, p. 32; *Principles of Philosophy*, p. 216.

84. Gottfried Wilhelm Leibniz, *Philosophical Papers and Letters*, translated and edited by Leroy E. Loemker, Dordrecht: D. Reidel, Second Edition, 1969, p. 454.
85. G. W. Leibniz, *Mathematische Schriften*, edited by C. I. Gerhardt, Bd. VII: *Die mathematischen Abhandlungen*, Hildesheim: Georg Ohms, 1962, p. 18.
86. G. W. Leibniz, *Der philosophischen Schriften*, edited by C. I. Gerhardt, Hildesheim: Georg Olms, 1965, Vol. IV, p. 467. For a discussion, see John Sallis, *Force of Imagination: The Sense of the Elemental*, Bloomington: Indiana University Press, 2000, p. 134.
87. See also the remarks on the mathematical issues in metaphysics in GA36/37: for example, 29–30, 31, 33, 35, and so on. There are also some important remarks in the early lectures on Hölderlin. For an analysis, see Elden, *Mapping the Present*, Chapter Two, and, for example, GA39, 195, 255.
88. This appears on the dust-jacket of the German version, and has been picked up by, for example, Parvis Emad, 'The Echo of Being in *Beiträge zur Philosophie – Der Anklang*: Directives for Its Interpretation', *Heidegger Studies*, Vol. 7, 1991; and George Kovacs, 'An Invitation to Think Through and with Heidegger's *Beiträge zur Philosophie*', *Heidegger Studies*, Vol. 12, 1996. See also Reiner Schürmann, 'Ultimate Double Binds', in James Risser (ed.), *Heidegger Toward the Turn: Essays on the Work of the 1930s*, New York: State University of New York Press, 1999, pp. 243–68.
89. See GA8 213–14/210–11; and GA28, 30.
90. Cited in Plato, *Theaetetus*, 152a.
91. For earlier discussions, and more straightforward readings, see GA22, 86–7; GA27, 154; GA41, 45/46–7. In the last (1935–36) Heidegger declares that 'the *polis* was the measure for the Greeks. Everyone today is talking of the Greek *polis*'. Appendix 8 of 'The Age of the World Picture', apparently composed but not delivered in 1938, prefigures the 1940 argument in some important ways, particularly in terms of the relation to Descartes. See GA5, 102–6/77–80. See also GA90, 65–70.
92. See Ingo Farin, 'Heidegger's Critique of Value Philosophy', *Journal of the British Society for Phenomenology*, Vol. 29 No. 3, October 1998, pp. 268–80.
93. Descartes, *Regulae ad Directionem Ingenii*, Vol. X, pp. 377–8.
94. For a discussion, see David Farrell Krell, *Nietzsche and the Task*

of Thinking: Martin Heidegger's Reading of Nietzsche, PhD thesis, Pittsburgh: Duquesne University, 1971, pp. 53–9.

95. Heidegger had made a similar point many years before: 'For Husserl, a definite ideal of science [*Wissenschaft*] was prescribed in *mathematics* and the mathematical natural sciences. Mathematics was the model for all scientific disciplines. This scientific ideal came into play in that one attempted to elevate description to the level of mathematical rigour [*Strenge*] . . . Fundamentally, one does not even realise that a prejudice [*Vorurteil*] is at work here. Is it justified to hold up mathematics as a model for all scientific disciplines? Or are the basic relations between mathematics and other disciplines not thereby stood on their heads? Mathematics is the least rigorous of disciplines, because it is the one easiest to gain access to. The human sciences [*Geisteswissenshaft*] presuppose much more scientific existence than could ever be achieved by a mathematician . . . To bring mathematics into play as the model for all scientific disciplines is unphenomenological – the meaning of scientific rigor needs rather to be drawn from the kind of object being investigated and the mode of access appropriate to it' (GA63, 71–2; see GA9, 104/83; GA21, 8; GA27, 43).

96. See Victor Klemperer, *The Language of the Third Reich: LTI – Lingua Tertii Imperii: A Philologist's Notebook*, translated by Martin Brady, London: Athlone, 2000, pp. 98, 142–3; John Wesley Young, *Totalitarian Language: Orwell's Newspeak and its Nazi and Communist Antecedents*, Charlottesville: University Press of Virginia, 1991, p. 71.

97. For a critique of the Nazi view of science, particularly in relation to worldview, see also the excerpt from a 1938 seminar, Martin Heidegger, 'Die Bedrohung der Wissenschaft', in *Zur philosophischen Aktualität Heideggers*, Band 1, edited by Dietrich Papenfuss and Otto Pöggler, Frankfurt am Main: Vittorio Klostermann, 1991, pp. 5–27. For a discussion, see Trish Glazebrook, *Heidegger's Philosophy of Science*, New York: Fordham University Press, 2000, pp. 148–52.

98. Indeed, as Jean Greisch suggests, the publication of the *Beiträge* was brought forward from the plan Heidegger outlined at his death precisely to 'allow the insinuation that until the end of the war and perhaps even beyond he had been a Nazi wolf disguised in the shepherd of being's clothing to be refuted'. See Jean Greisch, 'Études Heideggeriennes: Les «Contributions à la

philosophie (A partir de l'*Ereignis*)» de Martin Heidegger', *Revue des Sciences Philosophiques et Théologiques*, Tome 73 No. 4, Oct 1989, pp. 605–32, p. 605. The original plan had been to publish the *Beiträge* only when all the lecture courses had appeared. See Friedrich-Wilhelm von Herrman, 'Nachwort des Herausgebers', GA65, 512–13. A contrary view of the political importance of the *Beiträge* is taken by George Kovacs, 'The Leap (*der Sprung*) for Being in Heidegger's *Beiträge zur Philosophie (Vom Ereignis)*', *Man and World*, Vol. 25 No. 1, Jan 1992, pp. 39–59.

99. On Heidegger and the Four Year Plan, see Theodore Kisiel, 'Heidegger's Philosophical Geopolitics in the Third Reich', in Richard Polt and Gregory Fried, *A Companion to Heidegger's* Introduction to Metaphysics, New Haven: Yale University Press, 2001, pp. 226–49, pp. 242–3, 324–5 n. 22.

100. For a discussion of the translation of this term in Freud and Reich's psychology, see the translator's note in Philippe Lacoue-Labarthe and Jean-Luc Nancy, *Retreating the Political*, edited by Simon Sparks, London: Routledge, 1997, pp. 167–8 n. 15. On the relation of *Seyn* to *Maß*, see also GA66, 318.

101. See also the much later comments about the domination of *ratio* being the 'rationalisation of all order, as standardisation, and as levelling out in the course of the unfolding of European nihilism' (GA9, 388/293).

102. For discussions of *Gleichschaltung*, see Klemperer, *The Language of the Third Reich*, pp. 154–8; Berel Lang, *Act and Idea in the Nazi Genocide*, Chicago: University of Chicago Press, 1990, p. 93; and Gordon A. Craig, *The Germans*, Harmondsworth: Penguin, 1982, p. 326.

103. See Kisiel, 'Heidegger's Philosophical Geopolitics in the Third Reich'.

104. Ernst Jünger, 'Die Totale Mobilmachung', in *Werke*, Stuttgart: Ernst Klett, ten volumes, 1960, Vol. 5; translated by Joel Golb and Richard Wolin as 'Total Mobilisation' in *The Heidegger Controversy*.

105. The notions of 'military service' and 'labour service' play a central role in Jünger's *Der Arbeiter* (in *Werke*, Vol. 6). As discussed in Chapter Two, Heidegger utilises them and sets up the idea of 'knowledge service' in his Rectorial Address.

106. The fullest discussion of the early years of the war and the philosophical issues at stake can be found in the manuscript 'Κοινόν. Aus der Geschichte des Seyns', GA69, 179–214.

107. See, for example, GA65, 191–4, 207–8, 371–88.
108. Theodore Kisiel, 'Measuring the Millennial Moment of Globalization against Heidegger's Summer Semester 1935, and Other Politically Incorrect Remarks', *Current Studies in Phenomenology and Hermeneutics*, Vol. 1 No. 1, http://www.ereignis.org/csph/2000/kisiel.htm; Franz L. Neumann, *Behemoth: The Structure and Practice of National Socialism*, London: Gollancz, 1942; Guillaume de Syon, *Zeppelin! Germany and the Airship, 1900–1939*, Baltimore: Johns Hopkins University Press, 2002.
109. See also the marginal note in *Wegmarken*: 'calculating: domination – ordering to place [*Bestellung*]' (GA9, 309/236 n. a).
110. See also the comments reported by Theodore Kisiel from the seminar 'On the Essence and Concept of Nature, History and the State', in 'In the Middle of Heidegger's Three Concepts of the Political', in François Raffoul and David Pettigrew (eds), *Heidegger and Practical Philosophy*, Albany: State University of New York Press, 2002, pp. 135–57, pp. 148–9.
111. See Kisiel, 'Heidegger's Philosophical Geopolitics in the Third Reich'; and 'Measuring the Millennial Moment of Globalization'.
112. See Stuart Elden, 'Missing the Point: Globalisation, Deterritorialisation and the Space of the World', *Transactions of the Institute of British Geographers*, Vol. 30 No. 1, March 2005, pp. 8–19.
113. See also the discussion in GA77, 6ff; and GA66, 16–25; GA67, 146, 150.
114. See also the seminars on Nietzsche collected in GA87; and GA66, 173–8.
115. Ten years later, Heidegger would make this explicit: 'Modern science and the total state, as necessary consequences [*Folgen*] of the essence of technology, are also attendant [*Gefolge*] upon it' (GA5, 290/217).
116. A few pages on, he writes '*Machination (poiesis – tekhne – kinesis – nous)* has a correspondence which was long held back and only now finally emerges with "*Lived-experience*"' (GA65, 132).
117. Klemperer, *The Language of the Third Reich*, p. 244: 'The word utilised most powerfully and most commonly by the Nazis for emotional effect is "*Erlebnis* [experience]"'.
118. In GA34, 140, Heidegger notes that, in relation to lived-experience, 'the Greeks knew no such thing, thank God'. See also

GA9, 324/247; and GA20, 375, for an early discussion of the problem of 'experiencing' [*Erleben*], and 'lived-experience' [*Erlebnis*], and the equally problematic 'decision' [*Entscheidung*]. On life more generally in the *Beiträge*, see Chapter Six of David Farrell Krell, *Daimon Life: Heidegger and Life Philosophy*, Bloomington: Indiana University Press, 1992.

119. Heidegger, 'Wilhelm Dilthey's Research and the Struggle for a Historical Worldview (1925)', in *Supplements*, p. 163.

120. On the use of 'es gibt' in the *Kriegsnotsemester*, see Theodore Kisiel, *The Genesis of Heidegger's* Being and Time, Berkeley: University of California Press, 1993, especially p. 42. The term appears in GA2, 212; and numerous other places in Heidegger's work.

121. See also GA65, 70; GA40, 121–2; and GA45, 177–81.

122. See also the comments in *Martin Heidegger in Conversation*, edited by Richard Wisser, India: Arnold Heinemann, 1977, especially pp. 42–3.

123. This is one of the very few places Heidegger even mentions the economic. For a valuable critique and elaboration, see Michael Eldred, 'Heidegger's Restricted Interpretation of the Greek Concept of the Political', www.webcom.com/artefact/untpltcl/rstrpltc.html

124. Indeed, in one of the essays appended to the lectures in the Nietzsche volume, which dates from 1941, Heidegger suggests 'machination (*Das Ge-stell*)', as the final stage of a history of being (GA6.2, 429).

125. I have in mind particularly the scandalous comparison of mechanised agriculture with the Holocaust, famine and hydrogen bombs. Heidegger suggests they share the same essence (not that they are in essence the same). What they share is the essence of modern technology; what distinguishes the first from the subsequent is a particular conception of the political – although Heidegger does not make this at all clear. See GA79, 27, and compare to the published GA7, 16. For a discussion, see Elden, *Mapping the Present*, pp. 74–8.

Taking the Measure of the Political

Following the Allied victory, Heidegger was brought before a denazification commission at the University of Freiburg. He was forbidden to teach and refused Emeritus status. The details of the tribunal, the evasions he gave to try to hold onto his job, and the damning letter from Karl Jaspers that probably swayed the decision have been well explored in numerous works, and need not concern us here.[1] Although Heidegger's sentence is insignificant compared to the enormity of the crimes and punishments of Europe as a whole, the denial of an audience for his ideas was surely considerable for one who so clearly valued teaching as a means to research. We should note that almost all of Heidegger's published works after *Being and Time* derive from lecture material.

But Heidegger did not retreat into silence. Not long after the war, in late 1946, while his position was still undecided, and recognising the impact his ideas were having, particularly in France – Sartre's *Being and Nothingness* appeared in 1943; Merleau-Ponty's *Phenomenology of Perception* in 1945[2] – he agreed to respond to some questions posed to him by Jean Beaufret, who had been a correspondent since 1945.[3] This text, the *Letter on Humanism*, is one of Heidegger's most interesting pieces, a *tour-de-force* of clarification, summary and future programme, particularly orientated around positioning himself against the 'existentialist' interpretation. If a detailed reading will be eschewed here, one particular passage neatly illustrates a number of the problematics that this book has been concerned with.

Following an orientation of the European problem around the alternatives of Communism and Americanism, Heidegger declares

> Every nationalism is metaphysically an anthropologism, and as such subjectivism. Nationalism is not overcome through mere internationalism;

it is rather expanded and elevated thereby into a system. Nationalism is as little brought and raised to *humanitas* by internationalism as individualism is by an ahistorical collectivism [*geschichtlosen Kollektivismus*]. The latter is the subjectivity of human beings in totality [*des Menschen in der Totalität*]. It completes subjectivity's unconditioned self-assertion [*unbedingte Selbstbehauptung*], which refuses to yield. Nor can it be even adequately experienced by a thinking that mediates in a one-sided fashion. Expelled from the truth of being, the human being everywhere circles around himself as the *animal rationale*. (GA9, 341–2/260)

There is a lot going on here. Nationalism, *every* nationalism, is problematic, because of its buying into notions of anthropology and subjectivity. Internationalism, though, is not a solution, it does not *overcome* nationalism, but simply expands it [*erweitet*], enlarges it, extends it, moves it up a scale, elevates it [*erhoben*] to a system. The essence of humanism – that is, that issue that Beaufret had asked Heidegger about, that is, the point of the letter – cannot be attained simply by expanding or elevating, by quantitative increase, by addition. A straightforward move from individualism to collectivism is similarly flawed as a means of access. And this is a particular kind of collectivism, a *geschichtlosen* collectivism, one that lacks or is blind to history, history not understood as a school subject, but history in the sense of destiny or a sending.

Ahistorical collectivism [*geschichtlosen Kollektivismus*] is, again, simply the totality, the addition, the collecting of, individual subjectivity. A sum. A completion of a process, the completion of an absolute self-assertion. We can note here that Heidegger uses *Selbtsbehauptung* in a critical context – the title of his Rectorial Address was 'The *Selbtsbehauptung* of the German University'. The human being has therefore come a long way from the Greek determination as *zoon ekhon logon*. It is misleading, as we have seen, Heidegger contends, to translate this as the rational animal, the *animal rationale*. As Heidegger notes, 'this definition is not simply the Latin translation of the Greek *zoon ekhon logon*, but a metaphysical interpretation of it. This essential definition of the human being is not false. But it is conditioned by metaphysics' (GA9, 322/245–6).[4] Indeed, Heidegger suggests the whole purpose of his *Beiträge* is concerned with the essential transformation of the human from the 'rational animal' to Da-sein (GA65, 3). Rather, the *zoon ekhon logon* must be understood as the being with speech, *Rede*.

What we have here is the critique of calculative politics brought to bear on the categories employed in Heidegger's political period, dependent on his earlier failure to think being-together-politically in an adequate way.[5] In terms of this book, it is the insights into calculation examined in Chapter Three related to the categories explored in Chapter One and the action in Chapter Two. It is an explicit rendering of what Chapter Three suggested: that thinking through the politics of calculation is a response to the political action, which itself was dependent on intellectual failings. In reading the notion of *logos* as speech rather than reason, Heidegger is also distancing himself from the way that *logos* became 'logic', became reason, *ratio*, and how this in turn became tied to number, that is, calculative thinking rather than speaking, language. *Ratio*, in its originary sense, is not necessarily numerical, but can be seen in terms of relation and balance. It comes to be determined through the notion of quantity: reckoned, computed, enumerated, accounted.[6] In this way, Heidegger distances the modern *animal rationale* from the Greek *zoon ekhon logon*; opens up the possibilities of another kind of calculus; and points out the problems of modern subjectivity, collectivity, nationalism and internationalism. Slightly earlier in the *Letter*, he had noted that Communism is not merely a party or a *Weltanschauung*, and Americanism more than just a lifestyle (GA9, 340–1/259); similarly, world events are not, for Heidegger, as we have seen, the expression of the 'caprice of "dictators" and "authoritarian states"' (GA51, 18), but again dependent on this general casting of being, 'the metaphysical essence of modern actuality in general' (GA53, 118).

In his own copy of this text, after the word 'subjectivity' in the phrase 'the subjectivity of human beings in totality', Heidegger adds the following handwritten marginal note:

> Industrial society as the measure-giving subject [*das maßgebende Subjekt*] – and thinking as 'politics'. (GA9, 341 n. d/260 n. b)

The essence of modern technology, itself nothing technological, is the foundation of industrial society, here viewed as the *maßgebende Subjekt*. In a colloquial sense, *maßgebende* might mean the proper, the authoritative, definitive subject, or better, the determining subject, and yet, as we have seen, the *Maß* derives from *messen*, to measure or gauge. This is the subject that provides the measure, the measure-giving subject. As a corollary, thinking becomes politics.

In his later works, Heidegger both pursues this insight, and turns back from politics to thinking. Indeed, Heidegger's post-war work can be thought of in two ways: as an examination of the possibilities of language, particularly through the works of poets: and as a continued study of the dangers of technology.[7] Both of these, as we have seen, are prepared for in his writings after 1934, and in many ways date back much further than this. As the preceding chapters have attempted to show, these are inherently political issues – which both opens up possibilities and calls for caution. There is no straightforward break in Heidegger's thought, no turn away from Nazism in any simple meaning, no turn in the straightforward understanding of a *Kehre* at all. Rather, there is a continued emphasis on thinking a few very simple questions – which means, of course, that they are among the most difficult to answer.

In the final lines of the *Beiträge*, Heidegger rehearses and develops some of the themes touched upon here:

> Language is grounded in silence. Silence is the most sheltered measure-holding [*Maß-halten*]. It *holds* the measure, in that it first sets up measures [*Es hält das Maß, indem es die Maß-stäbe erst setzt*]. And so language is measure-setting [*Maß-setzung*] in the most intimate and widest sense, measure-setting as essential essency of the jointure and its joining (pro-priation) [*Erwesung des Fugs und seiner Fügung (Ereignis)*]. And insofar as language [is] ground of Da-sein, the measuring [*Mäßigung*] lies in this and indeed as the ground of strife of world and earth. (GA65, 510)

Although it is usually only Heidegger's later work that is seen as a 'retreat' into poetry, Hölderlin, Rilke and others, his concerns can be traced right back to 1934, when he began the first course on Hölderlin, and from occasional writings even further back. In one sense, it is instructive to compare Heidegger's characterisation of the Nazi regime and modern metaphysics, and indeed, his own 1932 offer of 'providing the measure and rule' with Hölderlin's poetry, specifi-cally the piece known by its first line, 'In lovely blueness'. A crucial line, much cited by Heidegger, is the question 'is there a measure on the earth? There is none [*Gibt es auf Erden ein Maß? Es gibt keines*]'. Rather, measure comes from the divinity – 'Is God unknown? Is he manifest as the sky? This rather I believe. It is the measure of the human. Full of acquirements, but poetically, the human dwells on this earth'.[8]

In his work on poetic dwelling later in life, Heidegger develops the idea of measure-taking. The dwelling of humans is part of the fourfold of humans, gods, earth and sky. The human measures themselves against the god, on the earth, beneath the sky – they take a measure, rather than provide one. Their dwelling 'depends on an upward-looking measure-taking [*Vermessen*] of the dimension, in which sky belongs just as much as earth'. What this means is that this measure-taking 'not only takes the measure of the earth, *ge*, and therefore it is no mere geo-metry. Nor does it lightly take the measure of heaven [*Himmel*], *ouranos*, for itself'. This measure-taking is 'no science'. Rather, 'measure-taking gauges [*ermißt*] the between, which brings both heaven and earth to each other. This measure-taking has its own *metron*, and therefore its own metric' (GA7, 199). Once again it is not a question of understanding nature as *res extensa*, not a simple earth-measuring, geo-metry, just as it is not simply a geo-graphy, or earth-writing. Rather, it is a rethinking of measure.[9] While this is not the place to discuss the role of divinity or the last god within the *Beiträge*, let alone the problematic relationship of Heidegger to theology more generally,[10] there is something fundamentally important in how he seeks to rethink the notion of measure, especially in relation to the notion of *Ereignis*, as already hinted at in Chapter Three. As Heidegger declares in 1942, again in relation to Hölderlin:

> If we merely attempt, on our own authority, to set or seize upon the measure, then it becomes measureless and disintegrates into nothingness. If we merely remain thoughtless and without the alertness of an intimative scrutinizing, then we will again find no measure. Yet if we are strong enough to think, then it may be sufficient for us to ponder merely from afar, that, scarcely, the truth of this poetry and what it poetises, so that we may suddenly be struck by it. (GA53, 205)

Shortly afterwards, in his Postscript to the 1929 lecture 'What is Metaphysics?', he declared that

> Calculative thinking . . . is unable to foresee that everything calculable by calculation [*Berechenbare der Rechnung*] – prior to the sum-totals and products that it produces by calculation in each case – is already a whole, a whole whose unity indeed belongs to the incalculable [*Unberechenbaren*] that withdraws itself and its uncanniness from the claws of calculation. (GA9, 309/235)

He similarly insists that *Ereignis* does not allow itself to be measured in conventional ways: 'Immeasurable [*Unausmeßbar*] are the riches

. . . the fullness of *Ereignis* is incalculable [*unerrechenbar*]' (GA65, 7). This is no mere suggestion that riches are immeasurable, or that love is incalculable, but something that goes to the very heart of the matter. Indeed, it helps to bring together many of the key ideas in his thought as a whole. Heidegger suggests that overflow, or excess of measure [*Das Über-maß*], 'is no mere abundance of quantity, but the self-withdrawing of all estimating and measuring [*Schätzung und Ausmessung*]'. In a 1946 address commemorating the twentieth anniversary of Rilke's death, Heidegger suggests:

> The interior of unwonted consciousness remains in the interior space in which everything, for us, is beyond the numbering [*Zahlhafte*] of calculation and, freed from those barriers, can overflow into the unbarred entirety of the open. This overflowing beyond number [*überzählige Überflüssige*] springs up, with regard to its presence, in the inward and invisible of the heart. The last words of the *Ninth Elegy*, which sings of men belonging to the open, run: 'Existence beyond number [*Überzähliges Dasein*] springs up in my heart'. (GA5, 306/229)

As a response to the notion of quantity becoming a quality in itself, this notion of existence beyond number is an important issue. And yet, this is merely a poetic and somewhat disillusioned response he tries to grasp in the late part of his career, rather than a fully worked out option. Indeed, perhaps number alone is not what needs to be resisted, but the mode of thought that makes possible such mere enumeration.

> The humanity of humans and the thingness of things is dissolved, within the self-assertion of producing, to the calculation of the market value of a market that is not only a world-market spanning the earth but that also, as the will to will, markets in the essence of being and so brings all beings into the business of calculation, which dominates most fiercely precisely where numbers are not needed. (GA5, 292/219)[11]

For Heidegger, 'in this self-withdrawing (self-sheltering) being [*Seyn*] has its nearest nearness in the clearing of the there [*Da*], in that it ap-propriates [*er-eignent*] Da-*sein*' (GA65, 249). Dasein, that simultaneously most common and yet most resistant to translation of Heideggerian words, is inherently tied to this refusal of measure and the politics of calculation. Heidegger notes that 'in philosophical knowing a change in the man who understands begins with the first step, and not in a moral-"existentiell" sense, but with Dasein as measure [*sondern da-seinmäßig*]' (GA65, 14, see 316, 407). This is the point of the human being rethought in transition from the 'rational animal' to Da-sein (GA65, 3).

For, Heidegger then, 'overall the issue is to think, and thus to *be* historically [*geschichtlich*], instead of calculating historiographically [*historisch zu rechnen*]' (GA65, 505, see 421–2, 492–4; GA38, 87).[12] Thinking historically, thinking the notion of *Ereignis*, through a preparatory analytic of Dasein, can provide insight into the question of being that metaphysics and the calculative mode of casting beings cannot achieve. In a sense, this is Heidegger's work as a whole, the study of Dasein in *Being and Time*, through the history of being, the history of metaphysics – what he calls thinking being historically (see GA65, GA66) – to the other beginning anticipated in the *Beiträge* with its study of *Ereignis*. But *that* story, at least in the way it is usually told, rather than the way I have traced it, obviously leaves out most of what has been treated here. Those seeking to make use of it need to fully come to terms with its entanglement in the thought that preceded the practice.

If Heidegger's own thought is so riddled with the complexities of his political action that it is difficult to see a way to take his work forward, this clearly does not mean that the questions he wrestled with are unimportant. While I am unwilling to accept Heidegger's poetic phrase '*wer groß denkt muß groß irren*' – 'he who thinks greatly must err greatly' (GA13, 81) – as an excuse, I do think a detailed examination of the political aspects of his thought is a constructive step towards making sense of these problems. Overstating the case though he undoubtedly did, Derrida was onto something when he suggested that 'we cannot understand what Europe is and has been this century, what Nazism has been, and so on, without interrogating what made Heidegger's discourse possible'.[13] Of course, we should not understand this in the sense that only attempts to understand Heidegger can unlock the issues of the twentieth century. But a weaker, and more tenable, claim is that as the most important philosopher so closely associated with Nazism, examining Heidegger's writings of the time may shed some light on the wider political situation. The understanding of the calculative casting of being, reducing the world to a problem of number, of quantity, is an important contribution to our understanding of modernity. Extending that to an immanent critique (too immanent, of course) of the Nazi period provides valuable insights into what was *behind*, in an ontological sense, that regime. If it stops short of moral outrage and blanket criticism, we may actually learn more, for it is not really much of a challenge for us today to condemn Nazism; but to *understand* it, and what made it *possible*, is a more difficult task. Understanding Nazism through the lens of calculation, which Heidegger began but never worked through in any thorough manner, is one way in which Heidegger's thought can be employed for more progressive political aims than those he chose for it himself.[14]

In 1940, in a summary of a lecture in the course *European Nihilism*, Heidegger commented on a passage from Nietzsche's *The Wanderer and His Shadow*, entitled *'Premises of the machine age'*. The passage reads: 'The press, the machine, the railway, the telegraph are premises whose thousand-year conclusion no one has yet dared to draw'.[15] In reply, Heidegger does not simply look at the conclusions, much less their temporal duration, which has different implications following Hitler's projection of the Reich, but rather at the premises themselves. What, he asks, are 'the conditions of the technical "premises" of the machine-age [*Maschinenzeitalters*]? Where does the internal ground lie for the fact that technology could and had to become machine-technology, the machine the force-production-machine [*Krafterzeugungsmaschine*]?' Why too are the 'masses' given priority, and the increases in the population of the earth [*der Bevölkerungszahl der Erde*] seen as significant? Heidegger continues: 'it is not sufficient to explain the emergence of the masses and the proletariat from industrialization', because this is dependent, like machine-technology, on the same basic issue (GA48, 15).

In this attempt to go beyond consequences and events and look for conditions of possibility, Heidegger's work here bears careful comparison with – amongst others – Adorno and Horkheimer's *Dialectic of Enlightenment*, Foucault's analysis of racism in «*Il faut défendre la société*», and, more recently, Zygmunt Bauman's *Modernity and the Holocaust*.[16] All of these thinkers are in some way dependent on Heidegger's insights. In particular, as I have argued elsewhere, drawing on Foucault, there is a radical break in how racism was developed in the recent past. Racism clearly existed before, indeed versions that were non-biological, non-metaphysical; but this was recoded and utilised in the new scientific version. As thinking generally becomes more scientific, mathematical, calculative, so too does racism, taking on particularly biological and medical aspects.[17]

The projects of many other European thinkers are indebted to Heidegger's work, but the better among them have realised that his philosophical insights cannot be straightforwardly detached from his

political commitments. Indeed, many of the leading French thinkers of
the late twentieth century – among them Bourdieu, Janicaud, Lyotard,
Nancy, Lacoue-Labarthe and Derrida – were inspired to confront this
issue head-on, inevitably in the wake of Farías' work, in the late
1980s.[18] But three thinkers of an earlier generation – Foucault,
Lefebvre and Axelos – who I have discussed in detail elsewhere, were
far from blind to these political issues, and equally recognised the
importance of his ideas.[19] A necessary step to such employment is an
assessment of the political.

In *The Fundamental Concepts of Metaphysics*, Heidegger notes
several philosophers who have held mathematical knowledge to be
'the highest, most rigorous, and most certain knowledge'. Plato had
the slogan 'let no-one who is not well-versed in geometry, in mathematical knowledge, enter' inscribed above the Academy; Descartes
wanted to 'furnish philosophical truth with the character of mathematical truth and wrest mankind from doubt and unclarity'; Leibniz
claimed that 'without mathematics one cannot penetrate into the
ground of metaphysics' (GA29/30, 23–4).

   In recent years, some of the most challenging and innovative work
at the intersection of politics, philosophy and mathematics has come
from Alain Badiou. In works such as *L'être et l'événement* and *Court
traité d'ontologie transitoire*,[20] Badiou has attempted to rethink the
question of the multiple and the one,[21] concerns which can be related
to this book's reading of Heidegger. Indeed, it has even been suggested
that Badiou's *Being and Event* is the most fundamental inquiry into
ontology since Heidegger's *Being and Time*[22] because, unlike many of
his contemporaries, Badiou does insist on thinking through to the
foundations of philosophy, to ontology. And yet Badiou's ultimate
claim is that ontology is mathematics, that if 'we abstract all pre-
sentative predicates little by little, we are left with the multiple, pure
and simple . . . being-as-being, being as pure multiplicity – can be
thought only through mathematics'.[23] For him, set theory – 'a consistent theory of inconsistent multiplicity'[24] – with its nine key axioms
of extensionality, subsets, union, separation, replacement, the void or
the empty set, foundation, the infinite and choice, is the supreme
means of access into these fundamental issues.[25] This leads to the
conclusion that 'every element of a set is itself a set . . . every multiple
is a multiple of multiples, without reference to unities of any kind'.[26]

   The problem, as he himself identifies, is that 'ontology has
to explain why science operates but ontology is mathematics, so

mathematics has to explain how mathematics operates'. But this is a dual sense of mathematics – both as the mathematics of mathematicians and that of 'thinking being itself'. Only philosophy, he claims, is able to organise that discussion between 'science on the side of specific production and science as part of the thinking of being *qua* being', science itself is unable.[27] For Badiou, philosophy is not an interpretation of science, and science is much more than a possible mode of access to the question of being. Indeed, this requires philosophy to humble itself 'before mathematics by acknowledging that mathematics is in effect the thinking of pure being, of being *qua* being', and that in so doing 'philosophy unburdens itself of what appears to be its highest responsibility: it asserts that it is not up to it to think being *qua* being'.[28] This position is therefore part of an irreconcilable difference between Badiou and Heidegger's thought.[29] Badiou admits that 'deep down I am Cartesian',[30] and in Hallward's helpful phrasing, mathematics as the determination of the being of beings is 'disastrous according to Heidegger . . . [but] nothing less than an emancipation for Badiou'.[31]

One of the key differences is that, for Badiou, mathematics is in no way indifferent to the complexities of a world that, for Heidegger, is radically irreducible to number. For Badiou, mathematics is 'always richer in surprising determinations than any empirical donation whatsoever',[32] for example our existence in three or four dimensions is radically limited compared to post-Euclidean geometry.[33] Heidegger would take an entirely different position:

> What does it mean to uphold mathematical knowledge as the measure of knowledge [*Erkenntnismaßstab*] and as the ideal of truth for philosophy? It means nothing less than making that knowledge which is absolutely non-binding and emptiest in content into the measure [*Maßstab*] for that knowledge which is the most binding and richest in itself, i.e. that knowledge which deals with the whole [*das Ganze*]. (GA29/30, 25)

This is not, he insists, to deny the validity of mathematical knowledge, which 'objectively comprises a great wealth', but to contend that 'in terms of its content', it is 'the emptiest knowledge imaginable, and as such is at the same time the least binding for man', and therefore 'cannot become the measure for the richest and most binding knowledge imaginable: philosophical knowledge' (GA29/30, 25). However, and this is the crucial point, Badiou's determination of mathematics as ontology does not mean that he embraces the quantitative measuring and statistical reading of the world. This works in two registers. First, he makes it clear that it is not ontology, founded on set theory, that is reducible to number, but that number needs to be understood from the foundation of the ontology of sets.[34] Second, in, for example, *Infinite Thought*, he goes out of his way to critique precisely those kinds of understandings: the 'obsession with calculating security', the human sciences 'in the service of polls, election predictions, demographic averages, epidemiological rates, tastes and distastes . . . this statistical and numerical information has nothing to do with what humanity, nor what each absolutely singular being, is about'.[35] For Badiou, and I take this to be a central theme of *L'être et l'événement*, if being can be determined mathematically, then the event is precisely that which escapes it.[36] While Badiou's notion of the event is not a Heideggerian *Ereignis*, his view of mathematics is equally very different from that of the tradition Heidegger criticises. We can see in this a potential for reading Badiou and Heidegger together to common purpose, even if at the fundamental, ontological level – and at many others – there are profound differences.

Mathematics is not, then, in itself bad, precisely because it removes itself from any prior ethics or politics, but it is dangerous. As a complement, it can have many uses, but when used alone, when the world is reduced to numbers, a measure, to what is calculable and laid before us; when humans are summed, aggregated and accounted for; then much remains forgotten, unsaid, concealed.[37] The 'against' in the contrast between 'speaking' and 'number' is therefore to be understood in the sense Heidegger argues we should think of the Greek *polemos*, not so much a struggle, a *Kampf*, but as an *Auseinandersetzung*, a setting-apart-from-another, a breaking of the mode of connection. It is in that sense, then, contingently, historically, and mutably, and as a thinking through of the three crucial Greek terms, *logos, polemos, arithmos*, that Heidegger's thought can be understood as a speaking against number.

Notes

1. See, in particular, Hugo Ott, *Martin Heidegger: A Political Life*, translated by Allan Blunden, London: HarperCollins, 1993, pp. 319ff.
2. Jean-Paul Sartre, *L'être et le néant: Essai d'ontologie phénoménologique*, Paris: Gallimard, 1943; Maurice Merleau-Ponty, *Phénoménologie de la perception*, Paris: Gallimard, 1945.

3. See the letter from Heidegger to Beaufret, 23 November 1945, in Martin Heidegger, *Questions*, Paris: Gallimard, four volumes, 1966–76, Vol. IV, pp. 129–30.
4. For an extensive late discussion, see GA8.
5. An early hint of this is the series of questions posed against a quotation from Hitler (GA66, 122–3). As Alain Badiou perceptively notes, using the notion of being-together as a basis for a 'democracy of human rights', or as Arendt does, is to 'fail to grasp the political essence of Nazism . . . nobody desired the being-together of the Germans more than Hitler'. See his *Ethics: An Essay on the Understanding of Evil*, translated by Peter Hallward, London: Verso, 2001, p. 65.
6. For a late reading of the term *ratio*, see especially GA10, 148–55/ 100–3; and on measure more generally, Martin Heidegger, *Zollikoner Seminare*, edited by Medard Boss, Frankfurt am Main: Vittorio Klostermann, 1987, pp. 127–44.
7. On language, see especially GA12, and the earlier GA85.
8. Friedrich Hölderlin, 'In lovely blueness . . .', in *Selected Verse*, translated by Michael Hamburger, German–English version, Harmondsworth: Penguin, 1961, pp. 245–6. For a discussion, see Werner Marx, *Is There a Measure on Earth? Foundations for a Nonmetaphysical Ethics*, translated by Thomas J. Nenon and Reginald Lilly, Chicago: University of Chicago Press, 1987.
9. For a reading of this work, see Stuart Elden, *Mapping the Present: Heidegger, Foucault and the Project of a Spatial History*, London: Continuum, 2001, Chapter Three.
10. See, however, Laurence Paul Hemming, *Heidegger's Atheism: The Refusal of a Theological Voice*, Notre Dame: University of Notre Dame Press, 2002; and, in addition to the *Beiträge* itself, GA66, 229–56.
11. See also the essay 'The Thing' in GA7, 167–87.
12. This relates to the distinction between calculative thinking and mindful thinking [*das besinnliche Nachdenken*] (GA16, 520; see also GA34, 224; GA9, 309/236 n. a; GA79, 66; GA13, 146). For a discussion, see Babette E. Babich, 'Heidegger's Philosophy of Science: Calculation, Thought and *Gelassenheit*', in Babette E. Babich (ed.), *From Phenomenology to Thought, Errancy and Desire*, Dordrecht: Kluwer, 1999, pp. 589–99.
13. Jacques Derrida, 'On Reading Heidegger: An Outline of Remarks to the Essex Colloquium', summary by David Farrell Krell, *Research in Phenomenology*, Vol. XVII, 1987, pp. 171–85, p. 178.

14. See, however, Berel Lang, *Heidegger's Silence*, Ithaca: Cornell University Press, 1996, p. 98, which describes taking Heidegger's analysis of technology 'as a basis for understanding the Holocaust itself' as 'a formulation that seems as dramatically revisionist as any other in Holocaust historiography'. See also *Act and Idea in the Nazi Genocide*, Chicago: University of Chicago Press, 1990; and *The Future of the Holocaust: Between History and Memory*, Ithaca: Cornell University Press, 1999. If I would resist attempts to explain this particular event, to understand Nazism more generally through an examination of Heidegger's work does not seem so problematic. While I appreciate what Lang is trying to resist, there is a danger that this falls into a version of what Foucault called the blackmail of the Enlightenment. In any case, this would inevitably be a partial explanation, Heidegger's account leaving no room for a moral account. For a fuller discussion, see Stuart Elden, 'National Socialism and the Politics of Calculation', forthcoming.

15. Friedrich Nietzsche, *Menschliches, Allzumenschliches II. 2 Der Wanderer und sein Schatten* § 278, in *Samtliche Werke: Kritische Studienausgabe*, edited by Giorgio Colli and Mazzino Montinari, Berlin and München: W. de Gruyter and Deutscher Taschenbuch Verlag, fifteen volumes, 1980, Vol. 2, p. 674; translated by R. J. Hollingdale as *The Wanderer and His Shadow*, in *Human, All-Too-Human*, Cambridge: Cambridge University Press, 1986, p. 378.

16. Theodor W. Adorno and Max Horkheimer, *The Dialectic of Enlightenment*, translated by J. Cumming, London: Allen Lane, 1973; Michel Foucault, *«Il faut défendre la société»: Cours au Collège de France (1975–1976)*, Paris: Seuil/Gallimard, 1997; Zygmunt Bauman, *Modernity and the Holocaust*, Cambridge: Polity, 1989.

17. See Stuart Elden, 'The War of Races and the Constitution of the State: Foucault's *«Il faut défendre la société»* and the Politics of Calculation', *boundary 2*, Vol. 29 No. 1, Spring 2002, pp. 125–51.

18. Pierre Bourdieu, *The Political Ontology of Martin Heidegger*, translated by Peter Collier, Cambridge: Polity, 1991; Dominique Janicaud, *L'ombre de cette pensée: Heidegger et la question politique*, Grenoble: Jérôme Millon, 1990; Philippe Lacoue-Labarthe and Jean-Luc Nancy, *Le mythe nazi*, La Tour d'Aigues: Éditions de l'Aube, 1991; Jean-François Lyotard, *Heidegger et les*

'*juifs*', Paris: Galilée, 1988; Philippe Lacoue-Labarthe, *La fiction du politique: Heidegger, l'art et la politique*, Paris: Christian Bourgois, 1987; Jacques Derrida, *Heidegger et la question: De l'esprit et autres essais*, Paris: Flammarion, 1990. A number of texts in Philippe Lacoue-Labarthe and Jean-Luc Nancy, *Retreating the Political*, edited by Simon Sparks, London: Routledge, 1997, dating from an earlier period, discuss and build on the political issues in Heidegger.

19. See Elden, *Mapping the Present; Understanding Henri Lefebvre: Theory and the Possible*, London: Continuum, 2004; and 'Kostas Axelos and the World of the Arguments Circle', in Julian Bourg (ed.), *After the Deluge: New Perspectives on Postwar French Intellectual and Cultural History*, Lanham: Lexington Books, 2004, pp. 125–48. Of Axelos' work, see in particular *Marx penseur de la technique: De l'aliénation de l'homme à la conquête du monde*, two volumes, Paris: Éditions de Minuit, 1974 [1961]; and *Einführung in ein künftiges Denken: Über Marx und Heidegger*, Tübingen: Max Niemeyer, 1966. An interesting discussion from 1959 is Kostas Axelos, Jean Beaufret, François Châtelet and Henri Lefebvre, 'Karl Marx et Heidegger', in Kostas Axelos, *Argument d'une recherche*, Paris: Éditions de Minuit, 1969, pp. 93–105. A very valuable study is Dominique Janicaud, *Heidegger en France*, Paris: Albin Michel, two volumes, 2001.

20. Alain Badiou, *L'être et l'événement*, Paris: Seuil, 1988; and *Court traité d'ontologie transitoire*, Paris: Seuil, 1998. Much of the latter is translated in *Theoretical Writings*, edited and translated by Ray Brassier and Alberto Toscano, London: Continuum, 2004.

21. Hence his critique of Deleuze, who he thinks of as a philosopher of the one rather than of multiplicity. See Alain Badiou, *Gilles Deleuze: La clameur de l'être*, Paris: Hachette, 1997. For a discussion and critique, see Daniel W. Smith, 'Badiou and Deleuze on the Ontology of Mathematics', in Peter Hallward (ed.), *Think Again: Alain Badiou and the Future of Philosophy*, London: Continuum, 2004, pp. 77–93.

22. See Dominique Janicaud, 'France: Rendre à nouveau raison?', in Raymond Klibansky and David Pears, *La philosophie en Europe*, Paris: Gallimard, 1993, pp. 156–93, p. 187; Ray Brassier and Alberto Toscano, 'Editor's Note', in Badiou, *Theoretical Writings*, p. ix.

23. Badiou, *Ethics*, p. 127.

24. Alain Badiou, *Infinite Thought: Truth and the Return to Philosophy*, London: Continuum, 2003, p. 184.

25. See Badiou, *L'être et l'événement*, especially pp. 536–8; and, for a very useful discussion and summary, Peter Hallward, *Badiou: A Subject to Truth*, Minneapolis: University of Minnesota Press, 2003, pp. 83–90, 323–48.

26. Badiou, *Court traité d'ontologie transitoire*, p. 35; *Theoretical Writings*, p. 46.

27. Badiou, *Infinite Thought*, p. 184.

28. Badiou, *Court traité d'ontologie transitoire*, pp. 38, 55; *Theoretical Writings*, pp. 47, 97.

29. The best introduction to Badiou is undoubtedly Hallward, *Badiou*, which contains some useful indications of the relation and difference between Heidegger and Badiou. See also Hallward (ed.), *Think Again*, especially Jean-Luc Nancy's essay 'Philosophy Without Conditions', pp. 39–49; and Ray Brassier and Alberto Toscano, 'Postface: Aleatory Rationalism', which was omitted from Badiou, *Theoretical Writings*, but can be found at http://www.continuumbooks.com/(jmlavu554rgri0itjcekv145)/ TWpostface.pdf

30. Alain Badiou, 'Dix-neuf réponses à beaucoup plus d'objections', *Cahiers du Collège International de philosophie*, Vol. 8, 1989, pp. 247–68, p. 259, cited in Hallward, *Badiou*, p. 8.

31. Hallward, *Badiou*, p. 56. Hallward bases his reading of Heidegger particularly on a section of GA41.

32. Badiou, *Theoretical Writings*, p. 73.

33. Hallward, *Badiou*, p. 59.

34. Badiou, *Theoretical Writings*, p. 71; and see his *Le nombre et les nombres*, Paris: Seuil, 1990.

35. Badiou, *Infinite Thought*, pp. 41, 53.

36. See, for example, Badiou, *L'être et l'événement*, pp. 193, 199; and, more generally, *Petit manuel d'inesthetique*, Paris: Éditions du Seuil, 1988, for the contrast between mathematics and poetry.

37. For Badiou (*Theoretical Writings*, p. 73), 'the recurrent theme of the "abstract poverty" of mathematics when compared to the burgeoning richness of the concrete is an expression of pure *doxa*'.

Subject Index

Note: works referenced are by Heidegger unless otherwise indicated

Affect, affect, 29
against, 9, 72, 85, 180
aletheia, aletheuein, truth,
   unconcealment, 24, 28, 44, 45, 46,
   47, 48, 50, 55, 56, 58, 75, 77, 124,
   140, 141
Americanism, 8, 105, 170, 172
architektonike, 53, 54, 57, 59
arithmos, arithmein, arithmetic, 10,
   116, 118, 123, 124, 125, 126,
   127, 129, 130, 135, 137, 140,
   142, 180
Auseinandersetzung, 84–5, 117, 180

Basic Concepts, 154–6
Basic Concepts of Ancient Philosophy,
   123
*Basic Concepts of Aristotelian
   Philosophy*, 22, 27, 28, 36, 42
*The Basic Problems of
   Phenomenology*, 19, 43
Basic Questions of Philosophy, 150
The Basic Questions of Philosophy, 83
Behemoth, 146
Being and Event (Badiou), 178, 180
Being and Nothingness (Sartre), 170
Being and Time, 6, 8, 9, 10, 17, 19,
   20, 27, 28, 29, 30, 31, 33, 34, 36,
   37, 38, 40, 41, 42, 43, 44, 46, 50,
   56, 60, 72, 73, 74, 75, 83, 96, 104,
   117, 118, 119, 120, 123, 130, 137,
   139, 151, 152, 170, 176, 178

*Beiträge zur Philosophie: Vom
   Ereignis*, 4, 10, 75, 90, 91, 100,
   105, 106, 139, 142, 144, 145, 146,
   150, 151, 152, 156, 157, 171, 173,
   174, 176
Besinnung, 75
bios, life, 69n65
body, 17, 95, 96, 125, 127, 131, 132,
   133, 134, 136, 137
Bolshevism, 8, 148

calculation, the calculative, 4, 5, 8, 10,
   11, 72, 85, 94, 101, 105, 106, 116,
   118, 121, 122, 123, 124, 137, 139,
   140, 141, 143, 144, 146, 147, 149,
   151, 154, 155, 172, 174, 175, 177
Cartesian, 95, 131, 137, 141, 150,
   152, 179
Categories (Aristotle), 129
Communism, 105, 170, 172
The Concept of Number, 119
The Concept of the Political (Schmitt),
   85
The Concept of Time, 35, 42, 123
The Concept of Time in History, 119
Critique of Practical Reason (Kant), 74
Critique of Pure Reason (Kant), 20,
   74, 120

Dasein, *Da-sein*, 1, 17, 25, 26, 27, 28,
   29, 30, 31, 34, 35, 36, 38, 39, 40,
   41, 43, 46, 47, 48, 52, 56, 57, 59,

Leviathan, 146
logic, 9, 17, 18, 20, 21, 22, 23, 26, 28, 72, 74, 83, 90, 91, 92, 98, 172
Logic (Hegel), 20
Logic (Heidegger), 90
Logic as the Question of the Essence of Language, 90
The Logical Problem of the Question, 119
logos, 9, 17, 18, 19, 20, 21, 23, 24, 25, 26, 27, 28, 31, 32, 33, 35, 44, 45, 51, 57, 60, 72, 85, 86, 90, 91, 96, 117, 118, 120, 124, 140, 154, 172, 180

machination, 104, 139, 143, 146, 148, 149, 150, 152, 153, 156
Marxism, 105
mathematics, mathematical, 2, 3, 4, 10, 57, 83, 118, 119, 123, 124, 125, 126, 129, 134, 142, 178, 179, 180
measure, measurability, 1–3, 11, 76, 88, 90, 92, 94–6, 106, 107, 118, 121, 122, 124, 139, 140, 141, 142, 143, 144, 145, 148, 150, 151, 152, 153, 170, 172, 173, 174, 175, 179, 180
Meditations on First Philosophy (Descartes), 3, 131
megathos, stretch, 128, 129, 130
metaksu, the intermediate, 128
metaphysics, metaphysical, 20, 21, 36, 83, 84, 95, 100, 101, 103, 104, 106, 131, 140, 141, 142, 144, 148, 149, 154, 155, 156, 171, 172, 173, 176, 178
Metaphysics (Aristotle), 26, 28, 29, 36, 44, 53, 57, 126, 129, 138
Meteorology (Descartes), 132
Mitdasein, 33, 34, 35, 41
Miteinandersein, being-with-another, 28, 30, 32, 33, 34, 35, 38, 51, 88, 99, 128
Mitsein, being-together, 6, 8, 19, 27, 33, 34, 35, 36, 39, 42, 44, 56, 60, 72, 86
Mitteleuropa (Naumann), 103–4

Mitwelt, shared world, 43, 52, 117, 118, 119
Modernity and the Holocaust (Baumann), 177
Monadology (Leibniz), 137, 138
monas, unit, 125, 127, 129, 137
myth of the Cave, 10, 74, 77, 78, 79, 84, 87, 158

National Socialism, National Socialist, Nazi, Nazism, 5, 6, 7, 8, 10, 11, 76, 80, 81, 82, 83, 85, 86, 88, 90, 91–2, 98, 100, 101, 102, 103, 104, 105, 144, 145, 146, 148, 151, 157, 173, 176, 177
nature, 9, 94, 120, 121, 122, 123, 131, 132, 134, 135, 136, 138, 140, 143, 147, 148, 154, 156, 157
New Research on Logic, 19
Nicomachean Ethics (Aristotle), 8, 9, 17, 22, 28, 31, 32, 38, 43, 44, 46, 47, 50, 59–60, 73
Night of the Long Knives, 80, 98
number, 1, 2, 10, 85, 93, 100, 106, 116, 118, 121, 123, 124, 128, 129, 130, 137, 140, 142, 145, 146, 147, 149, 154, 172, 175, 176, 179, 180

oikonomia, householding, 32, 53, 54
Ontology: the Hermeneutic of Facticity, 151
Origin of the Work of Art, 99
Ort, locale, place, 121, 125

Peri Hermeneias (Aristotle), 23, 24
Phenomenological Interpretations to Aristotle, 22
phenomenology, 19, 23, 31, 119
Phenomenology and the Transcendental Philosophy of Value, 19, 141
Phenomenology of Perception (Merleau-Ponty), 170
Philebus (Plato), 43
philosopher, philosophy, 7, 19, 21, 22, 23, 25, 30, 49, 73, 76, 77, 79, 84, 87, 88, 90, 100, 101, 102, 106, 119, 122, 144, 153, 178, 179

Index of Names

Adorno, Theodor W., 177
Anaximander, 79
Arendt, Hannah, 49, 68n61
Aristotle, 6, 7, 8, 9, 10, 17, 19–33,
    36–8, 40–6, 48, 49, 50, 53, 55, 57,
    58, 59, 60, 62n13, 64n30, 67n58,
    72, 73, 74, 76, 77, 86, 104, 106,
    116, 117, 120, 123, 124, 125, 126,
    127, 129, 130, 138, 140, 146
Augustine, 123
Axelos, Kostas, 178

Badiou, Alain, 178–80, 181n5
Baliani, Giovanni, 135
Bambach, Charles, 7
Bauman, Zygmunt, 177
Baumgarten, Alexander, 83
Beaufret, Jean, 170, 171
Bernasconi, Robert, 98
Bourdieu, Pierre, 7, 178
Bröcker, Walter, 102
Brouwer, Luitzen, 119
Buchner, Harmut, 102

Chamberlain, Houston S., 100

de Bestegui, Miguel, 7
Derrida, Jacques, 6, 7, 176, 178
Desargues, Gérard, 134
Descartes, René, 2, 3, 10, 12n9, 83,
    94, 120, 121, 123, 130, 131, 132,
    133, 134, 135, 136, 137, 138, 139,
    140, 142, 143, 144, 145, 146, 147,
    149, 150, 152, 178

Dilthey, Wilhelm, 119
Duns Scotus, 19

Euclid, 136, 160n29, 164n73

Farías, Victor, 6, 178
Foucault, Michel, 2, 177, 178

Gadamer, Hans-Georg, 55
Galilei, Galileo, 121, 135
Gillespie, Michael Allen, 8
Guterman, Norbert, 114n66

Hallward, Peter, 179
Hardt, Michael, 2
Hegel, G. W. F., 19, 61–2n8, 62n9,
    73, 83, 99, 120, 123
Hellingrath, Norbert von, 99
Heraclitus, 77, 84, 85, 118, 140
Hilbert, David, 119
Hitler, Adolf, 8, 10, 32, 80, 82, 85,
    93, 147, 177
Hobbes, Thomas, 3, 19, 146
Hölderlin, Friedrich, 10, 85, 90, 91,
    99, 101, 173, 174
Horkheimer, Max, 177
Husserl, Edmund, 4, 19, 119, 166n95

Janicaud, Dominique, 7, 178
Jaspers, Karl, 170
Jünger, Ernst, 81, 146, 167n105

Kant, Immanuel, 10, 19, 20, 62n9, 73,
    74, 83, 101, 106, 120, 121, 122,
    131, 139, 144, 162n41